ANDI HAYMAN

76

DIVE WIGHT AND HAMPSHIRE

Also in this series:
DIVE KENT by Kendall McDonald
DIVE SUSSEX by Kendall McDonald
DIVE DORSET by John & Vicki Hinchcliffe
DIVE SOUTH DEVON by Kendall McDonald
DIVE SOUTH CORNWALL by Richard Larn
DIVE ISLE OF MAN by Maura Mitchell and Ben Hextall
DIVE ST ABBS AND EYEMOUTH by Lawson Wood

DIVE WIGHT AND HAMPSHIRE

A DIVER GUIDE

Martin Pritchard and Kendall McDonald

Underwater World Publications

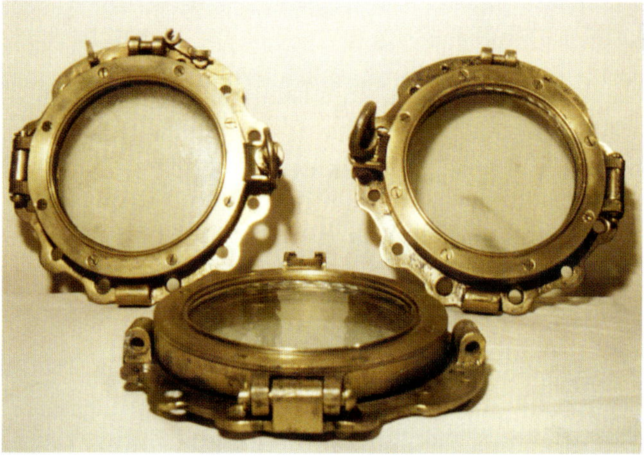

Above: Three bronze portholes recovered from the wreck of HMS P.12 (see Sites **137** and **158**).
Title page: Members of Shanklin SAC offloading kit after a dive on the Nab Tower.
Front cover: A diver studies the marine life on one of the many "wrecks" at Horsea Island (see Site **69**).

Copy-edited by Susannah Wight

Maps by Design IT, Liphook, Hampshire

Typesetting and editorial production by Martyn Yeo

Produced by **DIVER** Magazine

Published by Underwater World Publications Ltd,
55 High Street, Teddington, Middlesex, TW11 8HA

First published 1987
Reprinted with corrections 1991

Second edition 2001

ISBN 0 946020 30 2

Printed in the United Arab Emirates by Emirates Printing Press,
PO Box 5106, Al Quoz, Dubai

Contents

Looking east across Ventnor Bay.

Preface

The sea off Hampshire and the Isle of Wight provides some of the most rewarding diving in the whole of Britain. All the diver needs to get the best of it is a copy of this book, for these pages are packed with information and expertise from all the leading divers of the area.

The authors – and everyone who dives these waters – will wish to thank them all for their help, particularly:

- Martin Woodward, Isle of Wight salvage expert, underwater archaeologist and creator of the Bembridge Maritime Museum.
- Maurice Harknett of Portsmouth for his great knowledge of Hampshire waters.
- Alexander McKee who found the *Mary Rose* and before his death passed on to the authors much of his diving research and information about sites in the eastern Solent.
- Ray Mabbs, salvage expert, for detail about wrecks in the whole area.
- Richard Rimmer for identifying the *New Dawn.*
- Mike Walsh of Southsea who opened his logbooks to provide diving detail and wreck positions.
- Dougie Saunders of Ryde for an immense amount of detail about wrecks around the island, particularly the south-west coast of the Isle of Wight.
- Dave Ellison of Whippingham for diving detail and photographic research.
- Simon Dabell of Blackgang Chine Museum for access to his photographic collections, Tom Rayner of Ryde for more wreck pictures and Norman Taylor of Gosport for even more.

- Peter Street, skipper of dive boat Woodpecker, for detailed wreck information.
- Adrian Ponchaud for ship photographs.
- Paul Davies, dive boat skipper of Langstone, for help with local wrecks.
- The Southern Federation of Sub-Aqua Clubs and the Marine Conservation Society for use of some detail in their site register.
- The Wight Dolphins, BSAC, for a great deal of help with Wight diving.
- Lieutenant-Commander Nelson McEachan, Glynis Furse and Peter Gange, of the Wreck Section of the United Kingdom Hydrographic Office at Taunton, for their help and expertise.

Though the above named are those who made major contributions to the content of this book, there are scores of other divers who gave small, but no less vital, amounts of information and we are grateful for their help too.

MARTIN PRITCHARD
KENDALL McDONALD

Acknowledgements

The photographs on pages ii, 7, 9, 15, 19, 34, 35, 53 (inset), 60, 71, 89, 100, 104, 120, 121 (foot), 125, 129, 130, 137, 139, 142, 145, 156, 158, 160, 162, 166, 170, 171, 173, 180, 195, 199, 201, 202, 203, 204 and 206 were taken by the authors or are from their collections.

The photograph on the front cover was taken by Brendan O'Brien. All the remaining photographs were taken by Roy Smallpage except for the following, which are reproduced with grateful thanks and by kind permission of:

Beken of Cowes Ltd – page 121 (top)

Blackgang Chine Museum – pages 36, 38

A. Duncan – page 90

John Hammond – page 114

Imperial War Museum – page 111

Graham Mobbs – page 57

National Maritime Museum, Greenwich – pages 32, 99, 102, 153, 163

Adrian Ponchaud – pages 41, 59

Tom Rayner – pages 109, 113, 127, 138

Royal Navy Submarine Museum Photograph Archive – pages 94, 143, 159

How to use this Guide

The coastline of Hampshire and the Isle of Wight is divided into six areas, moving clockwise around the island. There is a chapter for each area, containing diving information, spot by spot, wreck by wreck. Each of nearly 250 dive sites is given a number and the sites can be located on the area map at the start of each chapter. Back-up information of vital importance to divers is given, including the location of launch sites, parking facilities, routes, and Admiralty chart and Ordnance Survey map numbers.

References to Ordnance Survey maps are to the Landranger 1:50 000 series. There are also useful Ordnance Survey maps published at the more detailed scale of 1:25 000. Relevant to this area are the Outdoor Leisure series Nos. 22 (New Forest) and 29 (Isle of Wight), and the Explorer series Nos. 119 (Meon Valley) and 120 (Chichester).

Appendix 1, Dive Services, has details of diving boats for hire, air supplies, equipment sales, hire and repair, and diving club branches.

Depths quoted in the text are given in metres, distances in yards and miles. Dimensions of ships are in feet; tonnages are gross. References to Admiralty charts are to the metric versions.

Dive sites are given a position in latitude and longitude; these are calibrated in degrees, minutes and decimals of a minute. Where possible, the positions given are those listed by the United Kingdom Hydrographic Office. These are based on the 1936 Ordnance Survey of Great Britain – OSGB 36. These positions are suitable for programming into Global Positioning System (GPS) receivers. However, it should be noted that GPS-generated positions are not based on OSGB 36 but on the data of the World Geodetic System 1984 – WGS 84. Therefore, for even greater accuracy, a correction can be applied to OSGB 36-derived positions to make them compatible with WGS 84-derived positions. For the area covered by this book the corrections are that 0.03 should be added to the latitude and 0.09 to the longitude

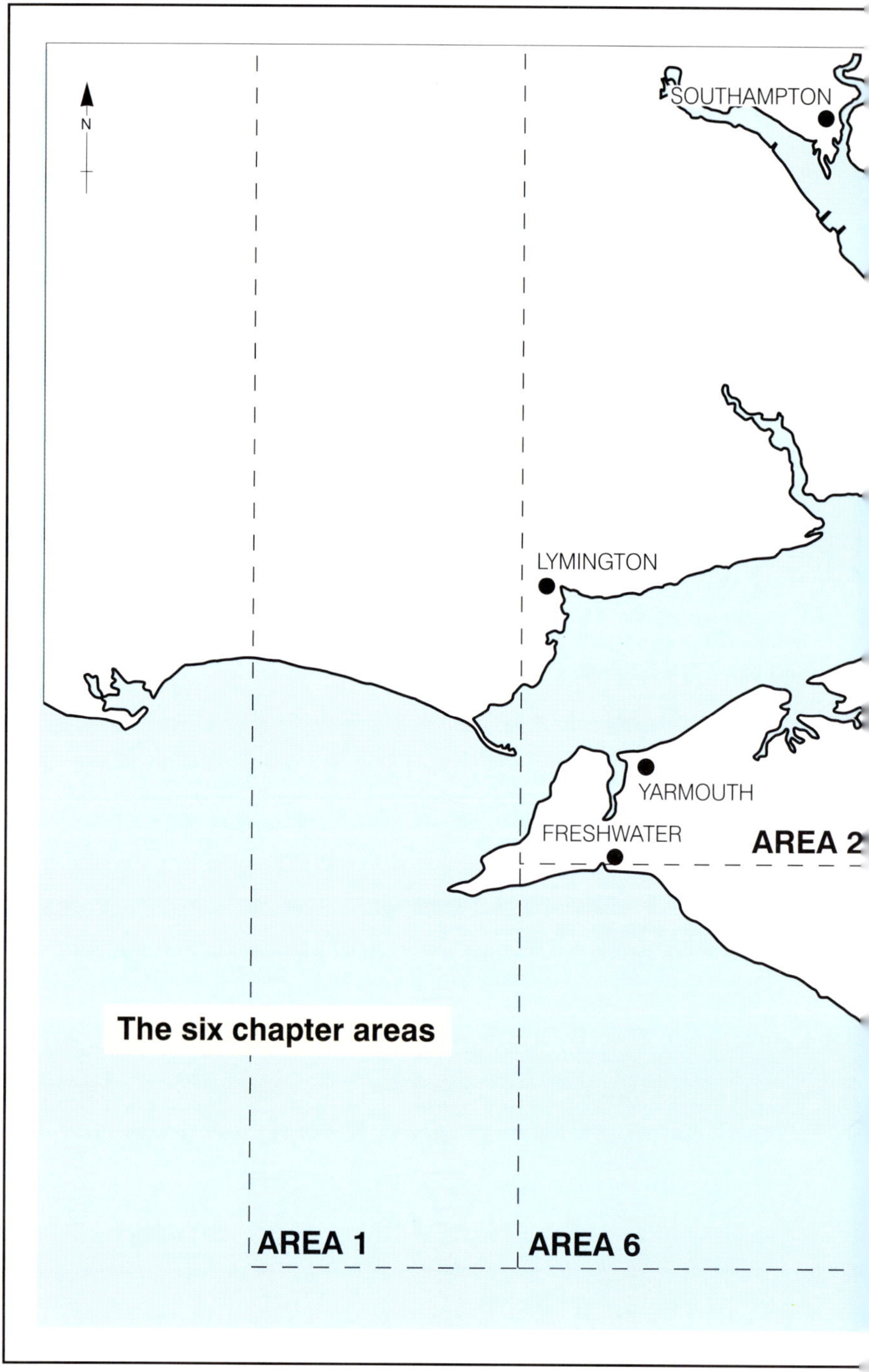
N
SOUTHAMPTON
LYMINGTON
YARMOUTH
FRESHWATER
AREA 2
The six chapter areas
AREA 1
AREA 6

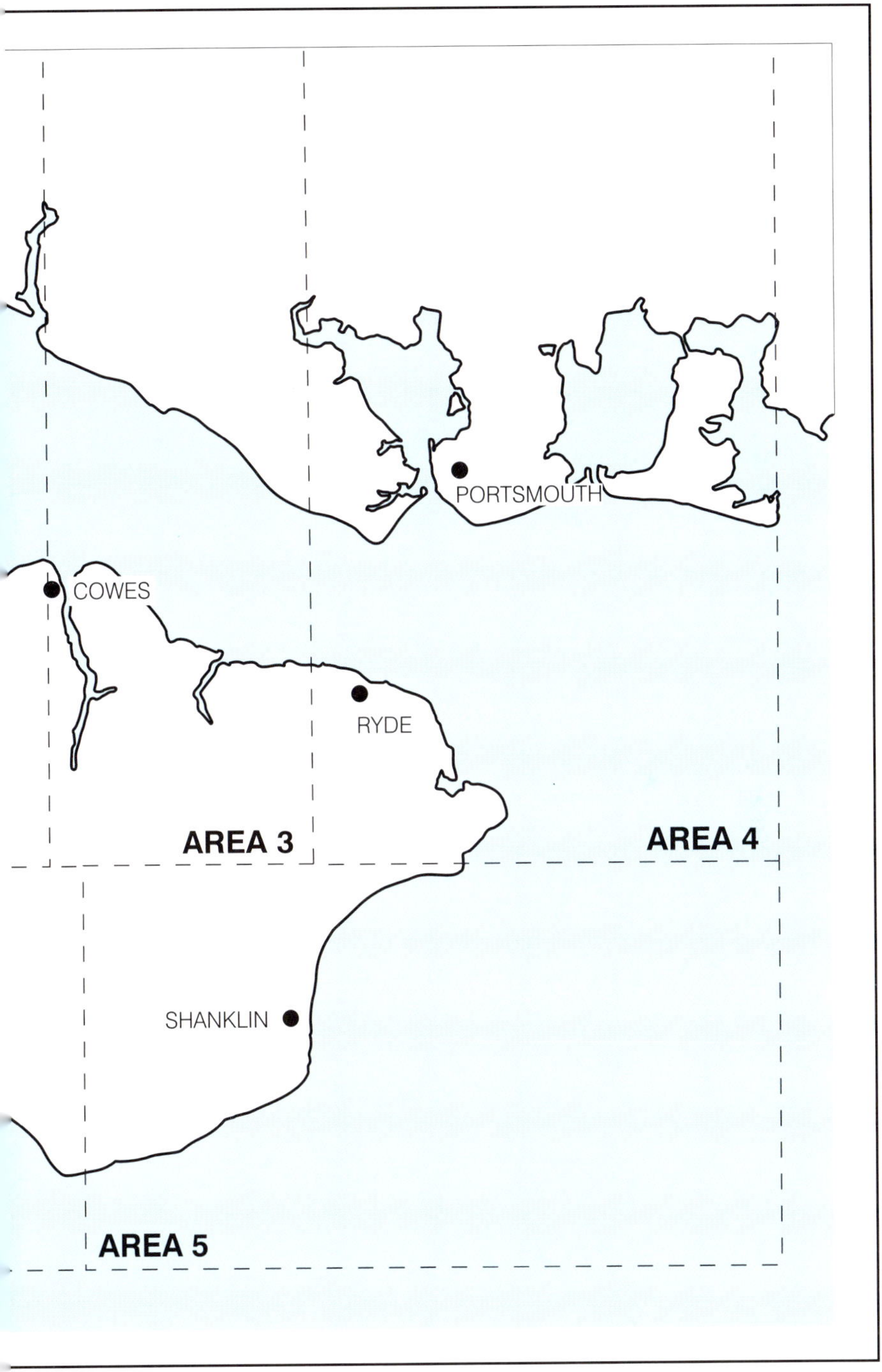
PORTSMOUTH
COWES
RYDE
AREA 3
AREA 4
SHANKLIN
AREA 5

Divers at Yarmouth.

measurements. For example, the position of the *Mendi* given in this book is 50 27.47N; 01 19.90W (OSGB 36). To correct this to a GPS value, add 0.03 to the latitude and 0.09 to the longitude measurements, which results in the following position: 50 27.50N; 01 19.99W (WGS 84). It may be possible to re-program GPS receivers, and many sets allow OSGB 36 to be selected, so that no further correction is required.

Most diving covered in this book is boat diving, particularly on the south-west coast of the Isle of Wight. Boat diving should be taken to mean inflatable and hard-boat diving. Not all boat diving sites are within safe inflatable range, however, and shore diving sites are intended only for a strong swimmer on a very calm day.

About Hampshire and the Isle of Wight

Some of Britain's best diving is packed into the sea off the coasts of Hampshire and the Isle of Wight. Although the Solent can be murky, it is not always so, except in the much boated areas. Visibility to the south of the Isle of Wight is just the opposite. Here the great cliffs, sometimes white, sometimes red, sometimes all the colours of the rainbow, soar up from clear seas and the diving beneath them is just as dramatic.

The waters covered by this book have carried the seaborne traffic in and out of Britain for more than two thousand years. The commercial port of Southampton and the naval base of Portsmouth have been the destinations of many an old-time ship – and these same waters have closed over many a long-lost wreck. Roman pottery has been found in the waters of the Yarmouth Roads; gold coins have been washed up on Isle of Wight beaches; the *Mary Rose* was found in the mud of the Solent; and in these waters are also the wrecks of more modern ships. Divers are making new discoveries every year, so there is still every reason to dive here.

Though this book covers the coasts of both Hampshire and the Isle of Wight, these coasts are separated not only by water, but also in their administration. HAMPSHIRE is run by Hampshire County Council in Winchester and is the largest non-metropolitan county in England and has a population of more than 1.2 million. The southern part of the county is the most densely populated and Portsmouth and Southampton are now unitary authorities. They are two of Britain's major ports and their naval links go back to the beginning of shipping. With its mild climate and long coastline – 145 miles – Hampshire is very attractive to divers and other watersports enthusiasts, with easy access to sheltered waters. Hampshire's borders run from Emsworth in the east to near Highcliffe in the west, where Dorset begins.

THE ISLE OF WIGHT, which likes to call itself "England's Garden Isle", is run by the Isle of Wight Council, a unitary authority based at Newport. The diamond-shaped island has some 480 miles of road and about 130,000 residents. It consists of 155 square miles and is 23 miles long from the Needles to Bembridge Foreland and 13¼ miles deep from Egypt Point near Cowes to St Catherine's Point in the south. The island's climate is mild, apart from occasional arctic aberrations, and the coastal scenery is often dramatic and beautiful. The island's motto is "All this beauty is of God" and there are 60 miles of coastline – over half of it designated "Heritage Coast" – for divers to explore.

Access by road

Access to Hampshire by road is easy, but access to the Isle of Wight by car can sometimes be difficult at the peak of the holiday season.

Hampshire can be reached from the south-west of England via the A35 or A303; from Wales and the west of England via the A36, from the Midlands and Oxford via the A34, and from the London area using the M3 or A3. From Sussex or Kent, or from the English end of the Channel Tunnel, Hampshire can be reached by using the A27 coast road; visitors arriving direct from continental Europe will probably chose the ferry terminal at Portsmouth. Once in the county, the M27 provides a fast link along most of the southern part of Hampshire.

Departure points for the Isle of Wight car ferries are Portsmouth for Fishbourne, Lymington for Yarmouth and Southampton for Cowes. Wightlink operates the

The Spyglass Inn at Ventnor is popular with divers.

This set of nesting troy weights was found off the south-west coast of the Isle of Wight.

drive-on-drive-off ferries from Portsmouth (Gunwharf Road) to Fishbourne. There is a very frequent service with a crossing time of 35 minutes. Wightlink also operates the Lymington to Yarmouth drive-on-drive-off ferry; crossing time is 30 minutes. Red Funnel operates the services from Southampton to East Cowes. Their drive-through ships take 1 hour for the crossing.

Taking cars to the Isle of Wight is not cheap, but a car is essential to travel around the island, especially with diving gear. It is best to book, but it is possible to turn up at the ferry and to cross without too much waiting. Do not delay in booking your return trip – in fact it is sensible to do it before driving away from your port of entry. Even in high season it should not present a problem to get a crossing mid-week; boats with very early or late afternoon and evening departure times are the easiest to book. Crossings on Fridays, Saturdays and Sundays are naturally the busiest.

There are three pedestrian-only routes to the island: by high-speed craft from Southampton to West Cowes, and the crossing takes 20 minutes; by hovercraft from Southsea to Ryde Esplanade the service is half-hourly in summer between 9am and 7pm, and the crossing takes 9 minutes; and by high-speed catamaran from Portsmouth Harbour Station to Ryde Pier the service runs between one and three times an hour from 6am to midnight, and the crossing time is 15 minutes.

Wrecks

A huge number of wrecks lie in Hampshire and Isle of Wight waters and readers will find many of them documented in this book; the shipwreck register in Appendix 3 notes many more. Few of these wrecks, in comparison with many documented losses, have been found or explored by divers. This makes the area of enormous interest to today's wreck hunter.

The most famous of all wrecks in these waters is that of the *Mary Rose,* located by the late Alexander McKee, excavated by teams of British amateur divers, and finally raised to be put on show near to HMS *Victory* at Portsmouth. There are also traces of many earlier ships. Divers have found amphora fragments in Yarmouth Roads in such quantity that there must be a wreck of Roman or earlier times buried somewhere in the soft mud of the area. Not far away a bronze mortar of the 16th century was found, together with pewter, and a full wreck site has been discovered, probably of the Spanish ship *Santa Lucia*, sunk in 1567. Four more Roman wrecks are suspected from net recoveries of pottery – all are to the east of the island. Very early gold coins have been washed ashore on the Isle of Wight and divers have found long narrow ingots of silver of ancient date. What else lies in the mud of the Solent remains for divers to find out. Certainly it is likely that ancient ships using the early trade routes may have been wrecked and long forgotten in these waters where fierce tides, combined with violent funnelling winds, can so easily bring disaster to any ship under sail.

The prevailing winds are, like the rest of the Channel, from the south-west, and gales from that direction have driven hundreds of ships to their doom, many on the south-west coast of the Isle of Wight. It is here that the Dutch frigate *Juno* was lost in December 1786. Earlier Dutch East Indiamen found another south-westerly gale laden with doom. The *Campen* was sunk in 1627 trying to get through the Needles into the comparative calm of the Solent, away from the storm in the open sea. The *Campen* was found in 1979 by Northampton BSAC. The Northampton divers found a considerable number of silver coins and other items from that wreck, but there were three other ships sailing with the *Campen* and two of them actually managed to get through the gap in the Needles. The *Vliegende Draeck* (Flying Dragon) was the other ship that failed to get through: she ripped her bottom out and sank somewhere in Alum Bay. Some of the ship was salvaged but divers have yet to discover her remains.

Over the years other ships have had reason to hate the Needles, where the tide runs at 7 knots on springs. For example, near the lighthouse, Goose Rock has the wreckage of four ships around it. HMS *Assurance* hit it in 1753; the *Pomone* went down on top of her in 1811; a schooner called *Dream* added to the sea bed tangle in 1837; and later, divers working on this mass of hardware found 17 Roman coins of AD 280 beneath it (Site **15**).

At the other end of the island and nearer the Hampshire shore lie other wrecks, like HMS *Impregnable,* lost in October 1799 (Site **100**), and HMS *Invincible*, lost in 1758 (Site **101**). Not far away are ships of much later wars such as HMS *Hazard* (Site **104**). All around are tank landing craft, British and German submarines of both wars, and the steamers that were the U-boats' victims. It is a wreck diver's paradise. Every year of diving brings new discoveries. Even so, while not seeking to dampen the wreck diver's ardour, some general words of warning must be given.

The Shipwreck Centre at Bembridge should figure on every diver's itinerary.

WARNING In some areas the sea bed is extremely soft and much silting has taken place of even the most modern wrecks. So it is extremely dangerous for divers to enter wrecks without some foolproof method of return to an exit point. A few fin strokes are enough to turn visibility in and around these silted wrecks to absolute zero.

In poor visibility the tangle or "wreck net" is another danger to the unwary diver. Though this part of the British coast was not one where wreck netting became extensive, some fishermen do use these almost invisible modern monofilament nets on sunken ships in the area. Divers must take care on all wrecks as many often have trawl and other nets wrapped around them.

Marine life

Sandwiched between Sussex and Dorset, this area might be thought to have a marine life that was identical with that of these neighbours, but in fact there are significant differences, and most areas teem with fish and shellfish. Every wreck in Hampshire and the Isle of Wight area is, like the lost ships of Sussex and Dorset, encircled with pouting and pollack. Those on the wrecks farther out are of enormous size. Skate, however, are not common here and there are many more seen in Sussex and Dorset waters by divers. Another flat fish that is cause for rejoicing when caught by local fishermen is the turbot, also uncommon in these waters.

Oysters are fished in the Solent. Some stray from recognised beds, and have been found by divers off Bembridge and round the Forts. Scallops are found in small beds (unlike the big concentrations in Dorset waters) and when found are usually smaller than their western neighbours. Sole and plaice are common and bass and mullet plentiful. Mackerel are seen in huge shoals and congers of enormous size haunt the deep wrecks. Sharks, threshers and porbeagles are known to be in St Catherine's Race off St Catherine's Point, when they follow the shoals of mackerel up the Channel. Gosport, Lymington and Isle of Wight ports all offer the tourists shark fishing. Few divers have come face to face with sharks in the water, however, though they are sometimes seen from the decks of the big dive boats.

The waters of Hampshire and the Isle of Wight are famous for their crabs, "brown", as the local fishermen call them, and edible by any name. These crabs, which make up the major part of the fishery in these waters, are usually large, with 5 to 6lb being the standard weight. Lobsters are common too, and in certain parts of the east end of these waters are more prolific than crabs. The Solent is excellent lobster ground, but is not extensively potted due to the amount of shipping traffic. As a result, some small wrecks are home to very large specimens.

Dive planning

Weather

If you believe, together with every other diver, that winds only exist to spoil the diving, then you will find the winds in this area particularly annoying. For here winds simply do not behave as they should. From the first glance at a map, it would seem certain that the great land mass of the Isle of Wight would protect much of the Hampshire coast from really bad weather. However, it does so only to a certain extent. The protection is far from complete, causing very strange wind effects: it is quite possible to have yachts sailing up the Solent under spinnakers from both east and west at the same time. This is the result of "wind bend", when winds from the south-west funnel into the Solent around the Needles from one end, but more of the wind hits the south side of the island. This wind bounces off the cliffs and literally bends round the great headlands like Culver Cliff until it is coming from almost the opposite direction from which it set out.

However, apart from these tricks, the weather of the Hampshire coast and Isle of Wight is not greatly different from that of the rest of southern England and will change without any warning. In winter, for example, spells of dull cloudy weather, wet with mild temperatures, can change quickly to brilliant blue skies, but with the temperature down below freezing. And in summer one of those lovely, long, hot, still spells can break almost overnight into chilly, wet and windy weather. One of the characteristics of the weather in this area of which you can be sure is that the weather to the east is drier than that of the west, as the area known as the "Back of the Wight" (the south-west coast) collects most of the prevailing wind and rain. It is these south-west winds that have accounted for most of the huge number of sailing ship wrecks under the massive cliffs of the Back of the Wight over the years.

The holiday resorts on the east of the island have tucked themselves into the shelter of cliffs out of the wind. It is not surprising that Shanklin has held the British annual sunshine record for more years than any other resort in the country. Even so, it is the prevailing south-west air stream that dominates even such sunny areas for long periods in the winter, bringing cloudy and damp conditions, with strong winds from December to February.

The following rules about the winds of the area will be of use to the diver coxswain:

> When the wind blows from the polar regions it arrives from the north-west and brings with it showers and bright periods. Coxswains should look out for squalls in these conditions.
>
> Winds from the east and south generally bring warm and dry weather from June to August, but very cold conditions in winter.
>
> Winds from the west are the most frequent throughout the year. Winds from the south-east do not stay long. North-east winds are most likely from March to May.
>
> Gales come most often out of the south-west and west and they usually last from 4 to 6 hours in winter, but not so long in the summer. Boat handlers should be warned, however, that just because a gale dies down suddenly, it does not mean that all is over. Whole series of gales have been recorded in the area with wind speeds of over 90 knots, which is more than hurricane force.
>
> Sea breezes are not always gentle. Along the Back of the Wight during warm summer days a sea breeze can combine with the predominant south-westerly and may boost the force by two points on the Beaufort Scale between late morning and late afternoon. This can make return to an open beach quite hazardous.
>
> Winds in the area are subject to funnelling down valleys and off hills. Dive boat skippers should expect wind forces to rise by as much as 20 per cent above the wind speed in surrounding areas at such times. Even some of the main ports in this area are affected by these boosted winds.

All this may sound a little gloomy, but in fact the whole area enjoys a temperature that is higher than average. During the summer the air temperature averages 15–20°C and a mild 8–12°C for much of the winter. This means that, on average, the air is colder than the sea from October to March and a bit warmer than the sea from April to August. In September there is no difference in temperature between them. At all times the difference between air and sea temperature is small and rarely more than 1°C.

Just as the wind affects diving everywhere, so the wind affects the temperature all round. You can safely say that south-west winds in summer will produce temperatures slightly below average, and in winter will keep things mild. North-west or north-east winds will do nothing much to summer warmth, but will bring cold weather in winter. East and south winds will give really warm weather in summer, but produce a very cold winter nip.

As well as sensing the wind, diver coxswains are advised to keep their eyes on the clouds. When big cumulonimbus clouds appear it may well be time to batten down the hatches – squally showers and hail with thunder can develop very suddenly. This weather, coupled with a swift change in wind direction and a sudden increase in wind speed, can put a small boat or inflatable at risk. Thunderstorms generally develop over France and drift north across the Channel during the night. The sudden squalls that come with them seem to be tied in some way with the appearance of solitary waterspouts.

Snow and sleet will be of interest only to the all-seasons diver; this more extreme weather occurs most often between January and March, with an average frequency of two days per month during this period. If you are thinking of such cold diving, ice can form in shallow waters to the east of the area in very severe winters. (In January 1963 ice in the harbours of Fishbourne and Lymington interrupted the ferries across the Solent.)

Fog, particularly in summer, can affect all divers and is particularly worrying for the dive boat skipper at sea, with divers down when the fog banks suddenly start to roll in. When the wind comes from the south-west extensive banks may form at any time of year. Sea fog is most likely when the wind veers westerly and it is most common in spring and summer because of the mild westerlies blowing over colder waters. These fogs are unlikely to last more than 6 hours, but can persist for as long as two or three days . The risk of sea fog declines from May and June when an average of three fogs occur to an average of one only in August and September.

Tides

Tidal streams through the English Channel are fairly straightforward. They run to the east for the flood tide and to the west on the ebb. The strength of the streams varies with the width of the Channel: they run more strongly in the narrow sections of the Channel and are weaker where it is wider. This becomes complicated when one starts to deal with tidal currents and streams in the area around the Isle of Wight, however. The western part of the English Channel is wide and as a result the tides are not particularly strong. But farther up the Channel to the east, approaching the waters of the Isle of Wight, the width of the Channel narrows dramatically with the distance between the island and the Cherbourg Peninsula coming down to a mere 55 miles. Then tidal streams speed up and springs can reach 3½ knots.

With tidal streams running both east and west around the Isle of Wight into the Solent strange tidal patterns emerge. Most Solent ports and harbours experience a double high water with the flood tide running in two stages, separated by a period of near slack water. The flood runs for about 7½ hours and the ebb for 5¼ hours. Generally, the ebb tides are stronger than the flood as the water that took 7½ hours to come in only has 5¼ hours to get out. The ebb also picks up speed quicker than the flood and this must be taken into account when diving on high water slacks.

There are several prominent headlands in the region, where deep narrow channels and tidal streams always run more strongly. Beware of inshore eddies where the tide may turn much earlier than the main stream. In the Solent these eddies are particularly prominent and are sought after by yachts racing against a foul tide. They can be seen quite clearly from a diving boat – there is a "tide line" about 6ft wide, full of assorted debris and floating weed between the two streams. Tidal heights range between 3.5m at high water on neaps and 5.lm on spring high water above chart datum.

Visiting divers have been swept away from their dive sites and travelled a considerable distance before being picked up – they do not appear to have anticipated the strength of local tides. The golden rule for "diving Wight" is to arrive on site early and wait for slacks to reach you. On offshore sites and wrecks, it is best not to anchor the dive boat, but to mark the site with a shot line and keep the boat free to pick up any divers who may be swept off the target.

More detailed tidal advice on tides will be found in the introduction to each area of this book. Tidal information is based on the time of high water at Portsmouth. The time of slack water has been averaged, but remember, it can vary with the strength of the tide and local weather conditions.

Visibility

Some divers say that the visibility in the Solent is always so bad that there is never any point in diving there. They are wrong. The truth is that the visibility varies considerably throughout the area, but is worse in the places where the sea bed is muddy and the tidal streams run at their strongest. In areas of rock and low tidal movement the visibility is bound to be at its best. As a general rule, visibility is better during periods of neap tides and periods of dry settled weather. Strong onshore winds reduce the visibility inshore of the 10m depth line very quickly indeed. Though the visibility varies from day to day, divers should find the following simple guide by each area covered in this book of use in their general dive planning.

AREA 1 In the open water sections of Area 1 visibility is usually good, an average of from 5 to 7m, and on occasions it exceeds 10m. Through the Needles Channel the best visibility is usually found around high water and can reach 6 to 7m. This reduces as the ebb tide starts to run out of the western Solent.

AREA 2 Throughout the western Solent the best visibility is normally found in the shallower sections averaging between 2 and 4m. In the deeper waters of the main channel it only rarely exceeds 2m.

AREA 3 Central Solent visibility is much the same as in Area 2. It normally improves to the east of the area.

AREA 4 Visibility usually improves quickly as the murky waters of the Solent are left behind. Off Portsmouth and around the Solent Forts it is between 3 and 4m. Farther south off Bembridge Ledges it can reach 5 to 6m.

AREA 5 Average summer visibility is around 5 to 7m, reaching 6 to 10m farther to the south. There are recognised dumping grounds to the east of this area and visibility in the immediate vicinity decreases drastically when they are in use.

Marine life is varied and prolific in the waters around the Isle of Wight.

AREA 6 Summer visibility is usually in the region of 6 to 10m. Inshore of the Back of the Wight strong onshore winds can stir up the sand over the Brook and Atherfield Ledges and reduce the visibility to zero. After a strong blow the shape and extent of the ledges can be seen very easily by looking down from the top of the cliffs, when the sandy-coloured water marks them.

Navigation

Diver coxswains should note carefully certain points about handling boats in these waters. For example, in this area buoyage follows the normal convention of red to port and green to starboard – with one exception. Within the eastern Solent the opposite applies: the red buoys are moored on the island side and the green buoys are on the Hampshire side.

WARNING The area is heavily used by shipping of all kinds and no diver can be too careful in these waters of deep channels and narrows. Once sailing in them, many ships cannot alter course because of their deep draught and they are unable to reduce speed quickly or to travel at very low speeds, owing to the loss of steerage. Divers must not get in their way.

Areas where the greatest care is needed are off the Needles between the Needles Bridge buoy and the south-west Shingles buoy and in the deep water channels of both the eastern and western Solent. Off Cowes, ships inward bound to Southampton from the east turn to the south after passing the Prince Consort buoy, then arc to the north to enter the Thorn Channel. Once ships have started this turn, they must continue, so keep well away from big ships making this manoeuvre (*see* Area 3).

Another place where great vigilance must be taken is the channel and entrance to Portsmouth. Big ferries and naval ships come and go all the time. Small boats must use the designated small boat channel through the entrance. After leaving Portsmouth, many ferries head south-east until they reach the Bembridge Ledge buoy where they turn to the south-west to pass inshore of the Princessa buoy on the west side of the Princessa Shoal. The reverse procedure is adopted when they are inward bound for Portsmouth, so keep a good lookout for them when diving in the locality.

In the area between Stone Point and Lepe on the Hampshire coast, and between Egypt Point and Thorness Bay on the island, there are high voltage cables and gas pipelines running across the Solent. Anchoring of any kind is forbidden in this area.

During the summer months large spherical yellow buoys blossom in Solent waters. They bear names such as Deck, Frigate, Keel, Porsche and Ratsey. These are marker buoys for yacht racing and divers nearby should proceed with caution. There are two particular yachting events to be avoided by divers. In June each year the Round The Island race attracts an entry in excess of 1,200 boats. They race from Cowes, heading west and circling the island to finish at Cowes again. This is a day the Solent and Wight diver might think would be better spent in a pub! The other big occasion to be aware of is Cowes Week, during the first week in August, a time when the Solent and other areas are packed with yachts.

Minimum sizes for fish and shellfish from 1 January, 2000 as laid down by the Southern Sea Fisheries District.

Fish	**Shellfish**
Sole – 24cm	Lobster (carapace length) – 87mm
Megrim – 20cm	Edible crab (width at broadest part of back)
Plaice – 22cm	males – 160mm
Brill – 30cm	females – 140mm
Turbot – 30cm	Spider crab (carapace length)
Herring – 20cm	males – 130mm
Haddock – 30cm	females – 120mm
Whiting – 27cm	Norway lobster (carapace length) – 25mm
Cod – 35cm	Crawfish – 110mm
Hake – 27cm	Velvet crab – 65mm
Pollack – 30cm	Whelk – 45mm
Bass – 36cm	Scallop (longest part of shell) – 110mm
	Queen scallop – 40mm
	Clam – 40mm
	Razor clam – 100mm

Rules and regulations

The restrictions on divers in Hampshire and Isle of Wight waters can be split into three main categories: diving in harbours, taking fish or shellfish, and the exploration of naval ships and military aircraft.

DIVING IN HARBOURS The area covered in this book includes huge ports and busy harbours. Most divers would not want to explore the murky waters of any of them, but those who do must ensure that they have the harbourmaster's permission, that they dive only in the area for which such permission has been given, and only at the times stated. Harbourmasters from whom permission to dive must be sought are noted in each section.

TAKING FISH OR SHELLFISH Divers who want to take any fish or shellfish for their supper must conform to the same rules as those that apply to professional fishermen. These mostly concern minimum sizes. Such sizes for the whole of the area are laid down by the Southern Sea Fisheries District, which covers the coastline for 3 nautical miles seaward from the Coastguard Station, Hayling Island, to the Dorset–Devon border. The district includes the waters around the Isle of Wight, the Solent, Southampton Water, Langstone Harbour, Portsmouth Harbour, Poole Harbour and Portland Harbour. The whole of this district is administered from a head office at 64 Ashley Road, Parkstone, Poole BH14 9BN (tel. 01202 721373); the Chief Fishery Officer of the district is Mark Whitley. The district has its own fisheries protection vessels: the 42ft *Southern Trident* is based at Poole or Cowes and the district operates three smaller boats.

The minimum sizes of fish and shellfish that may be taken are summarized in the table on page opposite. Full details of these and other Southern Sea Fisheries District regulations are available on a special wheelhouse card sent free to any diver who writes to their headquarters in Poole. A copy of the by-laws may be obtained from the same address.

WRECK EXPLORATION is covered by various Acts of Parliament: the Military Remains Act, the Merchant Shipping Acts and the Protection of Wrecks Act. Wreck divers should make sure that their diving does not breach these acts, brief outlines of which are given below.

The Military Remains Act

The Military Remains Act 1986 may in the future affect the wreck diver much more than it does at present. Its main drive is to preserve the sanctity of "war graves" – the wreckage of military ships and aircraft known to contain remains of service personnel.

The wreckage of all military aircraft of any nation is automatically protected, but ships will have to be designated by the Secretary of State and will need a statutory instrument to do so. This means that ships to be named as "war graves" will have to be named and approved by Parliament in the same way that ships to be protected as historic wrecks need a statutory instrument passed through Parliament.

There seems no doubt that those who passed the Act had little idea of the number of ships that could fall under its terms, such as a merchant ship with a Navy gunner aboard – was he among the survivors? – and as a result no ships have yet been named under the Act. This does not mean that ships are not covered by the general thrust of the Act and divers should therefore treat all possible "war graves" with total respect.

However, once these ships have been named, the diver commits an offence only by tampering with, damaging, moving, removing or unearthing remains, or by entering an enclosed interior space in the wreckage. The punishment on conviction of an offence is a fine. Nothing in the Act prevents the wreck diver from visiting the site, examining the exterior or even settling on the wreckage. An offence is only committed if the diver disturbs remains or enters a proper compartment of the wreck. The punishment on conviction is a fine.

This is of course only a brief description, and serious wreck divers should study the Act itself. Your library or HM Stationery Office should be able to supply a copy.

The Merchant Shipping Acts

The Receiver of Wreck is responsible for the administration of the Merchant Shipping Act 1894 and the Merchant Shipping Act 1906, which deal with wreck and salvage. It is a legal requirement that all recovered wreck (flotsam, jetsam, derelict or lagan – whether recovered within or outside United Kingdom territorial waters) is reported to the Receiver of Wreck. Coastguards act as the Receiver, and it is to them that recoveries should be reported.

Finders who conceal items are liable to prosecution, so any object – even if it appears to have no monetary value – should be declared as soon as possible. The Receiver of Wreck can then make a decision as to the future ownership of the property.

Wreck recovered from within United Kingdom territorial waters that remains unclaimed at the end of a statutory one-year period becomes the property of the Crown, and the Receiver of Wreck is required to dispose of it. This may be through sale at auction, although in many instances the finder will be allowed to keep unclaimed items of wreck in lieu of a salvage award. This, however, is at the discretion of the Receiver of Wreck, and each case is judged on its merits.

For further information contact: The Receiver of Wreck, The Coastguard Agency, Spring Place, 105 Commercial Road, Southampton SO15 1EG (tel. 023 8032 9474; fax 023 8032 9477).

Lobsters are common inhabitants of wrecks off the Isle of Wight.

The Protection of Wrecks Act

Divers who find a site that might be of historical, archaeological or artistic importance should leave everything as it is and report their findings, in confidence and as soon as possible, to the Department for Culture, Media and Sport (or its equivalent in Northern Ireland, Scotland or Wales). If appropriate, the wreck can then be designated under the Protection of Wrecks Act 1973, in order to control activities on the site.

Designated sites may only be dived or items recovered if a licence for that purpose has been granted; failure to comply with this is an offence and can result in a fine. All recoveries from designated sites must be reported to the Receiver of Wreck. For further information contact: The Secretariat of the Advisory Committee on Historic Wreck Sites, 5th Floor, Department for Culture, Media and Sport, 2–4 Cockspur Street, London SW1Y 5DH (tel. 020 7211 6367/8).

Contacting the Coastguard

The Solent Coastguard covers the area, the Solent District headquarters is at 44a Marine Parade West, Lee-on-the-Solent, Hampshire PO13 9NR. For information on sea and weather conditions and to report intended dive boat expeditions use their non-emergency number, tel. 023 9255 2100.

Diving emergencies

In the event of any life threatening or serious diving accident, such as a diver being lost or missing, a case of decompression sickness or an embolism, the coastguard must be contacted at once. For such diving incidents, all other coastguard matters of lesser importance will be put on hold. This will mean that help, often by helicopter, will be on its way to you within minutes of your call.

Always call the Coastguard first. At sea, contact them direct on VHF channel 16; on shore use your radio in the same way, or dial 999 and ask for the Coastguard.

If less dramatic symptoms of decompression illness occur inland, a GP or hospital casualty department (or the coastguard) should be contacted. Emergency transfer to the nearest available recompression chamber will be arranged for you if it is necessary. Make sure you carry the 24-hour telephone number of Portsmouth Naval Base (tel. 023 9281 8888), which you can pass to the doctor concerned so that specialist advice can be obtained from the Diving Medical Centre there.

Decompression illness and air embolism

Decompression sickness symptoms vary from those so sudden that immediate air evacuation to a chamber is vital, to those that may not become apparent for some hours. Some of these less dramatic symptoms, which may well be delayed, can be more serious and produce greater disability than the excruciating pain associated with a joint bend. Tingling and numbness are included in this category.

Air embolism or severe symptoms require prompt but careful transfer of the subject to a recompression chamber. Victims should be laid flat on their back and, if possible, should be given 100 per cent oxygen. If at sea, contact the coastguard for help immediately: in a small boat, any attempt at speed may bounce the victim and almost certainly worsen the symptoms rather than help the situation.

Divers and fishing nets

So far no diver has been reported as trapped in tangle nets in Hampshire or Isle of Wight waters, though this may be more a matter of luck than of any other significance. Certainly divers only a few miles away in Dorset waters have been caught up in these wreck nets and have been lucky to escape with their lives.

Wreck netting has not caught on so widely in Hampshire seas and around the Isle of Wight as it has elsewhere and the Southern Sea Fisheries District representatives have described the use of such nets as "not a major feature of the fishing effort". This must not be taken to mean that no wreck netting takes place. It does, and divers should be on the alert for these almost invisible killers on every wreck they dive. The modern tangle and gill net is made of a monofilament material, which is extremely difficult to see, hence its increased effectiveness over the older type of net whose knots stood out in even poor visibility. These nets are different from those used by trawlers, which often become draped on wrecks by accident. It is only in very recent years that nets have been deliberately placed on wrecks.

These tangle nets are known to fishermen as "wreck nets". The nets used are usually about 53m long with floats at 1m intervals. The bottom of the net is attached to a footrope weighted with galvanised steel rings. The footrope is designed to break so that the net can be torn free if totally snagged on the wreck.

This netting is generally for pollack, conger and sometimes cod, in fact any large fish that congregate around wrecks. Wrecks are usually fished on neap tides only and are left netted for 24 hours before being hauled. This means that there may be no sign of life when the dive boat arrives at the wreck and indeed the marker float may be submerged. (The fishing boat will have no difficulty in relocating the wreck and the nets with modern electronic gear.) The need for care is obvious. Wreck nets are usually laid in a fleet of three to five straddling the wreck.

The danger to divers is not only on wrecks. Nets are often set for bass. For many years an important fishery for bass, which fetch extremely high prices, has grown up inshore between Selsey Bill and Swanage using monofilament gill nets. The main concentration of this fishery is in the Solent and Southampton Water. In addition to the full-time professional fishermen, large numbers of part-time, casual and amateur fishermen are using gill nets. Set nets are also used close inshore for plaice and sole, a major part of the catch for the area, but the majority of the Solent sole catch is by trawling.

It is clear that in this area there is an enormous amount of net about and divers must be alert at all times. Worried about the threat of nets to the diver's safety, the British Sub-Aqua Club carried out special tests, deliberately entangling divers in this type of modern monafilament net. As a result their advice is to carry a small special knife or a pair of small stainless steel shears. BSAC found that the standard large diver's knife was ineffective, regardless of how sharp it had been kept. The diver and gear underwater present a multitude of points on which net can become snagged. A survey showed that the majority of divers who had become entangled had first got caught on their legs. Despite this divers tend to wear their knives on their legs, which presents a major snagging point. It would be better if a small knife or small shears were worn on the arm or in an easily accessible purpose-made pocket on the upper part of the suit.

If a diver does become entangled, the BSAC advises partial inflation of the lifejacket making the diver rise inside the net, pulling it under tension and making it easier to cut. Then the positive buoyancy should help to tear the diver free. If an ensnared diver has partners clear of the netting they should cut the victim out still enmeshed and finish the clearance on the surface.

Divers and pot fishermen

The major fishery in the area is for "brown" or edible crabs and these are obtained by boats of all shapes and sizes, with a fishing effort ranging in scale from the single pot to strings of well over 50 pots at a time. Unlike the neighbouring fisheries district, Sussex, the Southern Sea Fisheries District puts no limits on the number of pots per professional registered fishing boat. Some of the larger boats set their pots in mid-Channel and then land their catch in France. On the return trip they pick up another catch from the re-baited pots and land that in Britain, alternating in this way on each voyage.

Lobster landings are much smaller than those of crab, but are sometimes more profitable. This could make the area one of sensitivity, but on the Isle of Wight conflict between diver and fisherman is unknown and diver–fisherman relations are excellent. Even so divers should take every possible precaution to stay clear of fishermen's gear. Remember that fish landings in the district are over £25 million in value per year. Shellfish landings are made at many places, but are generally channelled through Portsmouth and Portland on the mainland or Bembridge and Wootton on the island.

Divers and "White P" (white phosphorus)

Divers exploring the wrecks of World War One period in this area should be aware that "wedges" of phosphorus are being found in increasing numbers on these ships. One very good description of them is that "they look like wedges of Danish blue cheese – just like you see in a supermarket". Divers should avoid handling these "wedges", which ignite spontaneously when exposed to air: one diver was burned after bringing up a stick of this white waxy substance and putting it in her pocket. White phosphorus was produced for the Allies in the First World War by a Midlands firm, whose output for the whole war was 6,083 tons. "White P" was used in a wide variety of munitions – for thermalite and phosphorus grenades, trench mortar bombs, 12-pounder aircraft bombs, as well as for a whole range of shells, including 6in, 4in and 3in incendiary and shrapnel naval shells.

"White P" can look yellow, almost veined like cheese, and comes in various shapes. Those seen so far are either "wedges" or little sticks. But whether it is cheese-shaped or looks like a fish finger, divers should treat it all the same way – do not touch it or bring it up. It not only burns, it is also deadly poisonous.

AREA 1:

Highcliffe to Hurst Castle and the Needles

Area 1 runs from 01 41.00W to 01 33.00W and stretches to the foot of Admiralty Chart No. 2045. It takes in a graveyard of lost ships – particularly those close to the chalk spikes of the Needles. It is here that the entry to the western Solent is most dangerous and many sailing ships, driven by south-westerlies, never made the entrance. Some ended up on the huge cliffs on the western side of the Isle of Wight and others were swallowed up by the Shingles, those great shifting banks of pebbles that stretch diagonally across the obvious route into the Solent.

This whole area can be a difficult one for divers and it is important to understand the tidal patterns, which vary dramatically from one part of the area to the other. The northern half, for example, produces very strong tidal streams. At the narrow entrance between Hurst Castle on the Hampshire side and Fort Albert on the Isle of Wight (the narrowest part of the Solent) the flood tide runs in a north-easterly direction and can reach speeds of 4 knots. The ebb runs south-west and can go even faster – up to nearly 5 knots.

It is surprisingly deep in the narrow straits, reaching over 60m very close in. Despite the depth there is often a great tumult on the surface. Much of this is caused by a strong stream running through the North Channel (between the Hampshire coast and the northern edge of the Shingles); through here the flood tide reaches 3 to 3½ knots in the deeper parts. Its speed increases as it reaches Hurst Castle and, where it finally joins the Needles Channel stream about 400yds south of Hurst Castle, violent eddies are often created. But on the ebb tide this main stream branches off at Hurst Castle where some runs through the North Channel to disperse into Christchurch Bay and the rest goes to the south through the Needles Channel into open water. On the ebb this movement causes a strong inshore eddy along the Hampshire coastline.

Off the Needles themselves, and the Lighthouse, the flood tide reaches 2½ knots and the ebb slightly more – up to 3 knots. Across the Needles Bridge rocks, when

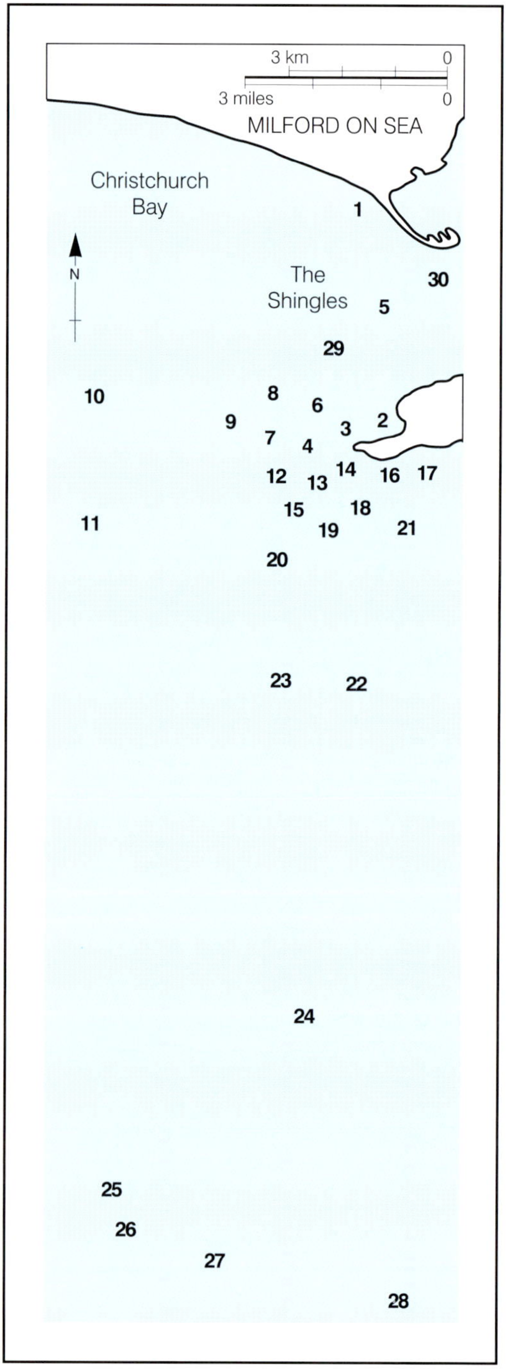

Dive sites in Area 1, which includes the Hampshire coast from Highcliffe to Hurst Castle and the western tip of the Isle of Wight. This area is covered by Admiralty Charts 2045 (Outer Approaches to the Solent) and 2219 (Western Approaches to the Solent); Ordnance Survey Landranger Maps 195 and 196.

the streams are strong and full, a line of disturbed sea is clear to see. This disturbed area becomes very rough when a strong westerly wind blows against an ebbing tide and then the seas can truly be described as mountainous.

The Shingles cover a large area stretching from a little south of Hurst Castle as far as the Needles Bridge buoy. These shingle banks are well marked by buoys. Although it is a shallow area, the tidal streams still run across them strongly and there always seems to be disturbed water over them. The banks are constantly shifting and at low water springs parts of them are exposed. The ebb tide, running against a strong westerly wind, will produce some spectacular and breaking seas and great care should be taken by anyone in a small boat.

In this area slack water occurs about 1 hour before high water and 5 to 6 hours after high water Portsmouth, and the slack lasts only for 10 to 20 minutes – depending on whether there are spring or neap tides. In the southern half of the area, well south of the western end of the Isle of Wight, the east-flowing stream can reach 2½ knots and the west-flowing stream about 3 knots. The general depths are between 30 and 40m and slack water comes 1 hour before high water and 5 to 6 hours after high water at Portsmouth. Here the slack period lasts for 15 to 45 minutes, once again dependent on neap or spring tides.

In Area 1 there is little diving from the shore. Diving in the area is all boat diving, except for Sites **1** and **2**, and the small boat launch sites are all on the Hampshire side.

Launch sites

Along the Hampshire coast from the Dorset border, near the luxury hotel of Chewton Glen, the A337 comes first to Barton on Sea where, though there is a splendid car park, access to the sea is confined almost entirely to windsurfing.

MILFORD ON SEA provides a launch site for small inflatables. Right on the front, with a magnificent view of the Needles and Hurst Castle, is a good car park. From this, a lift over a low wall and across a shingle beach will get small boats into the water. The shingle bank can be steep.

KEYHAVEN, farther to the east, provides even better launching from a good concrete slip right in front of Keyhaven Yacht Club. This ramp is usable by inflatables at all states of the tide except very low springs. Many speedboats with big outboards have come to grief within seconds of launching here as the coxswain opened up and headed for the widest part of the channel.

The left-hand side of the channel facing the sea is the shallower side, with sand banks – so keep to the right-hand side. Fishing boats in the area take sole and bass. This is a public launching site and there is parking for cars and trailers.

Above: Two of the slipways at Keyhaven. Below: Keyhaven and Hurst Castle Spit.

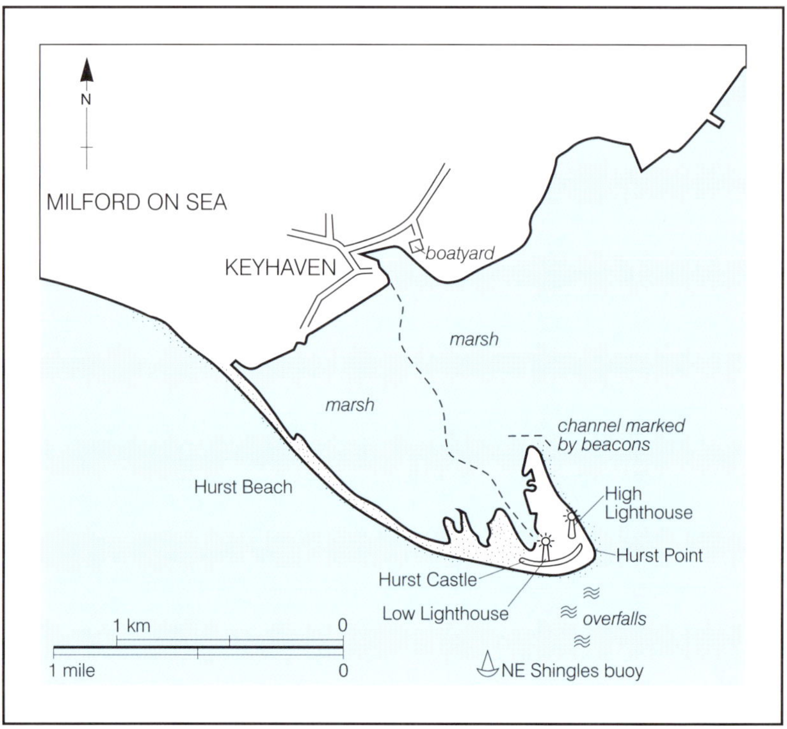

Shore diving sites (Hampshire)

1 Hurst Castle Spit This huge bank of pebbles runs out from the Milford shore for 1½ miles, reaching almost half way to the Isle of Wight. Though there is no exact point for this shore dive, those who find it interesting – for plaice – say that the farther along the Spit you carry your gear the better the dive, but most tend to go only a short way out along the barren pebble ridge. In places stone has been dumped in an attempt to stop the Spit being breached and prevent the flooding of the marshes to the east.

WARNING Divers anywhere in this area must be well aware of the vastly powerful tides that sweep through the Solent at its narrowest point. The closer to Hurst Castle – built by Henry VIII and famous as the prison of Charles I in 1648 – the stronger the tides.

HURST POINT has two lighthouses. Hurst Point Low Lighthouse is 16m high with a red, square tower and is sited on the Castle. Hurst Point High Lighthouse has a white, round tower and is 26m tall. It is 250yds behind the Low Lighthouse.

Shore diving sites (Isle of Wight)

2 Alum Bay This attractive bay lies between Needles Point and Hatherwood Point, the latter about a mile to the north-east. The bay is famous for its cliffs of many colours on the east side and these multicoloured sands are bottled and sold as souvenirs. Beach diving is possible. Two pylons support a chair lift down to the beach some 400yds south of Hatherwood Point. Unless you fancy a long hike down a wooden stairway from the car park at the top of the cliff, the chair lift is the best method for beach divers to get themselves and their gear down.

Some life is provided by the remains of an old sailing vessel, known as the "Alum Bay Pier Wreck". The wooden hull is covered with kelp and the depth here is less than 5m.

The "Tool Wreck" is not far from the remains of the old pier. The 50-foot wooden MFV *Enid* was wrecked here in a storm a few years ago. The wreck is only a few yards offshore, at the extreme southern end of the beach; many timbers stick up out of the sand. Divers have been surprised at the number of tools and electric drills found in the wreckage, which lies on sand in water less than 5m deep. Her cargo appears to have included cutlery, judging by the amount around the site. The whole sea bed of this bay is sand and shingle, but it gives way to rock and weed farther out. The maximum depth in the bay is 10m.

THE LONG ROCK, which dries, lies in the middle of the bay and in the centre of an area of foul ground that often has only 2m of water over it. The main rock area runs for 300yds to the west of the Long Rock. There is some shellfish life, though there are no reports of anything large. Boat cover is needed.

Five Fingers Rock is said to have five rock ridges running 300yds out from its centre. The main rock lies the same distance to the south-west of Hatherwood Point. It does not dry but is very shallow, and at low springs it can have less than 1m of water over it. There is much weed and small marine life.

Boat diving sites

3 Alum Bay South This is the area just inside Needles Point, with the best diving in the vicinity. A boat is essential; it is not a dive that can be attempted from the beach at Alum Bay. The dive is along the ridges and gullies at the foot of the huge chalk cliffs at the southern end of the bay. One particularly good patch is 400yds north-east of Needle Point, where the rocks come to within 5m of the surface. There are one or two small wooden wrecks here and a good deal of debris. The rocks and gullies under the cliffs are the home of large plaice and shellfish, and divers will see many bass. Because of their presence, some of the boats specialising in bass fishing will come right in to very shallow water, so diver coxswains should take care. The area is generally sheltered. The water is up to 15m deep.

4 The Needles This landmark – and seamark – is almost impossible to mistake for anything else. The Needles are all that is left of a chalk ridge that centuries ago ran without a break to the Old Harry Rocks north of Swanage. A change of sea level let the sea smash through the ridge to flood the old Solent River valley and form the Solent, more or less as we know it today.

The Needles form a narrow chalk peninsula rising up from the rocks to over 400ft. They too are not the same as they were. The slender pinnacle that gave them their name disappeared more than 200 years ago, as a result of erosion. This "needle" was 115ft high and stood slightly to the north of the main group. Locally it was called "Lot's Wife" and it fell into the sea in 1764. In the past there were five prominent stacks, one of which was joined to the mainland by an arch, but the arch collapsed in the early 19th century. The chalk peninsula has always been eroded by the sea, and probably will be for ever.

The Needles have often been a welcoming sight for those homeward bound. For others they have been a cause of great fear and, for some, the last sight they have seen. For they are more than just great white portals to the Solent standing out from the dark ground behind them. The rocks at their base extend a farther 400yds to the west of Needles Point; then the Needles Bridge, a deadly reef with depths varying from 2 to 8m over it, extends well over a mile to the west again. This reef is clearly marked by overfalls in rough weather and in flat calm there are still ripples to be seen – except at complete slack water.

Many ships have been lost on the Needles Bridge, in addition to those driven into the Needles themselves, and the rocks in the area have always been a hazard to shipping coming in and out of Portsmouth and Southampton. As long ago as 1781 merchants and ship owners petitioned Trinity House for a lighthouse. In January 1782 it seemed they were to get their wish: a light was to be erected "to be kept burning in the nightseason whereby seafaring men and mariners might take notice

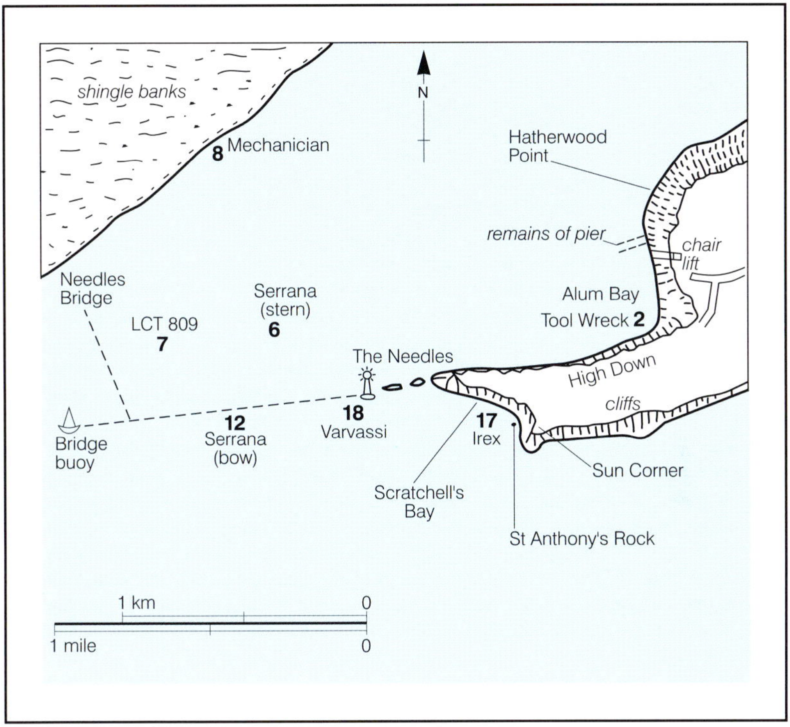

Alum Bay, The Needles and Scratchell's Bay.

and avoid danger ... and that ships and other vessels of war might safely cruise during the nightseason in the British Channel". However it was not until 1785 that Trinity House started work on the NEEDLES LIGHTHOUSE and it first sprang into light on 29 September, 1786. It did not work well. The tower had been erected on the top of a cliff overlooking Scratchell's Bay and was some 474ft above the sea. At that height the light was often shrouded in sea mist and fog.

In 1859, a new lighthouse was built on the outermost point of the chalk rocks, and near sea level. It was designed by James Walker and cost £20,000. The base was stepped unevenly to break the force of the waves and much of the rock at the base was cut away in building the foundations. This made it possible for cellars and storehouses under the lighthouse to be excavated from the chalk. The lighthouse is a circular granite tower standing 108ft high and its 35,000 candle-powered light, nearly 80ft above the sea, has a range of 17 miles. The lighthouse, with its distinctive red band and red lantern and gallery standing out against the white chalk background, used to be operated by a principal keeper and two assistants, but is now fully automatic. The light is a white, red and green grouping occulting twice every 20 seconds. The fog signal sounds twice every 30 seconds.

Diving the Needles needs good weather. Even in moderate winds there can be a very uncomfortable swell around the rocks and particularly over the Needles Bridge. Wind against tide is, of course, even worse. Divers must be aware that tides over the Bridge can reach speeds of up to 5 knots and that slack water periods are very short – only 20 minutes on neap tides.

Average depths over the Needles Bridge are 10 to 15m and the sea bed is almost entirely rock. The Bridge is a favourite area for angling boats and diver coxswains should expect to see anglers in the area during times when diving is possible.

Diving behind the shelter of the large white rocks of the Needles themselves is usually possible at any time but, though the tide run is greatly diminished, a nasty swell can build up in the shallow waters close in to the rocks where the depth is only 4 to 5m. The sea bed here is chalky rock with sand and shingle patches.

SCRATCHELL'S BAY is the name of the small area between the Needles Lighthouse and Sun Corner, ½ mile to the south-east. St Anthony's Rock stands ½ m high at low springs, 200yds to the west of the point of Sun Corner; another 200yds to the west two other rocks will be just awash at the same time. In the bay are the remains of the wreck of the *Irex* (Site **17**). Access is by boat only.

THE SHINGLES is a series of banks – or perhaps just one great bank – of shingle, sand and gravel forming the north-west side of the Needles Channel. Tides are tricky (see tidal information in the introduction to this area). The north-west side of the Shingles slopes gradually down to 25m, but the south-east side of the bank is very steep, racing up to only 10m from 30m, and looking in places like a hanging wall of shingle just about to topple down into the depths.

It is also a ship-swallower and whole ships have been known to disappear into the Shingles only shortly after being wrecked. But the Shingles move and the ships do tend to emerge from time to time. The Iron Ship (Site **5**) is a good example.

Parts of the Shingles is dry at times of low springs and can show as much as 2m above water, but there are many other patches that at the same time will only just be covered. Southerly gales are the ones that really set the banks on the move and the general drift is to the south-west.

Diver coxswains must take great care wherever they are on the Shingles. Overfalls appear suddenly on the south-east side on the flood; during the ebb a short sea can appear on the northern edge.

5 Iron Ship Yarmouth 3 miles; Lymington 4 miles. 50 41.55N; 01 34.35W. Depth: 7m. The site lies on the Needles Channel side of the bank, 1¼ miles south-west of Hurst Point.

This wreck was located by divers clearing some fishing nets after they had snagged on the edge of the Shingles Bank in 1983. The nets were found to be entangled in the wreck of some sort of coaster or barge, which is probably fairly old as there is evidence that it was steam powered. The wreck is around 200ft long with a 30ft beam and lies in an east–west direction. The bows appear to have sunk into the shingle or to have disappeared altogether into deeper water. Within the wreck are many copper pipes and the remains of the cargo, which seems to have been iron pyrites. The divers estimated that the wreck is from some time between 1890 and 1914; it is only now emerging from the shingle.

6 Stern of the Serrana Yarmouth 4½ miles; Lymington 6 miles. 50 39.88N; 01 35.68W. Depth: 20m. For details of the loss of the *Serrana,* refer to Site **12**. The stern is ½ mile away from the bows and is spread over an area of about 200ft. Though almost completely broken it is lying on the starboard side with some plates and ribs sticking up 2 or 3m. The site runs north to south with the stern to the north. The sea bed is sand and shingle with a few rocky outcrops. One of these is quite confusing to echo-sounders. It is a red sandstone needle jutting straight up from the sea bed to a height of 5m, and is close to, but not in, the wreckage. At one time a 14ft diameter iron propeller lay across some of the wreck at the northern end.

7 LCT 809 Yarmouth 5 miles; Lymington 7 miles. 50 39.69N; 01 36.38W. Depth: 17m. *LCT 809* was built in July 1943 by A. Findlay and Company of Old Kilpatrick on the Clyde, and was 187ft long with a beam of 39ft. This 611-ton Mk 4 tank landing craft returned to Southampton in June 1944 after being badly damaged on the Normandy beaches. The ship was under tow by HMT *William Brady* from Southampton to Poole when she foundered ¼ mile north-west of the Needles on 26 September, 1944. Dispersal operations took place in May 1946 reducing her height by 5m. This dispersal left the majority of the wreck standing less than 1m proud and very well broken.

There is a bit of a mystery about the wreck. It was first dived by Mike Walsh and Maurice Harknett in 1976. They found some bronze steam parts in the wreckage, which suggested that the wreck was that of a steamship. However, the site was surveyed in 1997, and the resulting report stated that the wreck was 40m long, 10m wide and stood less than 2m off the sea bed. She appeared to be in one piece with no evidence of scattered wreckage. This certainly ties in with *LCT 809.* The wreckage lies alongside a steep rock face of greater height than the wreck.

WARNING Very strong tide streams make this a difficult dive.

8 Mechanician Yarmouth 5 miles; Lymington 6 miles. 50 40.22N; 01 36.33W. Depth: 10m. It took two torpedoes from Kurt Stöter's *UB-35* to sink this armed escort vessel of 9,044 tons. The *Mechanician* was bound for Plymouth from London in ballast when the first torpedo hit her, 8 miles west of St Catherine's Point, on 20 January, 1918, but even after the second torpedo went home the ship still staggered on. Naval drifters tried to tow her in, but the *Mechanician* finally grounded on the edge of the Shingles at the entrance to the Needles Channel, with 13 of the crew dead. Her back broke and by October that year the ship was a total wreck and in two separate halves; later still the shingle closed over much of her.

Stöter and the *UB-35* did not last long either. On 26 January, nearly a week after it had attacked the *Mechanician,* it was depth charged and sunk by the destroyer *Leven* in the Dover Straits. None of the crew on board survived the depth charging, but six of the original crew did survive – they had been on board the Greek steamer *Epstatios* the day before as a boarding party from *UB-35,* when a Navy patrol boat appeared, drove off the submarine, and took the German sailors of the boarding party prisoner.

The *Mechanician* was 482ft long with a beam of 57ft and drew 31ft. Today parts of her are 3m clear of the shingle, though it is obvious that most of her is buried. The edge of the shingle bank here moves from time to time and some divers see more than others because of this. Diver Mike Walsh located the *Mechanician* after

The Mechanician was a victim of UB-35 in 1918 and now lies on the edge of the Shingles (Site 8).

getting a strong magnetometer reading. "When we dived, there was little to see – most of the wreck is buried in the shingle with only isolated parts sticking up through it," he says. But the shingle does move and this is a site worth checking after a good blow.

9 Concrete Barge Yarmouth 6 miles; Lymington 7 miles. 50 39.65N; 01 37.30W. Depth: 10m. This wreck is a concrete barge, around 70ft long, which sank while under tow of the motor tug *Pullwell* on 19 January, 1980. She lies in shallow water on the south-eastern edge of the Shingles Bank, approximately 60yds north of the south-west Shingle buoy, which is just over 1 mile west of the Needles Lighthouse. The barge lies north-east to south-west and is slowly being covered in shingle. There is not much to interest the wreck diver here, but it is a good hideout for crabs and lobsters. Being on the southern edge of the Shingles, a nasty sea can be kicked up, even in fairly light conditions, so care needs to be taken when diving this site.

10 Caroline Susan Yarmouth 7 miles; Lymington 8 miles. 50 40.40N; 01 40.67W. Depth: 15m. The *Caroline Susan* was a 23-ton British motor yacht, which foundered in this position on 13 June, 1940. One report suggests that the yacht hit a mine as there was an explosion at the time of her sinking. Diving information is needed.

11 Wreck, name unknown Yarmouth 8 miles; Lymington 9½ miles. 50 38.40N; 01 40.40W. Depth: 21m. A wreck or obstruction was located in this position during a survey in 1981. Little information was collected other than that it stood 1.8m high. This is very little to go on, but it should be worth locating and diving here to find out whether this is a natural feature or a new wreck.

12 Bows of the Serrana Yarmouth 5 miles; Lymington 6½ miles. 50 39.62N; 01 36.10W. Depth: 12m. The *Serrana,* which had been operated by Scrutton and

Sons, was built by J. Readhead and Sons in 1905. She was 353ft long with a beam of 48ft and her 399hp engines gave her a top speed of 11 knots. Torpedoed on 22 January, 1918, 10 miles west of St Catherine's Point, the *Serrana* struggled hard to reach port. Oberleutnant Stöter in a *UB-35* had hit her with one torpedo in the port side amidships, killing five men, but the 3,677-ton British steamer stayed afloat long enough to reach the Needles Channel. Patrol boats took her in tow. However, at 3.07pm the next day her voyage from London to Barbados – with 300 tons of general cargo and over 100 bags of mail – came to an abrupt end. As the *Serrana* started sinking, bow first, she grounded on the Needles Bridge, and just ½ mile from the Needles Lighthouse her back broke.

The stern section of the *Serrana* quickly broke away leaving her bow and holds firmly embedded where she struck. The stern wreckage drifted away before sinking to form another wreck site only ½ mile to the north-east (Site **6**). The bow section broke up swiftly under the pulverising effect of fierce tides and the heavy seas that build up on the Needles Bridge, and is now mostly a large pile of steel plates and girders. Among the wreckage can be found a large amount of her cargo – bricks, railway track and wagon wheels are scattered around. A few bits of the wreck stand up to a maximum height of 3 to 5m and there is a lot of fishing tackle to be found draped around them, for this is a very popular site for local boats taking out angling parties. The bottom here is of rock and sand.

WARNING Divers should plan dives on the bow section carefully as tides are exceptionally strong.

13 Millmer Yarmouth 6 miles; Lymington 8 miles. 50 39.50N; 01 34.00W. Depth: 6m. The shores of the Isle of Wight and Hampshire are littered with the wrecks of yachts. This is one of them. The *Millmer* burnt out and sank on 23 September, 1981, 1 mile east of the Needles Lighthouse and close inshore under the high cliffs. She is now totally broken.

14 Kylin Yarmouth 4 miles; Lymington 6 miles. 50 40.00N; 01 36.00W. Depth: 6m. The British Ballerina class sloop *Kylin,* 21ft long, sank on 25 September, 1977, after hitting a submerged object off the Needles. Diving information is needed. The wreck is bound to be well broken.

15 HMS Assurance, HMS Pomone, Dream Yarmouth 5 miles; Lymington 6 miles. 50 39.70N; 01 35.45W. Depth: 11m. There are three wrecks on one piece of sea bed here and this is a protected site. No diving is allowed within 200m of this position.

The *Assurance* was protected on 11 April, 1974. Discovered by Isle of Wight diver Derek Williams, she had struck a rock south-west of Needles Point, one that HMS *Pomone* was also to strike many years later. HMS *Assurance,* a fifth rate ship of 44 guns, captained by Carr Scrope, was homeward bound from Jamaica when she ran onto Goose Rock off Needle Point just after dawn on 24 April, 1753. Unlike the *Pomone,* the 133ft long *Assurance* did not ride right over the rock, but perched on it for several hours enabling the crew and the passengers – who included Governor Trelawney of Jamaica and his wife – to get ashore by boats before *Assurance* finally sank. The *Assurance,* the fourth to bear the name in Navy records, was built at the Heather Yard, Bursledon, and launched on 29 September,

HMS Pomone (Site 15) struck a rock just south of the Needles in 1811.

1747. At the court-martial, held aboard HMS *Tyger* in Portsmouth Harbour on 11 May, 1753, Captain Scrope was acquitted, but the Master David Patterson was sentenced to three months in the Marshalsea Prison in London for running the ship upon the rock. The wreck site consists of cannon and other artifacts, copper nails, sounding leads, clay pipes and some coins.

HMS *Pomone* lies in 12m. This British fifth rate of 38 guns was 150ft long and weighed 1,076 tons. She sank on 14 October, 1811, when coming through the Needles Passage in the dark and striking a rock about 400yds to the south-west of Needles Point. The ship went right over the rock and started to fill with water. The wind then pushed her on to Needle Point. Captain R. Barrie ordered the masts cut away and she stayed afloat long enough for her crew of 284 to escape without loss. Many of the guns were salvaged. As a result of this wreck, the Admiralty issued orders that Naval ships should not come through the Needles Passage at night. Some cannon and artifacts from the *Pomone* were found just south of Needle Rock by teams working on the protected wreck of HMS *Assurance*.

The remains of the 162-ton schooner *Dream* lie entangled with those of the protected wreck site of HMS *Assurance*. The *Dream* was built at Yarmouth in 1837–38 and a bell, clearly marked and dated 1838, has been recovered on the site of the protected wrecks. Presumably she too hit that rock off the Needles and sank on top of *Assurance* and *Pomone*.

It is possible that a Roman ship also hit the rock because 17 Roman coins have been found on the site underneath the other wreckage.

16 Campen Yarmouth 5 miles; Lymington 6 miles. 50 39.70N; 01 35.45W. Depth: 10m. This wreck is 30yds south of the Middle Needle, but may be dived only with the permission of the owners, the Needles Underwater Archaeology Group, and is watched over by the nearby Coastguard station.

Though not all that far from the Needles protected site (Site **15**) the *Campen* is a much earlier loss. Her story starts when a small fleet of Dutch East Indiamen sailed from Texel on 12 October, 1627. There were seven ships together – the *Prince William*, *Nassau*, *Wieringen*, *Vliegende Draeck*, *Vlielandt*, *Terschellingh* and the *Campen.* All were bound for the East Indies and they carried cargo for the settlements there – and gold and silver to buy cargo for the return voyage. This autumn fleet was soon in trouble in the Channel, fighting a south-westerly gale, which seemed to increase with every hour. Despite this, four of the ships kept together. Soon it was clear that they were losing ground to the gale and were being driven perilously close to the Needles – so close in fact that they took the amazing course of trying to "thread the Needle" and sail between the jagged peaks into the calm of the Solent.

Even in flat calm it is something that small boats do with great care. The fact that the Dutch ships tried it tells a great deal about the state they were in. The four ships were the *Vliegende Draeck*, the *Prince William*, the *Terschellingh* and the *Campen.* First to try were the *Prince William* and the *Terschellingh* and amazingly enough they went through clean as a whistle. The *Vliegende Draeck* was next and was nothing like so lucky. She struck a rock in the gap and ripped her bottom open. Even so she lurched through and foundered not far up the Solent. The *Campen* was the last to try. She too struck a shallow rock in the centre of the gap, stopped dead, swung round beam onto the wind and almost at once started to break up. There were about 160 men aboard, but they all reached the shore on makeshift rafts.

Some salvage was done on the Dutch ships almost immediately and large quantities of coin were raised – but not all of it by any means. When modern diving equipment became available practically every name in the business had a look for the *Campen,* but though we now know that many finned within a few feet of the wreck, it was left to members of the Northampton BSAC to find it by accident in June 1979. First they found piles of lead ballast ingots, then cannonballs, and then silver coins. These were either Spanish-American pieces of eight or Dutch lion

The Dutch East Indiaman Campen (Site 16) sank off the Needles in 1627.

dahlers, a rare coin minted for only a few years at the turn of the 17th century. In all the diving team recovered some 8,000 coins and many items of great interest to historians, such as lidded brass shot containers to hold a made-up charge of gunpowder and a cannonball all ready for firing – though the containers were known about, it was not thought that they were used at such an early date. All the coin now seems to have been recovered.

17 Irex Yarmouth 4½ miles; Lymington 6 miles. 50 39.55N; 01 34.95W. Depth: 6m. The *Irex,* a fully rigged iron-hulled sailing ship of 2,347 tons, was 302ft long. On 10 December, 1889 she left the Clyde on her maiden voyage to Rio de Janeiro, Brazil, with a cargo of pig iron, earthenware pipes and pots. The *Irex* was commanded by Captain Hutton, and carried a crew of 32. The voyage was plagued with bad weather, and it was not until New Year's Day, 1890, that the ship was able to stand away from the land. The south-west gales soon returned and blew for more than three weeks. On 23 January, after taking a battering that left her crew sick and exhausted, the weather cleared sufficiently to enable the position of the *Irex* to be determined as the Bay of Biscay. With many of his crew sick and injured, and the cargo unbalanced, Captain Hutton turned the ship to run before the wind back to the English coast. Hutton, like his crew, was exhausted; he had not been able to go to his bunk for 24 days.

On reaching the south coast he sailed along desperately looking for a haven from the storms. As he approached the Needles, he mistook the flashing red warning light from the lighthouse for that of a pilot boat. The *Irex* turned toward the light, and only at the last minute did Captain Hutton see his mistake. But it was much too late and his ship grounded heavily, smashing open her hull. The wreck was seen and

The Irex aground in Scratchell's Bay (Site 17).

rescue attempts started quickly. Finally, 29 men were lifted by breeches buoy to the high cliffs. The ship, however, did not move and, though a large amount of salvage work was carried out, the weather soon broke her up.

Today the rusting hull and the remains of her cargo can be found on the bottom of Scratchell's Bay. The site is 200yds off the beach, close to the west of St Anthony's Rock.

18 Varvassi Yarmouth 5 miles; Lymington 6½ miles. 50 39.67N; 01 35.52W. Depth: 10m. This Greek steamer, built in 1915 and of 3,874 tons, was bound from Bona, Algeria, for Southampton with a cargo of 7,000 tons of iron ore, 300 tons of tangerines, many large tubs of wine, and some cattle, which she took on at Algiers. After unloading part of her cargo at Southampton she was to go on to Boulogne.

At 10am on 5 January, 1947, in the middle of a bad storm, the ship entered the Needles Channel. Moments later, something went wrong and she ran aground on the Needles Bridge, 100yds from the lighthouse. A huge swell was running into her and it was clear that the *Varvassi* was in big trouble. But when the Yarmouth lifeboat arrived together with a tug its crew were surprised to be told they were not needed, so the lifeboat returned to Yarmouth Harbour. Meanwhile, a salvage officer who had boarded the ship from the tug found her hard aground and water in all her holds. He was so concerned about the safety of the crew that at 5pm he radioed for the lifeboat to return. In huge seas and with the wind rising the Yarmouth boat came back. She stood by for 4 hours before being told yet again that she was not needed. At 6.30am the next day the lifeboat was called out for the third time. This time no one sent her away and despite the fact that seas were breaking right over the steamer, the lifeboat managed to draw alongside. She had to do this time and time again as ropes broke, but in the end the crew of 35, the salvage officer and a pilot were safely taken off.

The *Varvassi* was finished. Soon her back broke and she was in two. The stern section, from some 36ft aft of the funnel, slid off the rocks and sank. The bow section remained firmly jammed, but finally could not be seen at high water. Bits of the wreck would reappear at low water, however, and over the years several small boats were lost by hitting them. Despite the damage to the *Varvassi* very early on, the cattle were all saved and so were some of the tangerines, though the wine seems to have floated ashore and been lost!

Divers will now find that some parts of the wreck still lie only a few metres below the surface. The engine, stern shaft and cast iron propeller lie alongside the rocks. The bow section has slid off the Needles Bridge into deeper water to the west of the stern. Most of the wreckage is well broken and scattered with some parts almost 100yds away from the actual site of the wrecking. The most recognisable parts are the two large boilers, which now stand on their ends, at the centre of this rummage dive. Great care must be taken to take advantage of slack water: tides are very strong.

19 Teamwork Yarmouth 5 miles; Lymington 6 miles. 50 39.68N; 01 35.57W. Depth: 4m. This British fishing vessel sank on 13 February, 1983, just 200yds from the Needles Lighthouse. The wreck is now very broken.

20 Wreck, name unknown Yarmouth 4½ miles; Lymington 6 miles. 50 39.83N; 01 35.58W. Depth: 14m. A very small obstruction was located in this position, ¼ mile

The Varvassi aground on the Needles Bridge (Site 18).

to the north-west of the Needles Lighthouse in 1965. It may be a small cabin cruiser. Diving information is needed.

21 Wreck, name unknown Yarmouth 6 miles; Lymington 7 miles. 50 38.28N; 01 34.18W. Depth: 26m. Though local fishermen have believed for many years that this is a rocky outcrop, divers have found a small steamer at this position 1½ miles south-east of the Needles. Most of the wreck is buried in the sand and mud of the sea bed. However, the bows are clear and about 2m proud. The stern is 1m clear. The highest points, at 3m, are the boiler and the small triple-expansion engine.

22 Albion II Yarmouth 8 miles; Lymington 9 miles. 50 36.62N; 01 34.73W. Depth: 30m. "Reindeer" is what local fishermen call her, but a bell recovered from this site, though badly worn, indicates that this is the *Albion II,* an Admiralty trawler of 240 tons, which was sunk by a mine off St Catherine's Point on 13 January, 1916.

The *Albion II* was one of four vessels sweeping to the south-west of the Needles when she stopped to untangle her sweep gear. As she did so, a mine caught up in the wires exploded 5ft from her port side and blew a hole in her hull. Skipper Clark Mead and his crew were all taken off by her sweeping partner *Zena Dare* before the *Albion II* sank, stern first. She was found by a salvage firm in June 1975 and was upright and complete. Much of her plating has corroded, leaving a skeleton of girders. She lies east–west, and is 160ft long. The remains stand 5m proud of the gravel and sand sea bed.

23 HMS New Dawn Yarmouth 8 miles; Lymington 9 miles. 50 36.47N; 01 36.33W. Depth: 33m. The 93-ton *New Dawn* was built of steel in 1908 as a sailing drifter, in the Glasgow yard of Mackie and Thompson. She was 86ft long with a beam of 30ft, with a small two-cylinder compound steam engine and one little boiler. She was requisitioned by the Royal Navy in January 1915, and fitted with a 3-pounder gun and two machine guns. The *New Dawn* was used as a minesweeper until she became the victim of a mine herself on 23 March, 1918, one of a field laid by the German U-boat *UC-17.*

For many years this site was believed to be that of the Norwegian steamer *Borgny* (see *Dive Dorset*), but diver Richard Rimmer positively identified the *New Dawn* when he found the brass letters of her real name from her bow. Richard Rimmer has now started his own diving business – The New Dawn Dive Centre!

Today the *New Dawn* is very broken. She lies approximately east–west along the tide on a sand and shingle sea bed. The highest point is the boiler, at 3m.

24 Azemmour Yarmouth 13 miles; Lymington 14 miles. 50 32.00N; 01 36.00W. Depth: 40m. This is only an approximate position for the 928-ton French steamer, but a search in the area should find her. The *Azemmour* was 206ft long with a beam of 33ft. She was formerly the *Wisteria* and was built of steel in 1909 by Short Brothers at Sunderland with a 3-cylinder triple-expansion steam engine and a single boiler giving 143hp.

There is no uncertainty about her loss. She was torpedoed by Kapitänleutnant Fritz Wassner from *UB-59* on the surface in the 4am dark of 20 March, 1918. It was on this patrol from 10 to 28 March that Wassner accounted for the *Tweed* (Site **234**), the *Venezuela,* and the *South Western* (Site **237**). At the time of the loss the *Azemmour* was owned by Cie Generale Transatlantique with a home port of St Nazaire. A 90mm gun was mounted on her stern. She was bound from London for Nantes with 716 tons of general cargo and sank within 4 minutes of being torpedoed. Captain Jean Guillaume and 23 of his French crew of 28 were rescued by the Admiralty yacht *Maid of Honour.*

A possible position for the *Azemmour* could be that thought to be the *Myrtle Grove (*Site **29**).

25 Eleanor Yarmouth 15 miles; Lymington 16 miles. 50 30.04N; 01 40.35W. Depth: 40m. This position was believed to be the site of one of the wrecks of the British steamer *Coquetdale* and the Dutch steamer *Ajax,* both sunk on 8 August, 1940, by German aircraft (Sites **27** and **224**). However, diving has shown that there is only one wreck here and that is of the 1,980-ton British steamer *Eleanor.*

The *Eleanor* was built in 1888 by H.S. Edwards and Sons of Newcastle who installed a 3-cylinder triple-expansion engine giving 186hp. She was 270ft long and had a beam of 36ft. She was requisitioned by the Royal Navy early in World War One to transport mines. When sunk she was on passage from Immingham, via Falmouth, to Malta with a cargo of 270 depth charges and 1,494 sea mines of various types. The *Eleanor* was torpedoed on 12 February, 1918, by the German submarine *UB-57*, which was responsible for sinking 53 ships totalling 153,150 tons before being mined on 14 August, 1918.

Second mate Barton Hunter was the only survivor of the *Eleanor.* He was asleep in his cabin when he was awoken by a huge explosion at 2.04am. The deck was a shambles with all the boats blown to pieces and the ship already going down. There was another explosion and he found himself in the sea. Something bumped against him and he grabbed one of the rafts that had been loose on deck. Despite the darkness, he was spotted by *UB-57* and felt it best to answer questions about his ship; these were shouted down to him from the conning tower. The submarine then submerged again. It was not until 6.30am that Hunter was picked up by the steamer *Carronmore* and taken to Poole by a patrol drifter. Today the *Eleanor* sits upright on shingle and is 5m proud.

WARNING A look inside the holds should be undertaken with great care – the mines, some complete with detonating horns, are still all there.

26 Wreck, name unknown Yarmouth 3 miles; Lymington 4 miles. 50 41.87N; 01 33.91W. Depth: 5m. Here is yet another Shingle Bank mystery. In 1989 a fisherman working in the North Channel above the Shingle Bank was amazed to see a weed-covered wooden hull emerging from the shingle as the tide fell. A subsequent survey of the area in 1994 confirmed that there was indeed a wreck here, and one of good size. The wreck is about 180ft long with a beam of 40ft and stands 2m proud of the sea bed. No diving information is to hand, but this should make a good shallow water dive project – if the shingle has not reclaimed her.

27 Coquetdale Yarmouth 14 miles; Lymington 15 miles. 50 28.90N; 01 38.40W. Depth: 35m. This British steamer of 1,597 tons was part of a small convoy running from St Helen's Road for Plymouth, though that was not to be her final destination. She was travelling in ballast from Portsmouth bound for the Clyde and is described as being "OHMS", which merely means that she was now under Government control, as was much of British shipping in the early stages of World War Two.

The *Coquetdale* was unfortunate in that she became involved in a new phase of the Battle of Britain on its very first day, 8 August, 1940. The Luftwaffe needed to destroy more Royal Air Force planes to put Fighter Command out of action. To draw the fighters up to them they launched major bombing attacks on convoys in the Channel using some 400 aircraft. The aircraft they used for these attacks on shipping were the slow Stuka dive bombers from Generalmajor Wolfram von Richthofen's 8th Fliegercorps stationed at Caen. These "decoy ducks" – even the Germans called them that – were meant to provide such a tempting target to the Spitfires and Hurricanes that they would be drawn into positions where clouds of escorting Messerschmitts could fall upon them. The Spitfires and Hurricanes came all right, but the result was not quite what was expected. The Stukas proved to be a costly liability and from 8 to 18 August, the last a day on which one German squadron alone lost 16 Stukas, they were so depleted that they were withdrawn from the Battle of Britain altogether. Not that the decision to do so came in time to save the convoy in which *Coquetdale* sailed – it was 15 miles west of St Catherine's Point when the Stukas fell down on them from the clear blue of the afternoon of 8 August.

The screaming sirens of the Stukas were intended to strike panic into those below, and had so unsettled troops in Poland and during the German conquest of France that the noise had almost overshadowed the real power of these dive-bombers. In the hands of skilled pilots they were a highly accurate means of pinpoint bombing. In the case of the *Coquetdale,* this was only too true. The first bomb struck her amidships and then the wing guns and those of the Stuka observer strafed her from end to end. Within moments the *Coquetdale* was sinking and the 23 men of her crew only just had time to get away in the boats before she disappeared completely from sight.

The *Coquetdale* was 245ft long with a beam of 37ft. She is upright and is 5m proud of a sea bed of large stones.

The steamer Terlings (Site 28) was sunk in 1940 with the loss of 10 of her crew.

28 Terlings Yarmouth 17 miles; Lymington 18 miles. 50 28.25N; 01 33.62W. Depth: 37m. This 2,318 ton British steamer had not long left Southampton heading, in ballast, for Sydney, Australia, when she was caught by German bombers on 21 July, 1940. She did her best with her single gun, but was hit and sank swiftly. Of her crew of 27 with one gunner, 10 were lost. The *Terlings* was 283ft long with a beam of 44ft. She now stands 8m proud of the sand and shingle sea bed. She is well broken.

29 Myrtle Grove Yarmouth 15 miles; Lymington 16 miles. 50 31.20N; 01 37.65W. Depth: 35m. This is probably the site of the 2,642-ton British steamer *Myrtle Grove.* Formerly named *Huelva*, she was built of steel by J. Readhead and Sons of South Shields in 1894 when she was fitted with a triple-expansion steam engine producing 252hp. She was 303ft long with a beam of 41ft.

On 23 November, 1917 the *Myrtle Grove* was in collision in thick fog with the Norwegian steamer *Mineral*, when 10 miles south-west of the Needles. The *Myrtle Grove* was the most damaged of the two and began to sink slowly. She was found by another Norwegian ship, the *Astrea,* which tried to tow her into Freshwater Bay, but the tow line broke. Soon afterwards she sank, stern first.

The *Myrtle Grove*'s cargo is listed as 1,187 tons of hay and six railway wagons. But though the hay is of course long gone, there is no sign of the wagons in the wreck, which is lying on her port side and 5m proud. The absence of any such rolling stock is causing divers to wonder about the identity of the wreck. Some believe that this is the site of the *Azemmour* (Site **24**). Only more diving will give a positive identification.

30 Beverley Ann Yarmouth 2 miles; Lymington 3 miles. 50 42.00N; 01 33.30W. Depth: 20m. This 32ft fishing boat sank near the north-east Shingles buoy on 19 November, 1969. The wreck is very broken and is often covered by shingle.

Divers at the slipway in Yarmouth Harbour. The Yarmouth–Lymington ferry can be seen in the background.

AREA 2:

Lymington to the Hamble; Totland to Egypt Point

This area runs from 01 33.00W to 01 18.00W and takes in most of the western Solent, Southampton Water and the River Hamble. It also includes the north-west coast of the Isle of Wight from Hatherwood Point at the south-west end of Totland Bay to Egypt Point, close to West Cowes.

As in Area 1, great care must be taken with the tides. Tidal streams in the western Solent are very strong, with the east-running flood reaching nearly 3 knots and the west-running ebb often reaching 3½ knots. In the main channels the diver coxswain will find that the streams turn at almost the same times.

Off Yarmouth Harbour the last of the flood tide eddies west towards Sconce Point where it turns out to rejoin the east-going flood. In the same area, to the north of Black Rock (which dries and lies 800yds west of Yarmouth Pier), a patch of very disturbed water can often be seen. This is known as Fiddlers' Race and it is believed to be named after a ship that was lost here with a band of musicians on board. The area should be avoided by small boats, particularly in bad weather.

Yarmouth has two high waters. After the first one, the tide falls a little for about half an hour, then rises again into the second high water. After that it ebbs to the west until low water. Slack water periods occur at about 1½ hours before and 4½ hours after high water at Portsmouth. They usually last for 15 to 30 minutes only, but are sometimes a little longer at low water slack.

There is little diving of interest from the northern side of the Solent, much of the land being marshy and the water very shallow, with poor visibility, but the Isle of Wight coast offers some more interesting sites. Indeed, in the Totland and Yarmouth area interested crowds tend to gather when divers appear. This makes a change from the mainland where the sight of divers is now so commonplace that no one gives them more than a passing glance.

Divers should note that much of this area falls under the jurisdiction of the Port of Southampton. The eastern limit of the Port is in the Solent, bounded by a line

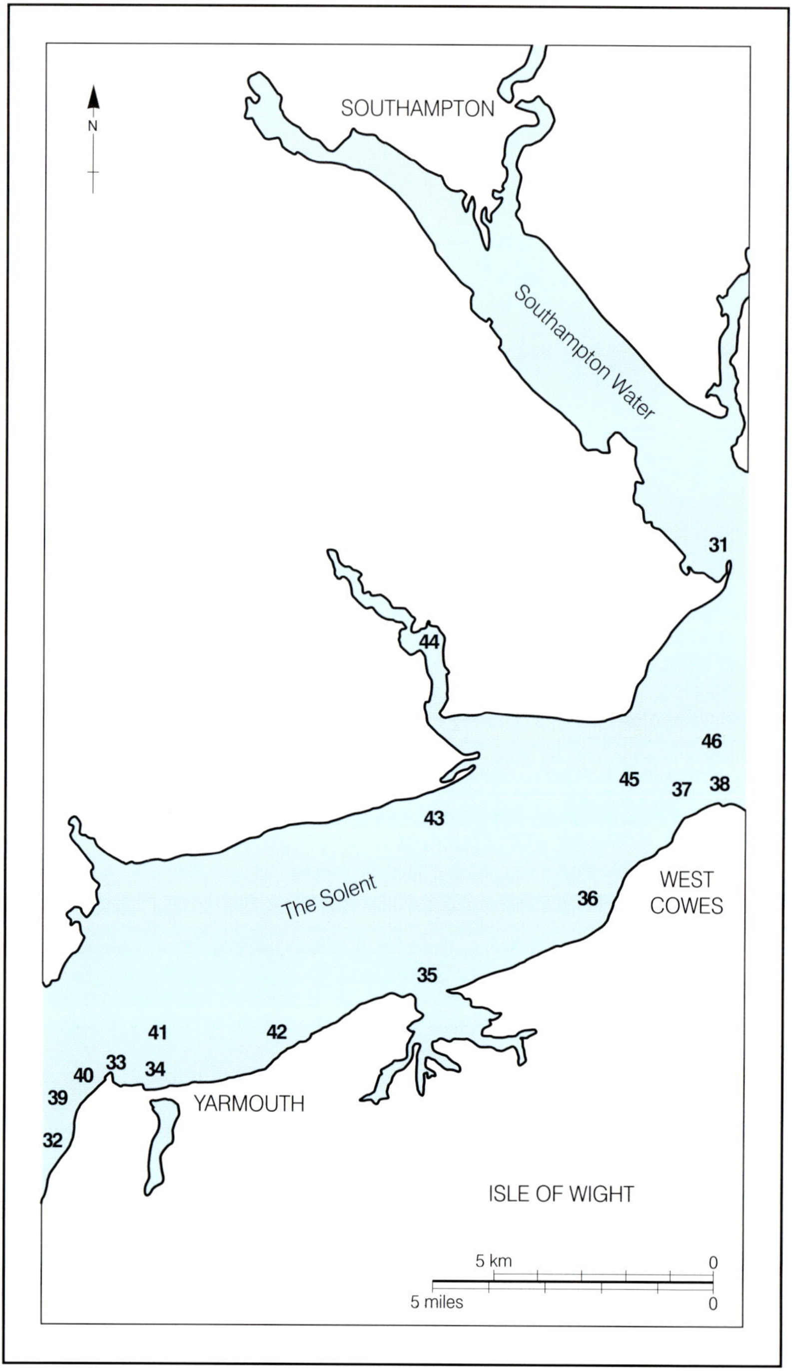
N
SOUTHAMPTON
Southampton Water
31
44
46
45
37
38
43
The Solent
36
WEST
COWES
35
41
42
33
34
40
39
32
YARMOUTH
ISLE OF WIGHT
5 km
0
5 miles
0

joining Old Castle Point, East Cowes (50 46.00N; 01 16.00W), with a point on the mainland 100yds south-east of Hill Head Beacon. To the west, the Port is bounded by a line joining Stansore Point (50 47.00N; 01 20.00W) with Egypt Point on the Isle of Wight. Those wishing to dive inside the Port of Southampton's limits must ask the harbourmaster's permission.

There is one wreck included in this section, the *Grace Dieu*, but the ship is protected under the Protection of Wrecks Act of 1973 and no diving is allowed. The designation order gives the area within which no interference must take place as anywhere within 75m of the OS grid reference SU 501 105 or the charted position 50 51.52N; 01 17.23W. Here, ¾ mile above Bursledon Bridge in the River Hamble, lie some of the timbers of Henry V's great clinker-built battleship. The *Grace Dieu* was built in 1418 and was huge for her time, being only a little smaller than Nelson's *Victory*. After being immobilised in the River Hamble, she was accidentally burnt in 1436 after being struck by lightning. Some of Southampton BSAC carried out an archaeological diving search of the stern in 1967 in appallingly muddy conditions, but found nothing except the ancient woodwork. Further archaeological surveys took place between 1980 and 1985.

Launch sites (Hampshire)

LYMINGTON This launch site is easily reached by leaving the M27 at Junction 1 and taking the A337 to Lyndhurst, Brockenhurst and then Lymington, a straight route through the New Forest. Once in Lymington, follow the signs for the Town Quay. The launch site is right beside a small car park in the centre of the town where a concrete slipway gives access at all states of the tide. There is a chain across the slip, but this is easily removeable by means of a twist shackle. There is no charge. The speed limit in the river is 6 knots.

WARNING Diver coxswains must take great care in this area. Lymington is an important yachting centre with marinas providing hundreds of berths for boats. In addition to these hazards, car and passenger ferries run from here to Yarmouth and all craft must give way to them.

The Lymington River exits through mud banks into the Solent 2½ miles north-east of Hurst Point. The whole of the river and the shipping activity around Lymington is controlled by the harbourmaster, who can be found at the Harbour Office in Bath Road, near the Royal Lymington Yacht Club. There is another slipway close to the Harbour Office, concrete on to shingle, usable except at extreme low water springs.

Opposite: Dive sites in Area 2, which includes the Hampshire coast from Lymington to the Hamble and the Isle of Wight coast from Totland to Egypt Point. This area is covered by Admiralty Charts 2045 (Outer Approaches to the Solent), 1905 (Southampton Water and Approaches), 2040 (The Solent – Western Part and Yarmouth Harbour) and 2793 (Cowes Harbour and River Medina); Ordnance Survey Landranger Map 196.

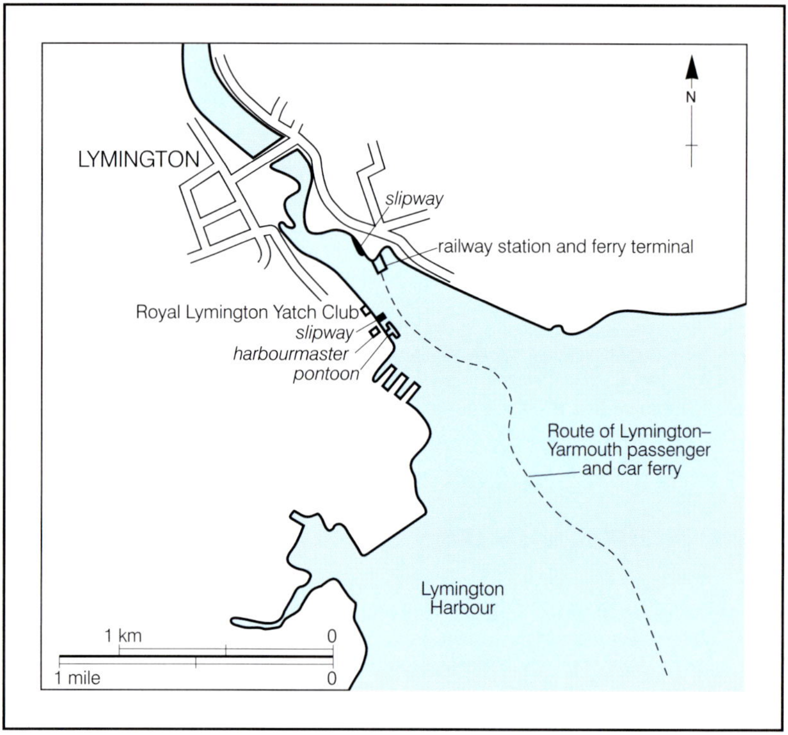

Lymington Harbour.

Parking is nearby. No anchoring is allowed within the approach channel or the harbour area.

There is no diving without the harbourmaster's permission and this will not be given except in cases of emergency. High water at Lymington is minus 55 minutes on springs and plus 5 minutes on neaps on the Portsmouth tables.

BUCKLERS HARD Bucklers Hard is unlikely to appeal to divers wishing to launch inflatables and small boats as it is some distance from the sea and a very popular yachting site. A powerboat could cost nearly £30 for a day launch and retrieve, and diving is allowed only at the harbourmaster's discretion. There is ample parking for cars and trailers nearby. The approach is by a private road off the road from Beaulieu. The Beaulieu River is under the control of Lord Montagu of Beaulieu and has a speed limit of 5 knots.

LEPE Lepe Country Park, on the road from Exbury to Calshot, has a large car park with toilets and there is a restaurant serving teas and snacks. This is an easy launch site over a low groyne, but involves a long pull over mud at low tide.

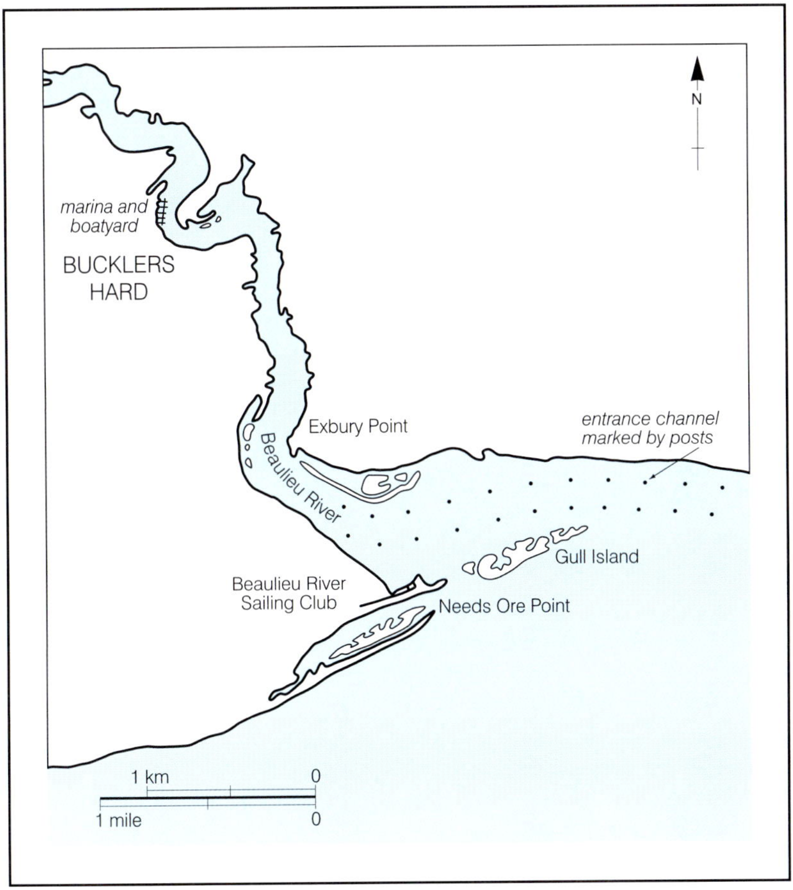

The Beaulieu River and Bucklers Hard.

CALSHOT SPIT Approach is made by the B3053; once in Calshot, follow signs for Calshot Activities Centre. Proceed along the road flanked by beach huts to the huge hangars of an old RAF flying boat base. Calshot was once the home of the RAF's High Speed Flight, which won the Schneider Trophy in 1931 and flew and developed the prototype of the Spitfire in time for the Battle of Britain.

The Calshot launching slips are magnificent – designed for flying boats, not inflatables – and are right under the eyes of the coastguard tower and Calshot Castle. An asphalt slip launches inwards towards Fawley; a concrete slip launches into Southampton Water towards Warsash. There is vast parking space at the Centre and slips can be used at all states of the tide. Toilets and showers are available, but there is a charge. Tides are strong; slack is 1 hour after high water at Portsmouth. Launching is controlled by Calshot Activities Centre.

The wide slipway at Calshot Spit, next to the coastguard tower, was designed for launching flying boats. The RIB belongs to the nearby Calshot Activities Centre.

FAWLEY Shortly after leaving the A326 for the B3053 turn left for Ashlett. In the village turn left at the hardware shop on the corner and follow signs for Ashlett Hard. The launch site, which is hard shingle, is right beside the Jolly Sailor pub. There is a launch charge for the slip, which is usable for 3 hours either side of high water. Parking is available nearby.

MARCHWOOD Turn off the A326 where signposted "Marchwood" and follow signs to a public hard at the end of Husbands Shipyard. It is very rough, with a mixture of shingle and mud, and has a tiny parking place above it. Beware of a group of rocks some 100ft from the edge of the slip. These show at low tide but catch propellers on exit at other times.

ELING WHARF After turning off the A35, follow signs for the village of Eling. The launch site is close to the Anchor Inn; it is shingle and steep, with a nasty drop at the end. There is a very muddy exit into the creek. The slip is available for 3 hours either side of high water.

SOUTHAMPTON (ST DENYS) From the city centre follow signs for St Denys Station, then for Priory Hard to the south of the railway station. The launch site is in Priory Road and there is parking nearby. Available at most states of tide, this concrete slipway is free. The launch is into River Itchen and the speed limit is 6 knots.

The public slipway at Eling Wharf in Southampton Water.

SOUTHAMPTON (WESTON) Follow signs for Weston off the A3025. Go down Weston Parade and the site is on Weston Shore. This site is available at most states of the tide; there is no charge and parking is nearby. The launch is into Southampton Water.

NETLEY Follow signs from the A3025 for Netley Abbey. The launch site is in Beach Lane, which is approached from Victoria Road. This is a concrete slipway, but it is usable for only 2 hours before and after high water. There is no charge. The slip leads to shingle.

There are many launch sites for small boats in the RIVER HAMBLE and they are well used. The sites give access first to the River Hamble, and so into Southampton Water, then from Southampton Water into the Solent.

There is a speed limit in the river of 6 knots. The river counts as a harbour and has a harbourmaster, whose office is in Shore Road, Warsash. The river is navigable at all states of the tide and high water is the same as at Portsmouth. No anchoring is allowed within the approach channel or harbour, which is just as well as the river is packed solid with moorings up to Bursledon Bridge and beyond. There are four major marinas too. No diving is allowed without the permission of the harbourmaster.

Launching sites are numerous. Listed here are just three of them, which the diver may find useful.

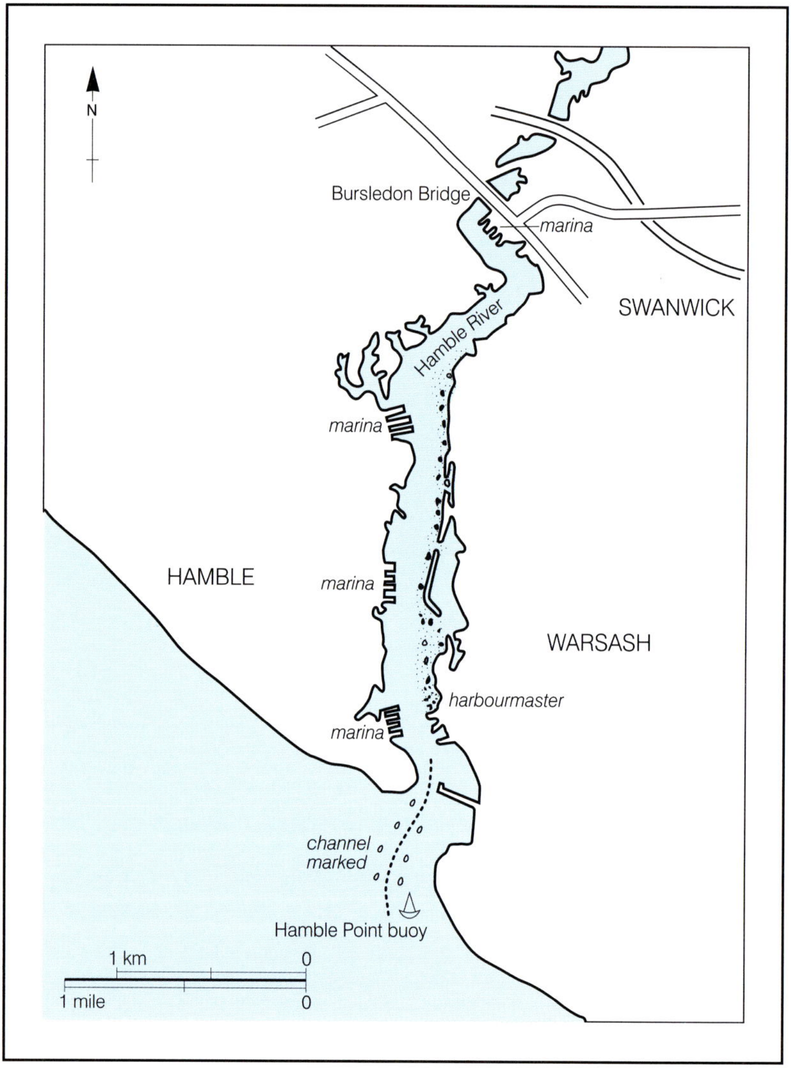

The River Hamble.

LANDS END PUBLIC HARD, BURSLEDON Turn off the A27 at Bursledon and look for Moody's Boatyard and the Jolly Sailor pub. Here the shingle foreshore is usable at all states of the tide. Park at the station ¼ mile away. There is no charge.

WARSASH PUBLIC HARD Leave the A27 and follow signs for Warsash. The shingle hard is close to the Rising Sun pub, with car parking nearby. It can be used at all states of the tide, without charge.

HAMBLE QUAY The concrete slip is close to the Bugle Inn pub at the end of the High Street and next to the Royal Southern Yacht Club. There is a car park nearby, but it fills quickly. There is no charge. The slip is usable for 4 hours either side of high water.

Launch sites (Isle of Wight)

COLWELL BAY Located at the end of Colwell Chine Road, off the A3054, a small concrete ramp leads on to a sandy beach, with good parking close by. The bay is privately owned and there is a charge.

YARMOUTH In the main harbour the former car ferry slip is now a public slipway and ideal for vehicle launching of boats. The slip is free and usable in most states of the tide. Access to the slip is through the harbour using the same route as car ferry traffic. Ferry staff will direct you. There is no parking in the harbour, but there is a large car park close by.

EGYPT POINT There is a small concrete slip at the junction of Egypt Hill and the Esplanade. It is usable for 3 hours either side of high water. Vehicle launch is possible and there is parking on the road next to the slip. There is no charge.

Shore diving sites (Hampshire)

There are not many shore dives on the Hampshire shore in this section; the best is at Calshot Castle.

31 Calshot Castle Diving here is from the Calshot Activities Centre. This area falls well inside the eastern limit of the Port of Southampton (as described in the introduction to this section) and all diving must be notified and permission obtained. Even so, any shore diving here must have boat cover, unless the divers are roped. The visibility is usually poor and the area is used by local clubs for novice training. Depths close offshore are down to 12m. However, close in to the east of the Castle is "The Hole", where the water is from 5 to 18m deep and there are said to be large conger eels. Tides are strong and eddies make the search for slack difficult. Official slack is 1 hour after high water at Portsmouth or 1½ hours after high water at Southampton.

A flying boat was found by the Southampton Harbour Board at this site, 700ft to the north of Calshot Light buoy, during a survey of the area in 1971. The aeroplane was dived by members of the Navy, who reported it to be upside down and almost buried in the mud. It appeared nearly intact apart from the tail section, which was missing altogether. Latest reports suggest that it is now very broken. 50 49.27N; 01 18.40W. Depth: 10m.

Calshot Castle stands at the mouth of Southampton Water.

Shore diving sites (Isle of Wight)

32 Totland Bay Totland bay lies between Hatherwood Point and Warden Point and is 1½ miles long. A pier, with a depth of 2m at full low, sticks out from the coast about 600yds south of Warden Point. It is the pier that seems to act as the centre of diving activity here and this is a favourite dive site for local divers. Parking at Totland is not usually a problem, but a charge is made in the summer months. Entry to the water is easy from the beach. At the time of writing the pier is closed beyond the café. Renovation work is being carried out by the new owner and when completed there should again be access to the end of the pier.

The sea bed is mainly sandy and flat with a maximum depth of 7m at high water. Just to the south of the head of the pier is an area where some fine old bottles have been found. This may well have been a dumping area, for the dates of the bottles vary too much for any one shipwreck. TINKER SHOAL, a rocky ledge with a depth to the top of about 2m, runs out some 800yds to the west of the pier. There is little marine life, but visibility in the area can be very good.

33 Fort Victoria Pier Fort Victoria lies ¾ mile to the west of Yarmouth and is one of many forts built during the 19th century to protect the Solent waters from French attacks. The pier is small and juts out into the Solent so that troops and their stores could be landed. Today it is in a poor state of repair. There is no direct access onto the pier, but the area directly below it makes a popular and interesting shore dive.

Above: The pier at Totland Bay, with the wooden slipway in the foreground.

Right: These bottles, jars and pots were found under the pier.

There is ample car parking at the fort and it is a short walk to the shingle beach. Access is simple and the site is well protected, except for winds from the north. Once in the water divers can follow the metal legs of the pier to its end. There is plenty of wreckage from the pier underwater, but there are also many small treasures – old bottles, stone jars and clay pipes are frequently found. Depths off the end of the pier quickly reach 10m and more. Within the fort there are other attractions for divers. A sunken history exhibition shows items recovered from many local shipwrecks, including the 16th-century wreck of the *Santa Lucia* (Site **41**). There is an aquarium with a conger eel pool, a planetarium and a café.

WARNING Tidal streams run hard here. The best diving is around 2 hours before high water on neaps.

34 Yarmouth This is a popular harbour, with a pier at its entrance. The pier, about 200yds long, has a depth of 3m at its head at low tide and is used by Solent cruise boats and anglers. There is some shore diving, but note that divers need

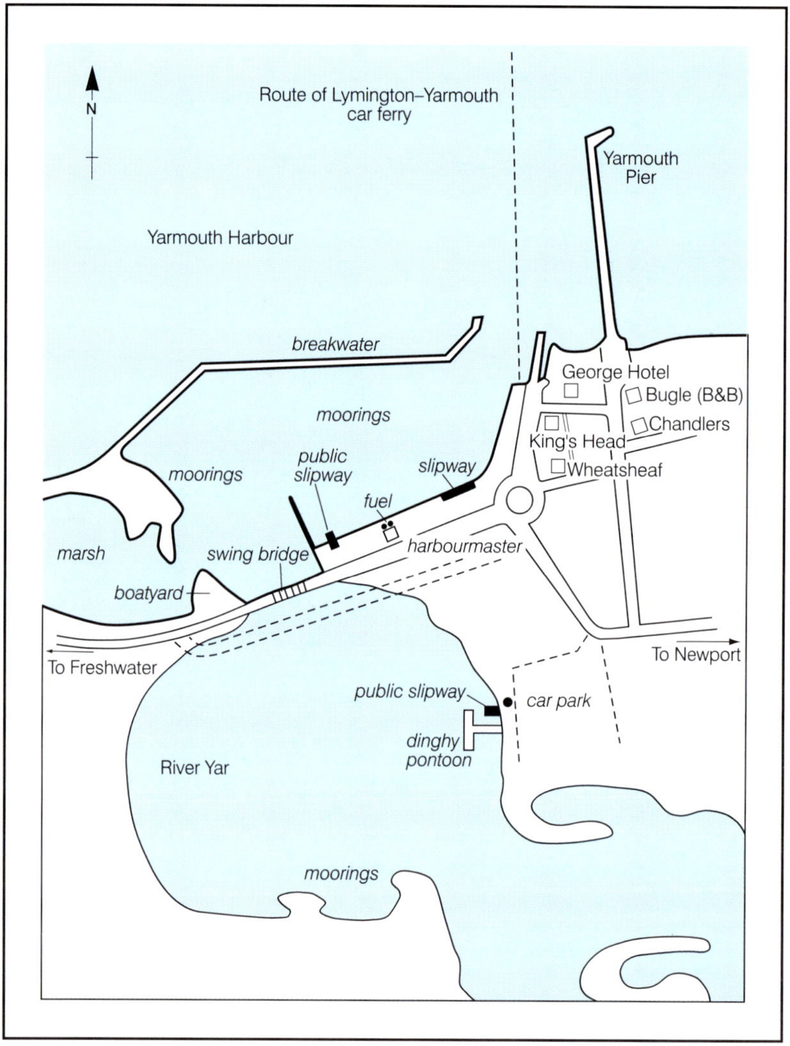

Yarmouth Harbour.

permission from the harbourmaster to dive here; the office is on New Quay. High water in the harbour is at minus 1 hour on springs and plus 5 minutes on neaps on the Portsmouth tables. Anchoring in the approach or harbour is not allowed. The sea bed is mostly mud with a covering of sand and shingle. Maximum depth is about 8m at high tide.

WARNING Strong tides run through the area and the large car ferries from Lymington pass very close to the pier every 30 minutes.

35 Newtown This small village is halfway between Yarmouth and Cowes on the north-western shore of the island and the area is dominated by the estuary of the Newtown River with 14 miles of narrow creeks and marshland. The estuary and the adjacent 4 miles of the Solent shore are owned by the National Trust and form an 800-acre nature reserve. Newtown, a thriving port in the 17th century, was once the capital of the Isle of Wight. It is now a favourite yachting site during the season.

The lakes formed by the NEWTOWN RIVER are shallow and muddy, but can be dived if permission is granted by the harbourmaster. Landing at Fishhouse Point at the entrance to the estuary is banned during the nesting season for seabirds, from April to June. On the Solent shore only shallow dives are possible. To the west of the harbour entrance the beach is shingle and runs steeply to the sea bed. To the east the beach is mainly sand and the sea bed is generally flat.

The main problem here for divers is access. There are no roads around the fingers of the estuary or to the shore, so diving means a long walk along pathways.

36 Thorness Bay Access to the beach at Thorness Bay is possible only through the Haven Holiday Centre. A road runs through the Centre to the mainly sandy beach. Permission to use it should be obtained from the Centre office. Diving is shallow, but can be interesting around the various rocky outcrops.

37 Egypt Point This is the most northerly point of the Isle of Wight. It is midway between the harbour at Cowes and the village of Gurnard. Access to the water here is easy, with plenty of car parking spaces on the main road that runs along the top of the beach. It is possible to walk from the car down the fairly steep shingle beach and straight into the water. Once in the sea, the steady downward slope continues with the shingle giving way to an area of weed at 8 to 10m. Within this weedy area is a small bank running parallel to the shore.

38 Junkers Ju 88 On the bank in the area of weed at Egypt Point are the remains of a German bomber shot down after bombing Portsmouth during World War Two. Pieces of aluminium sticking out of the weed give away the crash site at 50 00.20N; 01 18.70W. One engine was recovered some years ago, but the other engine has yet to be found; weed hides many parts of the aeroplane (which might be a Heinkel He 111 rather than a Junkers). Some of the items that have been found – a machine gun and one of the propeller blades – and a local artist's picture of the crash are in the possession of the previous owner of the nearby New Holmwood Hotel.

WARNING Although it is very close inshore here, the tide runs hard and it is easy to underestimate its effect. Slack water in the area is 1½ hours before and 4 hours after high water at Portsmouth and the longer slack is on the low water period.

A bronze cannon and other items from the Santa Lucia (Site 41) are on display at the Shipwreck Museum at Fort Victoria.

Boat diving sites (Isle of Wight)

39 Toccatina Yarmouth 2 miles; Lymington 3 miles. 50 42.20N; 01 33.00W. Depth: 5m. This British yacht was sunk on 10 August, 1977 just off Hurst Point, western Solent. The *Toccatina* is now very broken.

40 Jo-Anne Yarmouth ¾ mile; Lymington 2½ miles. 50 42.50N; 01 31.00W. Depth: 9m. The *Jo-Anne*, a 26 ft fishing boat, sank off Fort Victoria, Yarmouth, on 16 July, 1976, following a collision with a buoy. Although the *Jo-Anne* capsized, all the crew were saved. The wreck is now well broken and spread.

41 Santa Lucia Yarmouth ½ mile; Lymington 3 miles. 50 42.52N; 01 29.59W. Depth: 7m. This is another historic and protected wreck. It was known for years as the Yarmouth Roads Wreck, but is now believed to be the 600-ton 100ft Spanish carrack *Santa Lucia,* wrecked in 1567 while carrying wool to Flanders. A bronze saker gun made in Venice has been found, as well as pewter, pottery and ship's timbers; the recovered items can be seen at the Shipwreck Museum at Fort Victoria. Diving is banned within 50m of the above position, unless carried out under the guidance of archaeologists.

42 Margaret Smith Yarmouth 1 mile; Lymington 3 miles. 50 42.90N; 01 28.13W. Depth: 16m. The *Margaret Smith* is a modern wreck, a 300-ton gravel dredger, 141ft long with a beam of 21ft, built by J. Harker of Knottingley in 1943 for the Ministry of War Transport. At launch called *Empire Reaper*, the ship was renamed the *Margaret Smith* in 1972.

On 28 June, 1978, *Margaret Smith* was approaching Cowes Harbour when a series of big seas made her roll hard several times. This caused the cargo of gravel to shift – the dredger listed heavily to starboard and was soon out of control. An emergency call was sent out, and within a few minutes a rescue helicopter was on the scene. A crewman was lowered onto the tilting ship and told the crew to put on their lifejackets and to board the life raft. Just as the last man entered the raft *Margaret Smith* started to roll over. The helicopter crewman ran across the side of the ship to pull the life raft clear and later all the crew were safely winched up into the helicopter. The *Margaret Smith,* completely upside down but still floating, started to drift on the ebb tide down the western Solent. The local tug *Calshot* was able to secure a line and towed the ship to just outside Yarmouth, where she was secured to one of the Admiralty moorings. Shortly afterwards she sank.

Today the wreck is intact, and lies on her starboard side with the bows to the west. The port side is only 8m below the surface and there are even a few portholes still there, but they are well fixed. The hold is now empty and only a few small piles of gravel remain. The small box wheelhouse retains its radar scanner; behind the wheelhouse the door to the engine room hangs open, a home for conger eels. The 5ft diameter bronze propeller was in place for many years.

The site is fairly well protected from the prevailing winds and is a satisfying dive when the weather elsewhere is not so good. Beware strong tidal streams.

The dredger Margaret Smith, which sank just outside Yarmouth in 1978, is pictured here under way in the Solent.

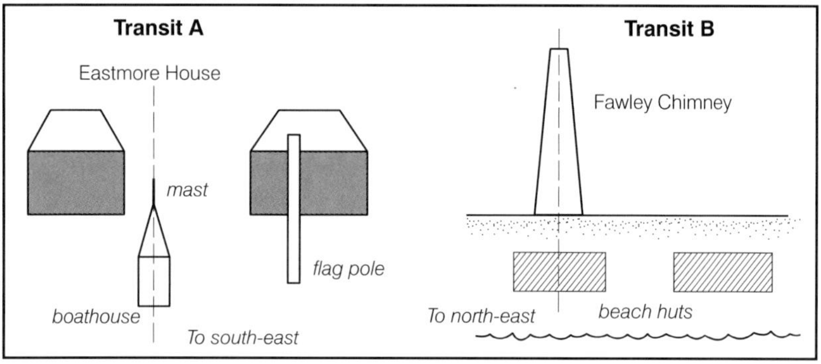

Transit marks for the Margaret Smith (Site 42).

43 Landing Craft Yarmouth 4 miles; Lymington 3½ miles. 50 45.77N; 01 25.80W. Depth: 5m. This wreck is a small landing craft upside down in shallow water approximately 1½ miles west of Needs Ore Point, near the Beaulieu River. It was found by Isle of Wight diver Dougie Saunders when helping a local fisherman to recover some fishing gear. He reports that the boat is upside down in the mud. The fishing nets were caught around the drive shafts and propellers; the bottom was wooden and fairly rotten. The wreck is very broken.

44 Minca Yarmouth 7½ miles; Lymington 7 miles. 50 48.27N; 01 25.05W. Depth: 2m. Known as the old Minca barge, this boat, which had metal fittings, was abandoned by the Army after World War Two when it broke free from its moorings and stranded up river. Reaching the boat involves not so much a dive as a mud bath.

45 Propeller Yarmouth 6 miles; Lymington 6 miles. 50 45.52N; 01 20.64W. Depth: 21m. A reported obstruction here turned out to be a ship's propeller when the site was checked by naval divers. The propeller had a diameter of 1.5m but there was no sign of any other wreckage in the area. The divers apparently failed to note whether the propeller was iron or bronze. It might be worth a dive to find out.

46 Algerian Yarmouth 7 miles; Lymington 7 miles. 50 46.00N; 00 01.32W. Depth: 24m. The *Algerian*, originally called the *Flintshire*, was built of steel by the Sunderland Steamboat Company in 1896. She was 364ft long with a beam of 45ft and was owned by the Ellerman Line. The ship had a three-cylinder triple expansion steam engine with two boilers, which gave a top speed of 10 knots. The *Algerian* was going at this speed, on her way from Cowes in ballast for Avonmouth on 12 January, 1916 when disaster struck. At 8.30am there was a mighty explosion as the 3,837-ton British steamer struck one of the mines that *UC-5* had laid the night before. The bang blew the hatch covers off the second hold and opened up a great hole in the steamer's starboard side. So bad was the damage that when Captain John Ring looked into the hold and saw the water streaming in, he thought the ship was holed on the port side too. Ring ordered his crew of 53 into the boats, but the

The Algerian struck a mine and sank off Egypt Point in 1916 (Site 46).

Algerian did not sink as quickly as he had expected. The captain's earlier distress signals were answered three Admiralty armed drifters and the Trinity House steamer *Warden*, which took his ship in tow. But at 2.30pm the bulkheads gave way and the steamer sank in the middle of the deep water channel, 1 mile west of Egypt Point. The high parts of the wreck were dispersed by explosives in 1920 and again in 1925. Despite this, the wreck still stands some 6m proud in places, but much of the plating is now flat on the sea bed. The strong tides have created a 1m scour around her. The wreckage lies north-east to south-west.

WARNING Great care is needed diving around the *Algerian* because of the strong tides and heavy shipping in this area.

Salvage diving off Cowes (date unknown).

AREA 3:

Warsash to Stokes Bay; Cowes to Ryde

The third area runs from 01 18.00W to 01 10.00W and covers a large section of the eastern Solent, which is one of the busiest waterways in the world, so great care must be taken if diving here. Much diving comes under the jurisdiction of the dockyard Port of Portsmouth, whose western limit begins where the eastern limit of the Port of Southampton ends (the limit runs in a straight line from Old Castle Point, East Cowes, to a point on the mainland 100yds south-east of Hill Head Beacon).

Once again, this is an area dominated by the tides. In the central and eastern Solent the streams are very strong. In Cowes Roads, for example, they reach 3 to 4 knots. In Cowes Harbour and the River Medina the tide floods for 6½ hours and ebbs for almost 5 hours. The ebb is particularly strong in the narrows where a floating bridge operates between East and West Cowes. Here it reaches 5 to 6 knots and many small craft are unable to enter the river until the stream has slackened. The run is strongest on the eastern side. On spring tides, after the first high water the tide falls a little and then a second high water occurs about an hour later. After this the tide ebbs away to the west until low water. On neap tides only one high water occurs. Slack water comes around 1½ hours before high water and 4 to 5 hours after high water at Portsmouth, and lasts between 15 and 30 minutes.

In the area of the Calshot Light buoy the tidal streams tend to be rotary. The last 2 hours of the ebb stream divide here and run east and west past the Bramble Bank. John Coote draws particular attention to the dangers of the Bramble Bank and advises: "Whether coming from east or west remember the Bramble Bank, situated in mid-Solent. In spite of being such a well-known danger, yachts still go aground on this shingle shoal, which may vary from year to year in depth and position. At lowest springs it used to be the scene of an annual cricket match organised by Uffa Fox." (K. Adlard Coles and J.O. Coote, *The Shell Pilot to the South Coast Harbours*, 6th edition, Faber, 1982, page 103.) There is at least one wreck on the edge of the Bank today – see Site **50**.

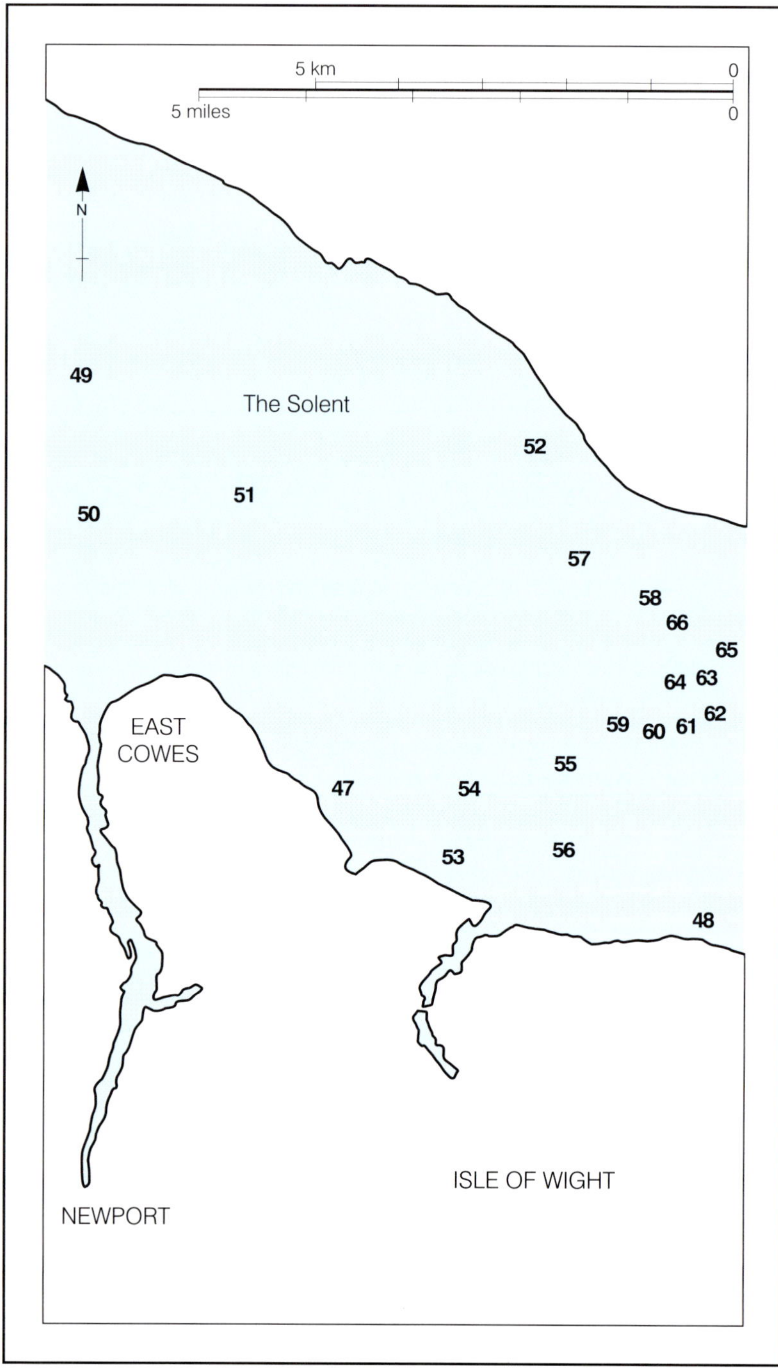
5 km
0
5 miles
0
N
The Solent
49
50
51
52
57
58
66
65
64
63
62
59
60
61
55
EAST
COWES
47
54
53
56
48
ISLE OF WIGHT
NEWPORT

All the tides in Southampton Water are tricky. On springs there are two high waters. The young flood rises for about 2 hours after low water. After that it becomes fairly slack rising only slowly for another 2 hours. Then the main flood sets in for almost 3 hours until high water is reached. After this the tide level drops a few inches for about an hour and then rises again for about 1¼ hours until a second high is reached. The second high is about the same height as the first. This long stand of high water was one of the reasons that Southampton became a major port as it allows deep-draught ships to manoeuvre for long periods. On neaps the high water stays for a long time with no appreciable drop in level. In fact, within Southampton Water there is little drop in level as long as the west-flowing stream is running through the Solent, but when the Solent stream turns to the east the water rushes out at high speed for about 3¼ hours. The most rapid fall is during the 2 hours after the second high water on springs. Within Southampton Water slack water occurs at approximately high water and there is little movement for up to 2 hours. A much shorter slack occurs at about 5 hours after high water at Portsmouth.

In the eastern part of the area – between East Cowes and Ryde on the Isle of Wight, and between Hill Head and Stokes Bay on the Hampshire coast – the streams follow the direction of the Solent. Their strength varies considerably, with up to 2 knots on the east-flowing and 2½ knots on the west-flowing run. The farther east one goes the slacker the streams get. Slack water is about 2 hours before and 4 hours after high water at Portsmouth, and lasts 15 to 30 minutes.

WARNING As a result of a number of incidents during which small boats hampered the movement of large ships in the main channel near Calshot Spit, the Southampton harbourmaster issued the following notice to mariners. Dive boat skippers should take careful note:

> Yatchsmen, mariners and owner/skippers of small recreational craft are advised of a new requirement when navigating in the vicinity of the main navigable channel in the Calshot Spit area.
>
> In view of the increasing movement of large deep-draught commercial vessels, which are severely restricted in their ability to manoeuvre while rounding the Calshot Turn, and the difficulties experienced with yachts and other small craft passing through the main channel, it has been found necessary to introduce a restriction in the following area – "That part of the main navigable channel defined on Admiralty charts Nos. 1905, 394 and 2040, which lies between a line drawn from Bourne Gap buoy to North Thorn buoy, and a line drawn from Castle Point buoy to the Reach buoy".
>
> The transit and movement of yachts and all small craft through this area is NOT PERMITTED AT ANY TIME. Failure to comply with this direction may lead to prosecution.

Opposite: Dive sites in Area 3, which includes the Hampshire coast from Warsash to Stokes Bay and the Isle of Wight coast from Cowes to Ryde. This area is covered by Admiralty Charts 2045 (Outer Approaches to the Solent), 394 (The Solent – Eastern Part) and 2793 (Cowes Harbour and River Medina); Ordnance Survey Landranger Map 196.

Launch sites (Hampshire)

LEE-ON-THE-SOLENT Take the B3385 to the seafront. A concrete slipway is usable for 4 hours either side of high water. There is no charge and parking is available close by.

STOKES BAY Take the B3333 and turn off to the seafront. Three concrete slipways are accessible at various points, which can be used for 4 hours each side of high water. Alternatively, a launch over shingle is possible at all times. There is no charge and parking is available nearby.

Note that there is speed limit of 10 knots within ½ mile of the shore.

Launch sites (Isle of Wight)

COWES Famous as the leading yacht racing centre of the world, this role being particularly manifest during Cowes Week, Cowes houses the headquarters of the Royal Yacht Squadron. It possesses the most convenvenient harbour of the Solent and is protected, except for winds from the north and north-east. The harbourmaster's office is on the Town Quay. There is a speed limit of 6 knots in the harbour and the River Medina, and no anchoring in the approach channel or

The public slipway at West Cowes is on the Esplanade next to the Customs House.

the harbour. There is no diving in the harbour without the harbourmaster's permission.

WARNING Diver coxswains should take great care when in this area – car ferries, passenger ferries and hydrofoils can make navigation difficult, even more so when yachts are racing. High water in the harbour is minus 15 minutes on springs and plus 15 minutes on neaps relative to the Portsmouth tables.

WEST COWES ESPLANADE There is a small concrete slipway at the far end of the Esplanade next to the Customs House. It is usable for 3 hours either side of high water. There is no charge and parking is available on the Esplanade.

RYDE There is a slipway into Ryde Harbour Marina that is usable for 2 hours either side of high water. There is no charge and there is ample parking close by. The harbour dries out, but is usable for 3 hours either side of high water. There are pontoon moorings available for visiting boats. Contact the Harbourmaster's Office, Ryde Harbour, Esplanade.

Shore diving (Hampshire)

There is little shore diving of any value on this section of the Hampshire coast, but some divers go off the shore in search of flatfish.

Ryde Harbour.

Shore diving sites (Isle of Wight)

47 Osborne Bay This bay offers some very shallow diving from the shore, but conditions are generally murky. Shore divers should be careful to keep close to the coast as the tide away from the shore is very fierce.

48 Ryde Few places can have had so many piers as the Isle of Wight. In the Victorian heyday of the pier, the island boasted no fewer than nine – one for every 6½ miles of coastline. Today only four of those piers remain. Ryde Pier is the largest and is the second longest in Great Britain, reaching out to sea for almost ½ mile. It carries trains and vehicles to the pier head, where high-speed catamarans from Portsmouth load and unload up to 450 passengers at a time. The pier is the base of the Ryde Pilot Station and the home of the Nab pilots, who are frequently seen

Cowes Harbour.

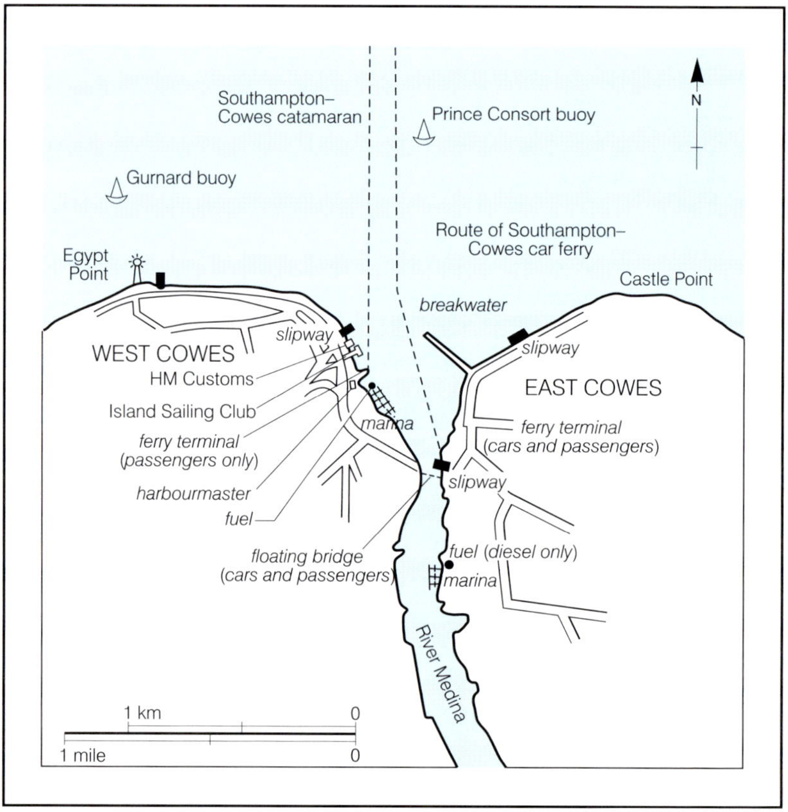

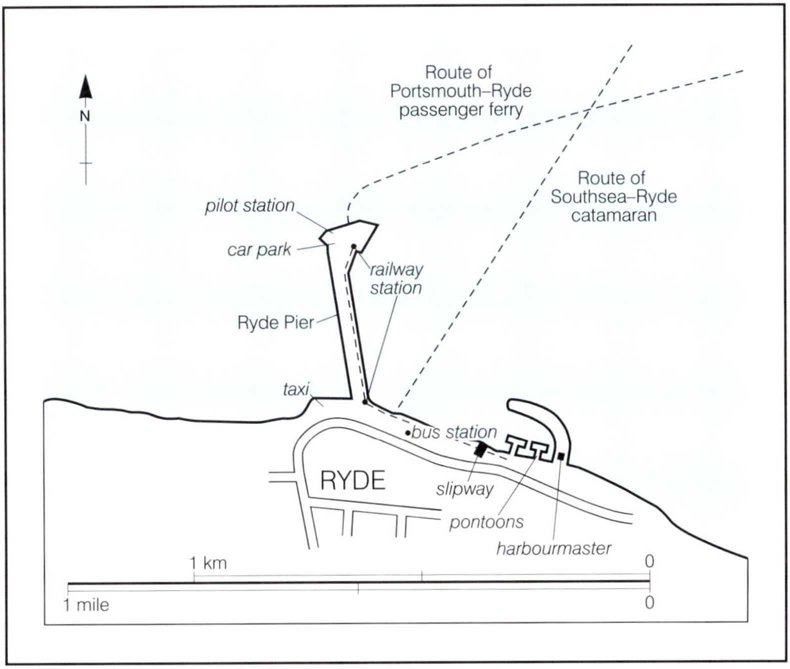

Above: Ryde Harbour.
Below: The long pier at Ryde.

being ferried out towards the Nab Tower to board inbound ships. During the summer months the pier is also busy with Solent cruise boats.

The pier had to be long to reach the deep water at the edge of the wide expanse of Ryde Sands. The diving straight off the beach is not very exciting, though it is a little more rewarding from the pier at low water. The business end of the pier is a different matter. The pier head covers a very large area and interesting diving can be had in and around the pier supports. The depth is 10m at high water. The sea bed is a mix of sand, mud and many years' worth of interesting items that have fallen from the pockets of those above or – in the case of the engagement rings – perhaps thrown in by disappointed or betrayed maidens. Entry and exit points here are few and not always available. Ask for permission to use them before diving.

Boat diving sites

49 Luciston Bembridge 10½ miles; Portsmouth 8 miles. 50 47.95N; 01 18.05W. Depth: 18m. Oberleutnant E. Steindorff's log shows that on his mission from Zeebrugge in *UB-74* on 24 December, 1917, he was near the Owers Lightship on his way west. Hull down in the dark, he spotted the 2,877-ton British steamer *Luciston.* He fired one torpedo, which hit the steamer on the port side. Despite this the *Luciston* struggled on, making for Southampton, but finally had to be beached near the entrance to Southampton Water, 1¼ miles from Calshot Point.

The slipway at Wootton Creek.

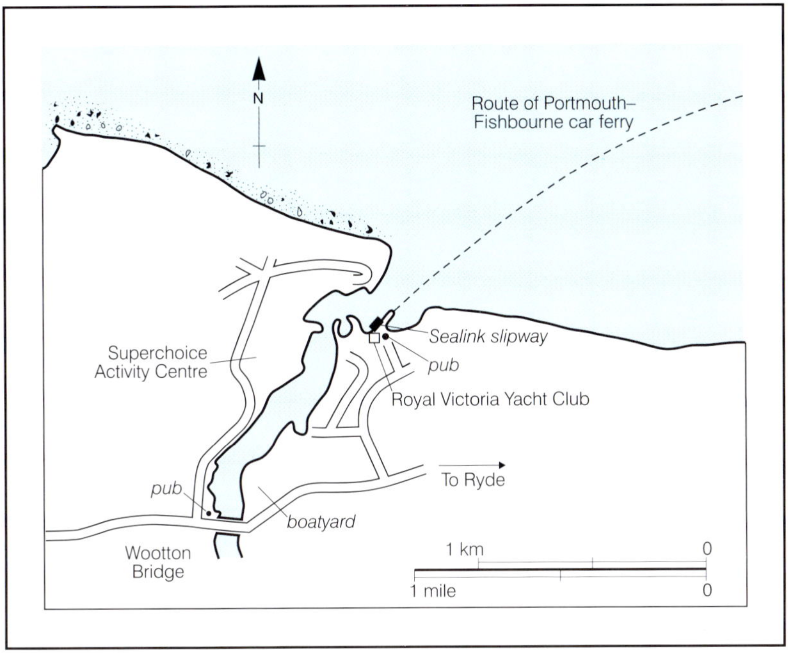

Fishbourne and Wootton.

There the *Luciston* stuck fast, despite all attempts at repairs. In 1922 a portion from the stern to the boiler room was blown away, but the rest of the wreckage remained, with 10m of water over her bow and 18m over her stern at low tide. Dispersal attempts went on for years, with the last recorded in 1963. As a result the wreck is well broken and lies on the side of a bank. This is a favourite angling site and abandoned anchors are plentiful!

Oberleutnant Steindorff lasted until 26 May, 1918, when he was caught off Portland Bill in the *UB-74.* There were no survivors from the U-boat when she was attacked by the anti-submarine yacht *Lorna.* After two depth charges were dropped, four objects bobbed up in the foam. Another depth charge went down and the explosion blew four German sailors into the air. That explosion killed three of them; only one was still able to cry "Kamerad" when picked up by the shocked crew of the *Lorna,* but he died from his injuries within 3 hours.

50 Chain Ferry Yarmouth 9½ miles; Lymington 9½ miles. 50 47.75N; 01 17.50W. Depth: 10m. An old chain ferry that used to operate on the River Medina between East and West Cowes sank in this position while being towed from Cowes to Southampton on 3 February, 1976. The position is close to the Bramble Bank about ½ mile south of the Calshot Light buoy. The wreck is very broken and muddy.

51 Florence Vivian Bembridge 10 miles; Portsmouth 7 miles. 50 47.63N; 01 16.27W. Depth: 3m. There is very little left to see of this fishing vessel, which sank in October 1923 on the East Knoll. Divers have been able to find only small pieces of wreckage.

52 The Bumps Bembridge 8 miles; Portsmouth 5 miles. 50 47.67N; 01 12.50W. Depth: 1–3m. This area is charted as foul ground, but apart from the very bumpy sea bed there seems no reason to give it this description and divers have found it a good area for big flatfish.

53 Peel Wreck Bembridge 6 miles; Portsmouth 5 miles. 50 44.87N; 01 13.37W. Depth: 5m. This Peel Wreck, also known as the Peel Bank Wreck, is 1 mile to the north-west of Wootton Creek. It was once described as a cube of concrete, but diving has shown that it is really a steel pontoon encrusted with barnacles, which give it the appearance of concrete, and that the wreck is much larger than originally reported. Its length is now given as 50 to 60ft and the beam as 15 to 20ft, the whole thing standing some 3m off the sea bed.

It is likely that the wreck is a section of Mulberry Harbour. Many units of the Harbour were anchored in this area prior to being towed across the Channel to France during the Normandy landings in June 1944. At low water there is not much cover over the site and on calm days the tide can be seen bubbling around it. The sea bed is mainly mud and shingle. The site is marked by a large red buoy marked "PEEL WRECK", which is to the north-east of the site.

54 Wreck, name unknown Bembridge 6½ miles; Portsmouth 4½ miles. 50 45.37N; 01 12.72W. Depth: 4m. This is a very small obstruction lying on the edge of a mud bank ½ mile to the east of the Peel Wreck buoy. It stands about 1.5m high and there is a scour around it of less than half a metre. It may be a small boat of some kind. There is no other information about the wreck, but it is in very shallow water and it would be a fairly simple snorkel dive to investigate further.

55 Unifloats Bembridge 6 miles; Portsmouth 4 miles. 50 45.55N; 01 12.02W and 50 45.53N; 01 11.77W. Depth: 18m. These unifloats are marked on Admiralty charts as separate obstructions alongside one another. The obstruction to the west is the larger section. It is approximately 100ft by 30ft and lies in a north–south direction. This unifloat, the remains of several unifloat pontoons, is mainly steel plates and ribs sticking out of the muddy bottom, and has a maximum height of 2m. Around the site are many bits of rope, wire, plates and bottles.

The second unifloat is a smaller section to the east. It lies north–south and is made up of five unifloat-type pontoons. The length is 65ft in all, with a beam of 30ft. The pontoons stand 3m high and were part of the Mulberry Harbour D-Day operations.

The whole site lies on the side of a mud bank on the southern edge of the shipping channel and is 1½ miles north of the entrance to Wootton Creek. The area is well protected from south-westerly winds and makes a good dive when the weather is bad.

56 Ibis Bembridge 6 miles; Portsmouth 6 miles. 50 45.75N; 01 11.60W. Depth: 16m. The *Ibis*, a British fishing vessel, was 26ft long and sank on 25 April, 1984.

A Mk IV tank landing craft of the same type as the one that sank off Stokes Bay in 1947 (Site 58).

The position given is that of her sinking, but local experts believe that the wreck may have moved a little with the tides from that point. Diving information is required.

57 RTC No. 9 Bembridge 5½ miles; Portsmouth 3 miles. 50 46.62N; 01 10.90W (bow); 50 46.60N; 01 10.65W (stern). Depth: 16m. *RTC No. 9* was an old steam-powered steel hopper barge, at one time owned by the River Tyne Commisioners. On 3 August, 1893, the *RTC No. 9* was in collision with HMS *Endymion*, ½ mile off Stokes Bay beach. The 317-ton barge was cut in two and sank. She measured 102ft by 28ft by 12ft.

The two sections of barge sank about 100yds apart. The larger section is the bow, about 65ft long; it lies in an east–west direction, standing almost 4m high. Most of the wooden decking is missing and the hold is well silted. The stern section is around 30ft long and stands 3m high. Within the wreckage can be seen the remains of a small steam engine; there is a deep scour around this section of some 2 to 3m, in the sea bed of mud and sand. The wreck was identified in 1972 when a diver recovered a bell, which had the inscription "SCREW HOPPER NO. 9".

For many years this wreck was known as the Weston Maid. The site is marked by a green wreck buoy.

58 Tank Landing Craft 1068 Bembridge 6 miles; Portsmouth 3 miles. 50 46.72N; 01 10.52W. Depth: 10m. This Mk IV tank landing craft was badly damaged by gunfire during ship target trials on 4 June, 1947. Two days later, while being towed across Stokes Bay by a salvage vessel, she sank just ½ mile off Stokes Bay Beach. All Mk IV landing craft were of 586 tons and measured 187ft by 39ft, with a draught of 5ft. They were powered by twin Davy Paxman diesels and fitted with two 20mm guns.

This wreck is broken into three parts on the sandy mud and shingle sea bed and lies in a north–west and south–east direction. The highest point of the wreckage is 3m proud, but much of it is buried. The parts that show are covered with dead men's fingers and anemones, and there appears to be a resident shoal of eelpout. This is a simple dive with an inflatable launch from one of the Stokes Bay slipways. Make sure of diving on slack – about 2 hours before high water at Portsmouth or 4 hours after.

59 Wreck, name unknown Bembridge 7 miles; Portsmouth 5 miles. 50 46.18N; 01 16.18W. Depth: 24m. This wreck was located during a survey in 1990 and is believed to be the remains of a small boat. She is fairly small, about 20ft long, and stands 1.2m proud of a mud and shingle sea bed. She lies north-west to south-east. Diving information is needed.

60 Steel Cylinder Bembridge 7 miles; Portsmouth 5 miles. 50 46.01N; 01 13.57W. Depth: 14m. First dived in 1997, this obstruction turned out to be a mysterious steel cylinder about 14ft long with a diameter of nearly 7ft. There is no obvious opening to the interior of the cylinder, which has slightly domed ends. The wreckage lies east–west on the mud and shingle sea bed.

61 Wreck, name unknown Bembridge 6 miles; Portsmouth 4 miles. 50 45.95N; 01 12.43W. Depth: 10m. A 1995 survey shows a wreck here. However, the site has not yet been dived and all indications are that the wreck is fairly small, at 25ft long, standing 1.2m proud of the mainly mud sea bed.

62 Cabin Cruiser Bembridge 7 miles; Portsmouth 5 miles. 50 45.72N; 01 13.18W. Depth: 19m. An cabin cruiser sank here during 1988. She was 45ft long, made of glass-reinforced plastic, and is starting to break up. The wreckage stands nearly 3m proud.

63 Picket Boat Bembridge 7 miles; Portsmouth 4 miles. 50 46.98N; 01 12.26W. Depth: 17m. Divers report a wreck at least 50 years old here, believed to be the remains of a 50ft steam picket boat lost many years ago in exactly this area. The boat was of steel and wood construction and is mostly upside down. Some of the wreckage stands 2m off the sea bed.

64 Motor Cruiser Bembridge 8 miles; Portsmouth 5 miles. 50 46.61N; 01 13.19W. Depth: 17m. Following an instrument survey a diver was sent down at this position. He reported a modern wreck of 36ft, with a beam of 7ft, and standing 1.5m off the sea bed. This is possibly the wreck of a Princessa 37ft motor cruiser, which burned out and sank in this area in August 1988.

65 Metal Box Bembridge 6 miles; Portsmouth 4 miles. 50 46.81N; 01 10.66W. Depth: 9m. When the first divers investigated here in 1997, they found a large rectangular metal box, some 33ft long with a width of 15ft.

The box stands 2.5m proud. The top is open with one strut across joining both sides and the interior is heavily silted to about half its height. There is 1m scour around the object, which lies north–south.

66 Wreck, name unknown Bembridge 7 miles; Portsmouth 5 miles. 50 47.06N; 01 12.65W. Depth: 16m. This wreck is about 39ft long with a beam of 16ft. Amid mostly wooden wreckage is what appears to have been a small mast. The highest point is 1.5m off the sea bed. The boat lies east–west and the wreckage has a ½m scour around it.

There is excellent snorkelling and diving in Seagrove Bay (see Site 72).

AREA 4:

Gosport to Hayling Island; Ryde to Culver Cliff

Area 4 runs from 01 10.00W to 00 56.00W at the border with West Sussex, and south to 50 40.00N. It takes in a great deal of exciting diving and includes the Nab Tower, the Solent forts, and a mass of highly diveable wrecks.

The diver who wants to explore this section must take the strong tides into full account, particularly when wreck diving. At Spithead and to the west of Spithead the west-going stream runs for about 5 hours, which is between 2½ hours before and 2½ hours after high water at Portsmouth. The east-going tide runs for 7 hours with no appreciable slack at the end of the run. In the outer approaches to Portsmouth the first 4 hours of the flood tide is fairly slow, with the last 3 hours rising faster. The ebb stream runs for 5 hours, starting slowly but gaining speed once the east-going tide stream picks up at Spithead. The later part of the ebb is the strongest, reaching 4½ knots on springs between the 3rd and 4th hour.

At the entrance to Portsmouth Harbour the first 4 hours of flood runs across the Channel towards Langstone Harbour, then for 1 hour it makes towards Southsea Castle, then turning directly into the harbour entrance. The ebb first sets to the west, then south-west, then finally south-east, running between 2½ and 3 knots for 3 hours. Within Portsmouth Harbour the flood tide runs in two periods reaching speeds between 1 and 3½ knots. The ebb runs in one period, reaching 5 knots through the narrows. The strength of streams drops quickly farther inside the harbour. There are frequently eddies on either side of the harbour entrance. There is a small boat channel on the western side of the entrance for use when entering and leaving the harbour. The only true slack water off the entrance occurs at 1 hour after high water at Portsmouth.

In the entrances to Langstone Harbour and Chichester Harbour the tidal streams are very strong, reaching up to 6 knots on spring tides. Offshore, the west-going stream starts at around 2 hours before and the east-going stream around 3 hours after high water at Portsmouth. In the southern part of this area, to the east of

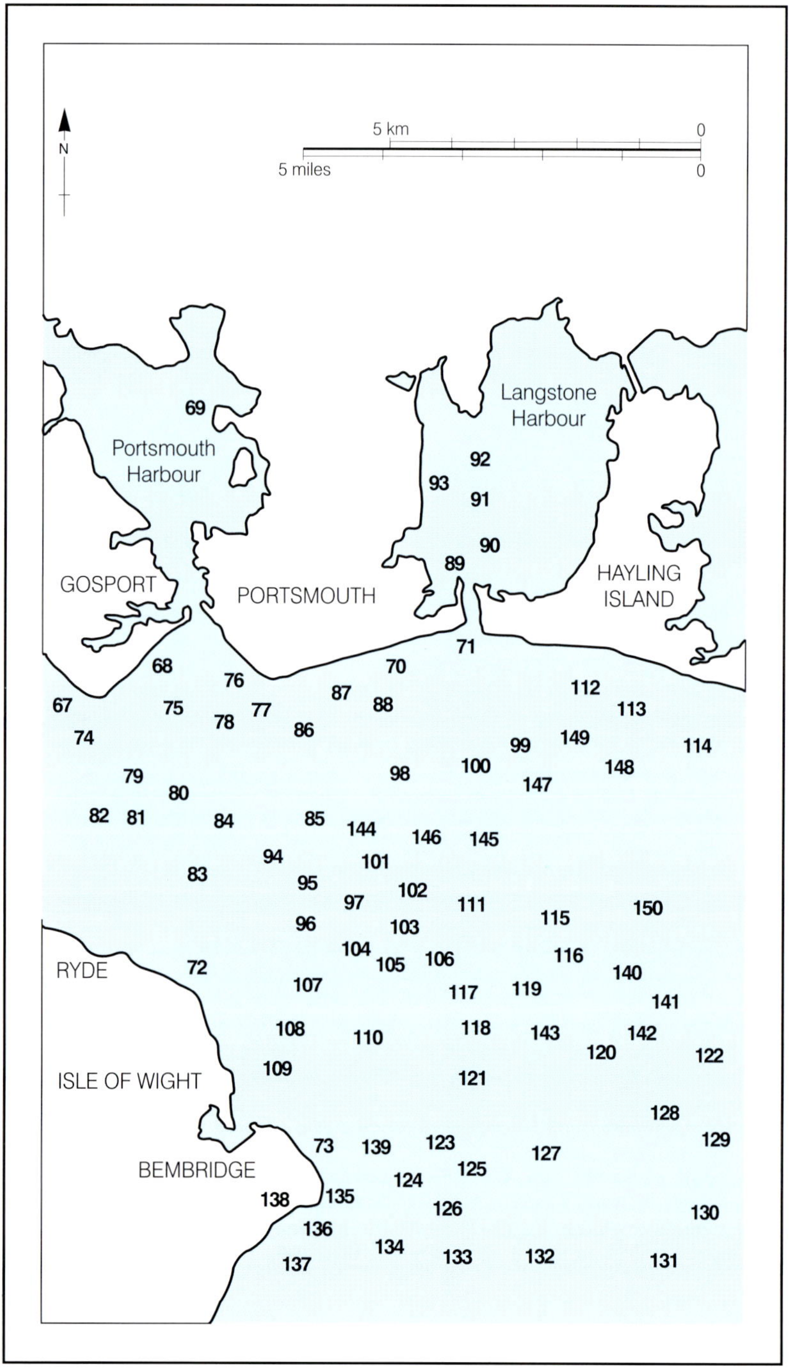
5 km
0
5 miles
0
N
Langstone Harbour
Portsmouth Harbour
GOSPORT
PORTSMOUTH
HAYLING ISLAND
RYDE
ISLE OF WIGHT
BEMBRIDGE
67 68 69 70 71 72 73 74 75 76 77 78 79 80 81 82 83 84 85 86 87 88 89 90 91 92 93 94 95 96 97 98 99 100 101 102 103 104 105 106 107 108 109 110 111 112 113 114 115 116 117 118 119 120 121 122 123 124 125 126 127 128 129 130 131 132 133 134 135 136 137 138 139 140 141 142 143 144 145 146 147 148 149 150

The slip at Hardway, Gosport, gives access to the inner part of Portsmouth Harbour.

Bembridge, the flood tide runs south-east through the Solent and north-east around the Isle of Wight shoreline. The flood and ebb are strongest running along the eastern side of the Isle of Wight, reaching 2.4 knots on the flood and 2.7 knots on the ebb. Slack water occurs at around 1 hour before and 5 hours after high water at Portsmouth. Inshore, the ebb can start around 2 hours before high water at Portsmouth.

Launch sites (Hampshire)

HARDWAY, GOSPORT Close to Hardway Sailing Club and Priory Road, this is a concrete slipway available for 2 hours either side of high water. Use is free and there is parking nearby for cars and trailers.

HASLAR MARINA, GOSPORT There is a public slipway in the marina, usable at all states of the tide.

Opposite: Dive sites in Area 4, which includes the Hampshire coast from Gosport to Hayling Island and the Isle of Wight coast from Ryde to Culver Cliff, south of Bembridge. This area is covered by Admiralty Charts 2045 (Outer Approaches to the Solent), 394 (The Solent – Eastern Part), 2625 (Approaches to Portsmouth) and 3418 (Langstone and Chichester Harbours); Ordnance Survey Landranger Map 196.

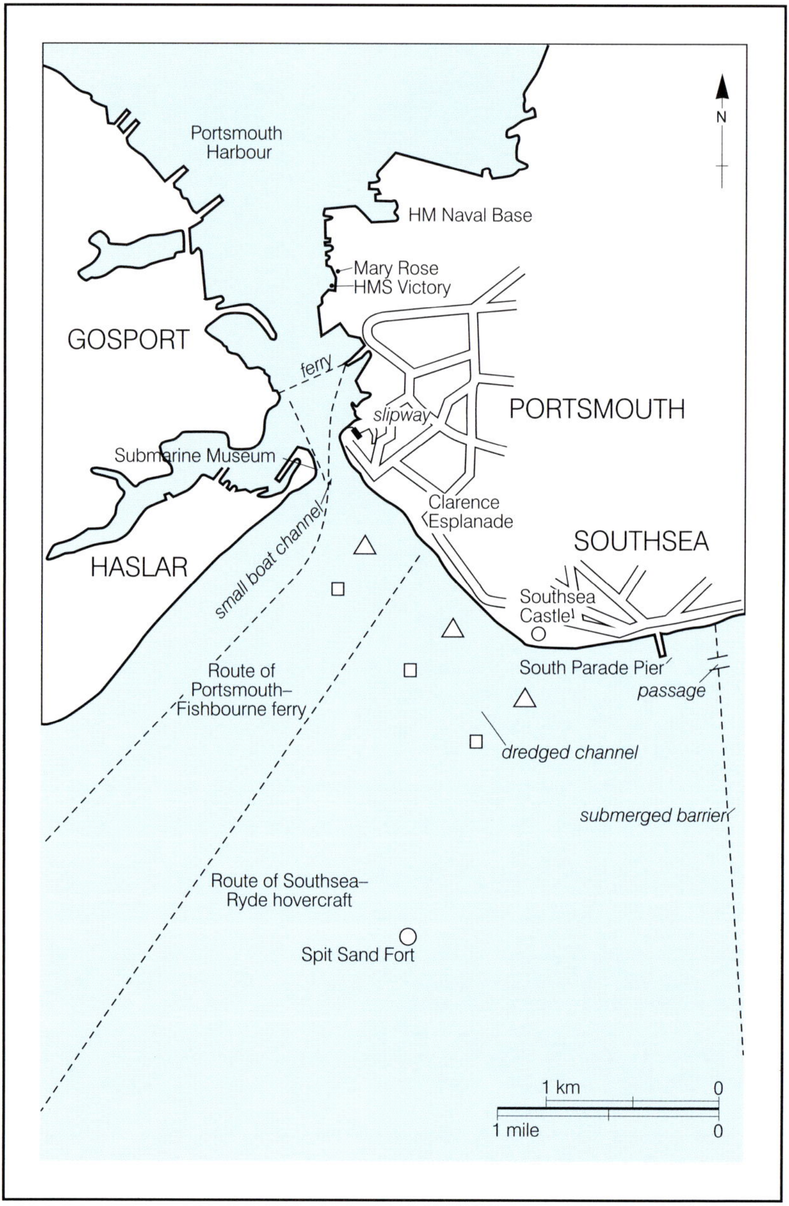

Portsmouth Harbour and the busy ferry routes. The dredged channel for the largest ferries is marked with square and triangular symbols.

PORTSMOUTH HARBOUR There is a speed limit of 10 knots inside the harbour. No diving is permitted in the harbour or within 150m of any Royal Navy ship. Portsmouth's jurisdiction to the east stretches from near Hayling Island to Sandown Bay on the Isle of Wight but the harbourmaster, whose office is in the dockyard, does not enforce the no-diving rule outside the actual harbour limits.

The entrance to the port is extremely busy and diver coxswains must take great care in this area.

CAMBER QUAY, EAST STREET Camber Quay has a wide, concrete, former ferry slip that is the best small boat launch site in Portsmouth. Launching is possible at all states of the tide, but the barrier can be locked after 5pm on weekdays, and at weekends. There is ample parking for cars and trailers, with charges.

WARNING Diver-coxswains should be very aware of the big car ferries that may come in nearby at speed. They can send a great surge of water up the slip.

LANGSTONE HARBOUR Two launch sites enable divers to explore the sheltered waters of the harbour and the shallow wreck sites.

Langstone Harbour separates Portsea Island from Hayling Island.

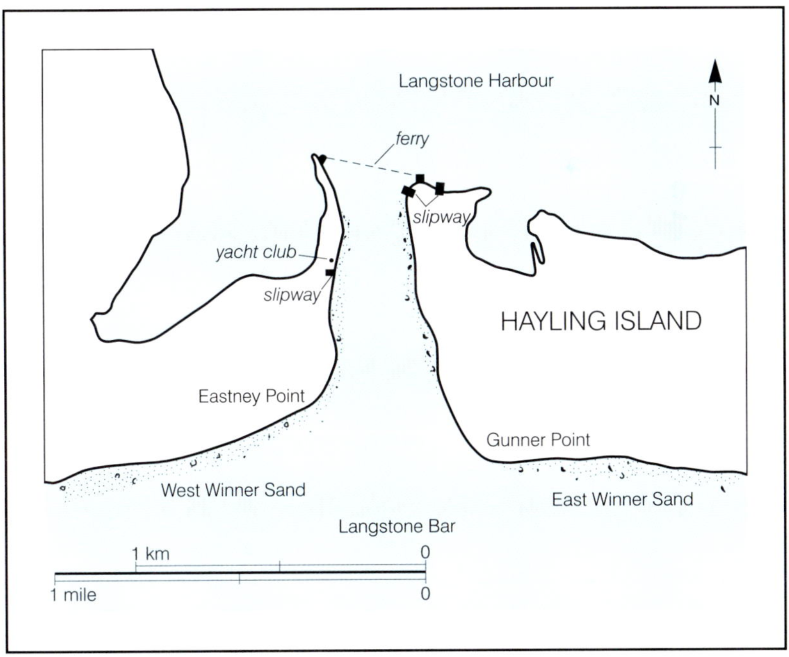

Above: The concrete slipway at the Ferry Boat Inn on the western side of Hayling Island. Below: The slipway at St Helens. The white building in the background is St Helens Church.

EASTNEY From the A2030 follow signs for the Hayling Island Ferry. Close to the Eastney Cruising Association clubhouse is a concrete slip available at all states of the tide. There is ample parking for cars and trailers. No charge is made for the slip.

HAYLING ISLAND There is a wide concrete slipway, usable at all states of the tide, near the Ferry Boat Inn and the Harbourmaster's office on the western tip of the island. There is no charge. Parking is available nearby.

Launch sites (Isle of Wight)

SEAVIEW There are three launch sites at Seaview. At the end of Pier Road there is a good concrete slip on to the beach. Vehicle launch is possible at high water, but parking is very limited. At the junction of the High Street and the Esplanade a small concrete slip curves down to the beach. Vehicle launch is impractical and there is only limited parking. On the Esplanade next to the Seaview Yacht Club is another concrete slip. It is usable for several hours either side of high water, but is only really suitable for small boats. Vehicle launch is not possible; parking is very limited.

ST HELENS There is a slipway at the bottom of Duver Road. It is usable for around 2 hours either side of high water and gives access to the channel leading into Bembridge Harbour. Vehicle launch is possible around high water.

BEMBRIDGE This shallow harbour is protected from westerly and southerly winds. A speed limit of 6 knots is enforced by the harbourmaster, who can be found at the Harbour Office. High water is the same as at Portsmouth. There is no anchoring within the approach channel or harbour and there is no diving without the permission of the harbourmaster. Launching is by means of private slips, for which there is a charge. Usable for 2 hours either side of high water, one of these slips is at the premises of Bembridge Outboards, and another at the A.A. Coombes boatyard.

Shore dives (Hampshire)

67 Stokes Bay Pier This ruined pier is at the eastern end of Stokes Bay at 50 46.60N; 01 08.94W and 700yds to the north-west of Gilkicker Point. There is a maximum of 7m at high water. The area is often used for training. Around the piles of the pier there is plenty of debris and there are flatfish on the sand away from the actual pier remains. Entry is from the beach, with a short swim to the pier. Take care as there are frequently windsurfers and small boats: use SMBs. If you are unlucky enough to coincide with an angling competition – go somewhere else!

68 The Glasshouse This is Army slang for the detention centre at Haslar, near which the dive takes place. There is a car park beside the golf club and close by is an easy entry point via the steps in the sea wall. Take care if you enter elsewhere – that sea wall is steep and slippery. This is primarily a dive for novices and instructors. The site is shallow down to 5m. The bottom is sand and gravel with a few small rocks. Marine life is scarce.

69 Horsea Island This man-made saltwater lake with a mud bottom inside Portsmouth Harbour was dug by convicts in the 1880s for testing early torpedoes. Later it has been the setting for the tough training of marines and other soldiers. Today it is used by the Defence Diving School to train Royal Engineers and Navy divers. Spare capacity makes it ideal for civilian sports divers to use the big lake for training, too, and it is well booked by clubs, who often travel long distances to dive here. This interest is not surprising for the lake bottom is the scene of an amazing collection of "wrecks" – a helicopter, a Range Rover, old ambulances, a recompression chamber, and a boat or two. There are also some large guns, used by Service divers in lifting exercises. Four days in the week are available to sports divers and bookings are controlled by the Horsea Island Dive Centre, which provides changing facilities and air fills (see Appendix 1).

The lake is 1100yds long and its depths vary from 6 to 9m. It is cut from chalk and comprises 97% sea water. A project to stock the lake with marine life is under way. Crabs and lobsters are already there, and must be left well alone.

70 West Winner The stretch of coast from the submarine barrier near Lumps Fort to the big bank of the West Winner has been the site of many beach dives. Most were made by Southsea spearfishermen in snorkel gear and there have been many catches of flatfish and other species, including bass. The fit spearfisherman can swim out to the site of the wreck of the *Roway* (Site **88**), which has a post alongside it, but the scuba diver will find this too much. Most beach diving takes place from around the Pier in Clarence Way, and along the blocks. It is shallow, but there are lobsters to be found here.

71 Fravis 50 47.16N; 01 01.37W. Depth: 3m. The *Fravis* is an old dredger, only a few yards offshore and just qualifies as a shore dive. Now there is only a boiler and small wreckage left. Note that the wreck is close to a sewer outfall. The tide through the harbour mouth can be very strong.

Shore dives (Isle of Wight)

72 Seaview Excellent snorkelling and diving can be had in Seagrove Bay. The most popular area is at the end of Pier Road. To find it, approach Seaview from the village of Nettlestone, turn into Seaview Lane on the B3340, and then turn right into Old Seaview Lane. As you approach the shops, Pier Road is on your right. It is a cul-de-sac, but there is turning room at the end. There is a good concrete slipway onto the beach, but car parking is limited. Heading south along the beach you can walk down to Horestone Point.

The sea bed here is mainly sand and rocky outcrops. A short way out are some gullies, much weeded, with plenty of sea life. Visibility is usually good and the area is well protected from the predominant south-westerlies.

73 Bembridge Lifeboat Station The Lifeboat Pier at Bembridge in Lane End Road is a favourite site for local divers. The area is well protected from the predominant south-west winds so there is nearly always calm water close inshore. Visibility is also usually good. These conditions make this an ideal area for novice dives or training exercises. There is a car park above the beach and a slipway suitable for launching small boats.

The Lifeboat Pier is around 150yds long and about 2yds wide, with the boat shed and slip at the seaward end. The piles of the pier are set into 1m square concrete blocks and the sea bed is a mixture of sand and shingle. About halfway out the bottom becomes more rocky, with many large stones and boulders, most of which seem to be an anchor for the abundant long strands of seaweed that grow here. The strands stretch right up to the surface of the water. This band of weed is around 15 to 20yds wide, stretches north and south of the pier, and is home to many small fish and lobsters. At the end of the pier the sea bed becomes rocky again and the maximum depth is around 6 to 7m. Most diving is carried out 1 to 2 hours before high water at Portsmouth to ensure a reasonable depth of water, although at this time there is usually a slight tide set to the south, which can sometimes be stronger close in by the beach than farther out.

WARNING The Bembridge lifeboat – a Tyne class boat – must never be obstructed in any way. There is also an inshore inflatable rescue boat on site.

The lifeboat station at Bembridge is at the end of the pier (Site 73).

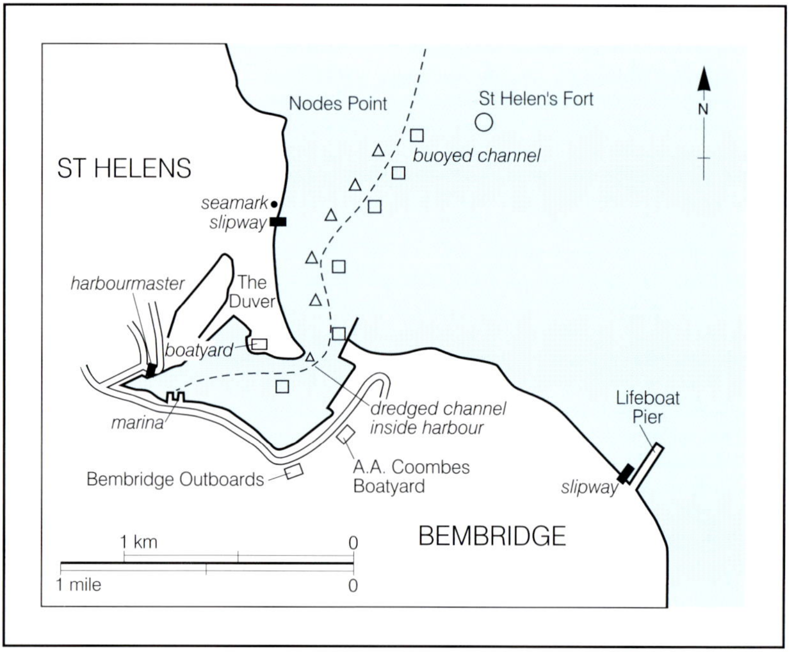

Below: St Helens and Bembridge.

Bembridge, apart from its harbour, has yet another attraction for divers. Up the hill from the harbour in the centre of the village is the Bembridge Maritime Museum. This is a "must" for any diver, with crowded displays of wreck recoveries. The museum is the creation of Martin Woodward, a former North Sea diver who was forced to give up oil-rig diving when a bell was dropped by accident with him in it, damaging his spine. He still dives from his own boat around the Isle of Wight, knows more about wrecks in the area than anyone and is Bembridge RNLI coxswain. Martin is without doubt the leading wreck, archaeological and salvage diver in the area; he is always willing to help amateur divers with marks and wrecks for them to explore.

Boat diving sites

74 Duddon Bembridge 5 miles; Portsmouth 2½ miles. 50 46.70N; 01 09.58W. Depth: 8m. This wreck is the remains of the old lighter *Duddon*, which broke in two during salvage operations near the end of Stokes Bay Pier in March 1924. The largest part was to be dispersed with explosives by the Navy, but unfortunately the buoy that was used to mark the site was lost and could not be relocated. Later attempts to find the wreck were of no avail. The Navy assumed that as the lighter had been empty the remains had probably drifted away on the tide.

It was not until 1981 when a local fisherman reported an obstruction ¼ mile offshore, saying that he could stand on it as it nearly broke surface, that anyone was sure where the *Duddon* had gone. Diving has confirmed that the wreck lies east–west and is upside down with a curved stern. She is 60ft long with a beam of 7ft and stands 2m proud of a sand and mud bottom.

75 Wreck, name unknown Bembridge 2½ miles; Portsmouth 3 miles. 50 44.52N; 01 06.75W. Depth: 17m. This unidentified wreck is of a very old ship of about 130ft long with a beam of 22ft, lying north–south. She stands 2m proud of the side of a steep mud bank. Local diver Mike Walsh has studied the site and has unearthed many lumps of concretion, pieces of iron and an extremely old iron anchor.

76 HMS Boyne Bembridge 4 miles; Portsmouth 1½ miles. 50 46.20N; 01 05.33W. Depth: 10m. The *Boyne*, with 98 guns, was a three-decker commanded by the Honorable George Grey. On 4 May, 1795, she was at anchor at Spithead, provisioned and with enough powder and shot for 4 months at sea. Not all of her 750 crew were aboard, though her marines were all there, practising musketry. They were drawn up on the poop deck, firing and reloading by numbers. Somehow a spark from this shooting blew away and landed in the Admiral's cabin. It was shortly before noon and the spark set light to some packages. In 5 minutes the rigging was ablaze and the fire out of control. News quickly spread around Portsmouth that a ship was on fire and crowds poured down to the waterside to watch.

So great was the excitement that a court-martial aboard one of the other ships in the anchorage was suspended and all but the prisoners went on deck to watch the blaze. However, other ships, closer to the *Boyne*, moved away – they knew how much ammunition she had aboard. By 2pm the *Boyne* was a complete mass of flames. Every now and then one of her guns went off from the heat. Then the cables to her anchors burned through and she drifted with the tide towards the harbour. Finally she ran aground off Southsea Castle. The crowds watching now numbered thousands and obviously had little idea of the danger they were in.

The *Boyne*, like most warships of her time, had one main magazine, lined with felt and situated below the waterline. In addition to this she had small "ready-use" magazines fore and aft. At 5pm the fire reached the aft magazine. The magazine may have been small but the explosion was huge. Portsmouth shook and a great cloud of smoke shaped like a palm tree rose thousands of feet in the air. Out of the smoke came a hail of debris – wood, cannonballs, bits of iron, and unidentifiable pieces of the ship herself. Some debris fell into the sea, some into the crowd of spectators. Yet oddly enough, the only casualties on shore were among a flock of sheep grazing on the common. Fourteen people died on board, including the Captain's clerk, four women and three children.

The wreck of this 1,800-ton ship, nearly 180ft long, obstructed the main channel into Portsmouth for many years, so in September 1838 it was blown up to reduce the danger to navigation. Today the Boyne buoy still marks the site of the wreck and on a great mound of shingle 200yds to the east of the buoy are various pieces of ironwork and concreted remains, including the odd cannonball. It is possible that quite a large amount of the ship is still intact under the mound.

WARNING Divers should take great care if diving this site not to stray into the main channel.

77 Mary Rose Bembridge 4½ miles; Portsmouth 1½ miles. 50 45.80N; 01 06.17W. Depth: 10m. Of course, the *Mary Rose* – Henry VIII's battleship, which sank in 1545 and was recovered in 1982 – is not here, but on display in Portsmouth very close to HMS *Victory*. However, the ban on diving for 300m around this position still stands, as there may well be more archaeological treasures buried under the mud. The fact that the stern and the bowcastle have never been recovered is sufficient to make this remain an historic wreck site with full protection. Every diver should pay the *Mary Rose* a visit, to see her and the splendid exhibition of items that came out of her. The exhibition shows the sort of objects that lie buried under Solent mud!

78 Solent Forts Spit Sand Fort: Portsmouth 1.2 miles, Bembridge 4.4 miles. St Helen's Fort: Portsmouth 5.2 miles, Bembridge ¾ mile. The Solent forts were constructed during the 1860s to protect the approaches to Portsmouth and the Navy anchorage at Spithead from attack by French warships. Work on constructing the forts, which were designed by Captain E. H. Steward, began in July 1861, but was halted during 1862 because of political problems, and restarted in 1865. The foundations were made of huge stone blocks, which were shaped in Stokes Bay and transported to the sites by barges. At the sites screw piles had been sunk into the sea bed and topped with staging on which a railway track was mounted, so that a steam crane could lift the blocks from the barges and then move them around the site and deposit them in the correct place on the sea bed, with assistance from divers. These foundations, an amazing 59ft thick at the sea bed, were finished in 1869. The forts were fully completed by 1880. The larger forts measured 240ft at the sea bed and around 200ft at the top.

A French invasion never materialised, but the forts were reactivated during World War One, although they were not used in action. During the inter-war years they were neglected but again refurbished and re-armed at the beginning of World War Two, when they were used against attacking aircraft. The areas between the two main forts and the seashore at Ryde and Southsea were protected by an anti-submarine defence system made up of large concrete blocks with pillars above water, and a boom of large concrete cylinders was stretched between the forts themselves. Many of these are scattered around the sea bed today.

After the war the forts were deactivated. In 1963 they were put up for sale, but it was not until 1982 that Spit Sand Fort was sold. It has now been renovated and opened to the public as a museum. No Man's Land Fort (Site **85**) and St Helen's Fort have been sold.

Diving is not recommended here as Spit Sand is a very busy place with many boats running back and forth. St Helen's Fort is situated at the entrance of the channel leading into Bembridge Harbour and is also very busy. It is shallow, with numerous rocks strewn around the base and a maximum depth of around 5m.

79 Obstructions Bembridge 5 miles; Portsmouth 1 mile. 50 46.75N; 01 07.30W. Depth: 20m. There are a great many obstructions in the area between the Harrow and Haslar Banks. The obstructing items are about the same size as oil drums – they might be oil drums, of course – and are believed to be part of the anti-submarine defences of World War One. Most are within a radius of 200yds of the above position. All are less than 1m high.

80 HMS Royal George Bembridge 3½ miles; Portsmouth 2 miles. 50 45.43N; 01 06.75W. Depth: 22m. This is not so much a wreck site as a burial mound. The *Royal George* was the flagship of Rear Admiral Kempenfelt, which capsized at Spithead on 29 August, 1782, with the loss of nearly 900 lives. That huge death toll included the Admiral and many women and children. The reason for the tragedy seems to have been that as the 100-gun first rate was about to sail with the rest of the British fleet to relieve Gibraltar, which was being beseiged by the French, a last-minute repair was necessary to a fitting that was just under water. To heel the ship and bring the leaking point above water, the crew moved the guns from one side to the centre of the ship. At the same time, stores for the voyage were being loaded and the ship was crowded with the women and children of the crew aboard saying their farewells. Old and rotten, the ship could not take the unbalanced load and something snapped. She went over suddenly and swiftly.

Salvage work was carried out over the years, notably by the Deane Brothers in 1836, and then by the Royal Engineers from 1841 to 1843. The *Royal George* was located again in 1965 by Alexander McKee during his search for the *Mary Rose*. McKee did not expect to find much of the *Royal George* as the Royal Engineers' liberal use of explosives in the course of raising her cannon from the wreck had been well documented. However, he did find her burial mound – of shingle – standing some 2 to 3m above the sea bed, complete with 32-pounder cannonballs and pottery from the ship. The area of the wreckage is large, for the *Royal George* was of 2,047 tons, 178ft long and had a beam of 51ft.

HMS Royal George (Site 80) capsized off Spithead in 1782 with calamitous loss of life.

81 Barge Bembridge 3 miles; Portsmouth 2½ miles. 50 45.07N; 01 06.17W. Depth: 30m. This wreck, 2 miles south of Southsea Castle, was found in 1978 and consists of the remains of a barge sitting upright on a mainly mud bottom. She is 100ft long and stands a maximum of 4m proud. The hold appears to be full of iron radiators and they are well silted in.

82 Yacht, name unknown Bembridge 3 miles; Portsmouth 2.4 miles. 50 45.07N; 01 06.42W. Depth: 30m. This is the intact wreck of a 30ft yacht. She was first dived in 1971 when her mast lay out to the port side. The wreck is now well silted, but lobsters can be seen clustering under the perspex hatch covers.

83 Hovercraft Bembridge 2 miles; Portsmouth 3 miles. 50 44.41N; 01 06.00W. Depth: 13m. The first diver to find this wreck on a drift dive was very puzzled about what he saw. He faced a mass of aluminium with some sort of rubber-compound sheeting on the top flapping about in the tide. It was only after other dives that he realised that what he was looking at was the skirt of a small upside-down hovercraft. The hovercraft is very broken, blunt in shape and quite small, some 40ft long. Gauges and filters have been recovered. This may be a hovercraft tested to destruction by the Royal Navy. She stands 3m proud and lies north–south.

84 Wreck, name unknown Bembridge 3 miles; Portsmouth 2½ miles. 50 45.28N; 01 05.13W. Depth: 13m. This wreck, first located ¾ mile north-west of Horse Sand Fort in 1977, was not dived until 1980. The divers reported finding a steel craft totally upside down. Twin shafts and propellers were visible. The hull was very corroded and was between 50 and 60ft long. She lies in a north–south direction with bows to the north. The wreck stands a maximum of 1m off the muddy sea bed. A dive in the late 1990s failed to locate the wreck, which may have been covered by mud during dredging operations.

85 Horse Sand Fort and No Man's Land Fort Horse Sand Fort: Portsmouth 3 miles, Bembridge 3½ miles. No Man's Land Fort: Portsmouth 3¼ miles, Bembridge 3 miles. These forts have a depth of about 8 or 9m around them at high water. They are popular as second dives and for training. The sea bed is mud well covered with shell and stones. The crevices in the foundations are homes for crabs and lobsters and there are a small number of scallops to be found nearby.

The forts can be dived at any time, as there is always a large area of slack on the lee sides. SMBs must always be used, as it is easy to move out into the tide run and be swept well away.

86 Pontoon Bembridge 5 miles; Portsmouth 3 miles. 50 45.60N; 01 02.22W. Depth: 10m. South of the *Roway* (Site **88**), this pontoon is 12ft square. It has big anchors on it and old pipes around it. It is a good site for lobsters.

87 Pearl Bembridge 4 miles; Portsmouth 2 miles. 50 46.55N; 01 03.97W. Depth: 3m. The *Pearl* was an old British sailing barge that foundered just to the east of the submarine barrier off Southsea on 25 March, 1922. The site lies ¼ mile off Southsea beach. The barge was quickly battered to pieces in the shallow water and very little remains today. Parts of the heavy wooden keel stand a maximum

Divers at No Man's Land Fort (Site 85).

of 0.2m off the sand and gravel sea bed. The site is sometimes used as a training place for divers.

88 Roway Bembridge 4 miles; Portsmouth 3 miles. 50 46.08N; 01 02.20W. Depth: 8m. The *Roway* was a 110-ton British dredger built in 1937. She was 90ft long with a beam of 19ft. She sank after being hit by a freak wave on 3 May, 1967, 1 mile south of Eastney Point on the Horse and Dean Sand.

In 1970 a contract was placed for raising the wreck, but the salvage attempt was unsuccessful. In 1978 the Portsmouth and Medway diving team from HMS *Vernon* carried out demolition of the upper part of the wreck that was very close to the surface and had been hit by several small boats. Today the remains of the *Roway* are fairly intact apart from her upper works. The hull is upright and full of sand and shingle. Parts of equipment used during the early salvage attempts can be seen close to the wreck. The site is easy to find as it is marked by a pile with a spherical topmark.

89 Prison Hulks Bembridge 6 miles; Portsmouth 3 miles. In Langstone Harbour. Depth: 12m. The hulks are relics of Napoleonic days; they housed prisoners of war and Navy prisoners but are now merely lumps of timber. The hulks were moored on both sides of the harbour entrance, one close to Eastney Lake and the other near the Ferry Boat Inn. Divers who groped around the moorings in the late 1990s recovered a number of stone jars.

90 Mulberry Unit and The Mask Bembridge 6 miles; Portsmouth 3 miles. 50 47.92N; 01 01.42W. Depth: 3m. This concrete unit has broken its back; the rate of break up seems to be accelerating and the unit is now in two sections. It dries and can be seen from the shore. At the northern end is the wreck of the *Mask*. This

72ft former dredger was used in her last days as a scrap recovery vessel. Her mast shows at all states of the tide, but she is very broken.

91 Excelsior Bembridge 6 miles; Portsmouth 3 miles. 50 48.02N; 01 01.72W. Depth: 12m. This was a small dredger, which sank at her moorings. She is upright and intact though becoming very fragile. The *Excelsior* is heavily silted, but can be good for shellfish. The wreck lies north–south with bows to the north. Her bell was recovered in 1970.

92 Irishman Bembridge 6 miles; Portsmouth 3 miles. 50 48.30N; 01 01.33W. Depth: 3m. The *Irishman* was a tug towing *Percy*, a barge carrying a crane, in Langstone Harbour on 8 May, 1941, when she ran into an aerial sea mine dropped earlier by a Heinkel 111 into the main channel. The 99-ton tug and the crane barge simply disappeared in a huge waterspout and the crew were killed. The remains of the tug and the barge lie just off Sword Point on the tip of the Sword Sand Bank. Part of the wreckage dries 2m at low springs and is marked with a beacon. This site was used for many years as a training dive area for Southsea BSAC. The most prominent underwater feature is a giant wheel that came from the crane, otherwise only the stern is recognisable.

93 Withern Bembridge 6 miles; Portsmouth 3 miles. 50 48.10N; 01 01.77W. Depth: 5m. The *Withern* was a bucket dredger and the wreck is marked by a beacon. She is very broken and lies on a sloping mud bank. This is a silty shallow dive, which might be good for trainees to accustom them to low-visibility diving!

The tug Irishman struck a mine in 1941 (Site 92).

94 Buoys Bembridge 2½ miles; Portsmouth 3 miles. 50 44.50N; 01 05.23W. Depth: 30m. Signs of a wreck in this position, ¼ mile north-east of No Man's Land Fort, were first found during a 1972 survey. Further surveys in 1975, 1978 and 1980 confirmed its existence. The 1980 survey also reported that the wreckage lay north–south and stood 4m off the sea bed, with 1m deep scour around it. There was some additional debris about 175yds to the south-south-west of the wreck. The site was dived in the late 1990s, but all that was found was a cluster of buoys and chain. It may be that this is all there is, or maybe it is debris from another wreck yet to be found by divers.

WARNING The site lies within the deep water channel so extra care should be taken when diving here.

95 Diadem of Bursledon Bembridge 2 miles; Portsmouth 3 miles. 50 44.45N; 01 04.15W. Depth: 30m. This wreck is probably the remains of the yacht *Diadem of Bursledon*, which sank ¼ mile north-west of the Horse Elbow buoy on 24 September, 1970. The site has been dived and divers report finding an old wooden yacht with 7m of the stern sticking out of the mud and standing a maximum of 3m off the bottom. The bows appear to be completely buried.

96 Torpedo Recovery Ship Bembridge 2 miles; Portsmouth 3½ miles. 50 44.17N; 01 04.88W. Depth: 28m. This wreck, ½ mile south-east of No Man's Land Fort, was first located in 1978. It was dived in 1980 and divers reported finding a torpedo recovery ship, the *460A*. The ship was 65ft long and stands upright on a muddy bed with a maximum height of 4m. Her bows are to the south-east. There is a fair amount of damage to the hull, particularly midships on the starboard side, probably from a collision. The hull is of wooden double-diagonal construction and of a semi-planing design.

Divers can see the tips of the twin propellers by lying on the bottom and looking under the stern. A derrick on the stern has now fallen. The binnacle has been recovered.

WARNING This site lies on the southern edge of the deep water channel leading into Spithead, so diver-coxswains must keep a sharp lookout for other shipping.

97 Cambrian Bembridge 3 miles; Portsmouth 3½ miles. 50 44.50N; 01 03.37W. Depth: 5m. This site lies ¾ mile south-east of Horse Sand Fort and is the wreck of the 388-ton 138ft *Cambrian*. This ship, built in 1924 and originally called *Lord Derby*, was requisitioned for Navy service at the beginning of World War Two. She was used as a boom defence vessel and patrolled the anti-submarine system rigged between Southsea and Ryde to prevent enemy submarines from getting into the Navy anchorage at Spithead.

The *Cambrian*'s active service did not last very long – on 30 May, 1940 she hit a mine. Although she sank in shallow water and was quite visible, the *Cambrian* was too badly damaged to salvage. Well clear of the main shipping channel, she was left to the elements. Over the years the wreck broke up into several sections and gradually disappeared from sight, though parts were only just below the surface. Because of this some demolition work was carried out in the late 1970s, which has left the wreck well scattered and spread over an area of 280yds radius around the green conical buoy that marks the site. Very little of the *Cambrian* is recognisable – she is mainly a pile of plates and ribs – but exploring the wreck makes a good shallow dive.

98 Pontoon Bembridge 5 miles; Portsmouth 4 miles. 50 45.73N; 01 02.22W. Depth: 4m. This is an old pontoon lying 1½ miles south of Eastney Point. Any planking that was on it has now disappeared and only the steel framework remains. It is about 10yds long and 2yds wide, lying in an east–west direction with a maximum height of 1m off the flat sandy bottom.

99 Margjagulin Bembridge 5 miles; Portsmouth 4 miles. 50 46.37N; 01 00.67W. Depth: 5m. The 50-foot yacht *Margjagulin* sank in this position, 1 mile to the south of Gunner Point on the southern tip of the East Winner Sand, on 5 February, 1977, after striking a submerged object by the old submarine barrier between Horse Sand Fort and Southsea seafront. The crew were saved. Very little remains as the yacht soon broke in two. The bows were washed ashore and most of the stern was salvaged from the sea bed.

100 HMS Impregnable 50 45.88N; 00 57.55W. Depth: 4m. Launched at Deptford in 1786, the 98-gun second rate man-of-war *Impregnable* was 178ft long, 49ft in the beam and drew about 25ft. The 1,887-ton ship carried a crew of 190 men.

The convoy of 12 merchant ships that the *Impregnable* had escorted home from Lisbon, without incident despite the war with France, broke formation off St Catherine's Point in the morning of 19 October, 1799, and started across Sandown Bay ready to turn into St Helen's Roads for the final leg into Portsmouth. The wind was blowing strongly from the south and the captain, Jonathan Faulknor, handed over charge of the ship to the master, Michael Jenking. The *Impregnable* was making her home run at a good 10 knots and at 6pm the cliffs of Dunnose were 2 miles off. At 6.30pm the crew could see Culver Cliff. It was getting dark and Captain Faulknor asked Jenking if it would not be better to stand out to sea for the night, but Jenking was determined to get home that evening. That was his undoing. Soon the great ship was aground and bumping heavily. Only in the dawn, when they had cut away the masts, could they see that they had bumped 1½ miles right across the Chichester Shoals to near the entrance to Langstone Harbour. The ship was bilged and became a total wreck, though everything that could be salvaged was taken out of her. None of the crew was lost. Jenking was dismissed from the Navy at a court-martial; Faulknor was acquitted.

This site is very close to that of *Caduceus* (Site **114**). Divers of 308 Sub-Aqua Association have found *Impregnable*'s massive keel, 4ft bronze pins weighing 30lb each, lead piping for bilge pumps, and mounds of cannonballs.

101 HMS Invincible 50 44.57N; 01 02.38W. Depth: 7m. This is a protected wreck site and has been since 30 September, 1980, when an order came into effect banning all diving within 100m of her position. She is marked by a spherical yellow buoy lettered "HMS INVINCIBLE WRECK".

The wreck was found in May 1979 when a Portsmouth fisherman, Arthur Mack, was hand-trawling over the Horse Sands. He snagged and hauled up a massive piece of oak – an old ship's timber. Diving revealed the warship, which, though its bow and stern had collapsed, was sensationally intact and well away from the recorded position of her sinking. At first, the site was thought to be that of HMS *Impregnable*, lost nearby (Site **100**), but a find by John Bingeman named her without any doubt. On the sea bed he unfurled a piece of canvas sail still intact and protected by the mud. Inside the canvas, written on a small wooden tag, was "Invincible. Flying Jib 26 x 26 No. 6".

The *Invincible*, a British third rate, 1,793-ton, 74-gun man-of-war was no ordinary ship: she was a prize. Built for the French Navy in 1741 by their master shipwright Morineau, she was far ahead of her time – better, faster and sounder than anything in service with the Royal Navy. She soon proved this, capturing HMS *Elizabeth*, winning odds of four to one. (However, even the *Invincible* could not cope when she was captured by an entire squadron off Cape Finisterre in 1747. Her capture is said to have led to a vital rethink in the building of British ships, without which Nelson would not have won at Trafalgar years later.)

The advanced design of the *Invincible* did not save her from a series of mishaps on 19 February, 1758. At 2.30am Admiral Edward Boscawen ordered the ship to take up anchor and sail for Canada, where she was to take part in the campaign to oust the French. The order seems to have upset conditions on board the man-of-war. The dark and the wind funnelling up the Solent from the east did not help, but soon there was no doubt that the *Invincible* was having serious problems. By 4.15am she had her anchor cables in a twist. By 4.45am it was finally raised and minutes later the ship set off on a north-east course to get some sea room on the fast ebbing tide, but then the rudder jammed and the *Invincible* sailed straight on until she grounded hard. All efforts to free her failed.

Three days later, with all the crew safely off and much of her cargo removed, a strong wind came out of the west; the ship heeled and went on heeling until she was on her side. Water rushed in and she sank into the silt. Her captain, John Bentley, was acquitted at the court-martial and the wreck was left there about 1½ miles south-east of Horse Sand Fort. Diving has recovered a host of items from the old ship and many can be seen in the Royal Navy Museum in Portsmouth.

102 MFV 118 Bembridge 2½ miles; Portsmouth 3½ miles. 50 44.43N; 01 03.32W. Depth: 6m. This wreck is probably the remains of the fishing vessel *MFV 118*, though the precise date of her sinking is unknown. There was a report of a wreck in this position in 1945. In 1976 divers reported that the wreck was an unidentified wooden craft, which lay north-east and south-west and stood about 1m off the sea bed. This was confirmed by diving. The site lies 100yds to the south-east of the Horse Elbow buoy and is very close to the wreck of the *Cambrian* (Site **97**).

103 Tank Landing Craft Bembridge 2 miles; Portsmouth 4 miles. 50 43.65N; 01 03.62W. Depth: 30m. This wreck was first located ¼ mile east of the Warner buoy in May 1967, and is a large landing craft. She is upright and intact, and lies north–south with her bows to the south. The wreck is about 150ft long with a maximum height of 7m. The stern is sunk well in, almost to the sea bed level of the soft mud.

Visibility here can be exceptional. "The viz was so fantastic that when I was up on the bridge I could see the bow ramp quite clearly," commented one diver. Be warned, however, it is not often like that.

104 HMS Hazard Bembridge 2 miles; Portsmouth 4 miles. 50 43.75N; 01 03.23W. Depth: 32m. The 1,070-ton HMS *Hazard* started life as a torpedo gunboat and was one of the Dryad class. She was launched in 1894 with measurements of 250ft by 30ft by 13ft and normally carried 120 men. Well armed, with two 4.7in guns, four 3-pounders and five 18-inch torpedo tubes, she was driven by two sets of vertical triple expansion engines producing 3,500hp and a top speed of 18 knots.

With the introduction of Holland class submarines into the Royal Navy in 1901, a tender ship was needed and *Hazard* got the job. On 28 January, 1918, she was rammed by the 2,937-ton casualty-clearing steamer *Western Australia* and cut in two. She sank very quickly, with the loss of three lives. A fourth man died later from his injuries.

The site is rarely visited by divers. The wreck is almost totally upside down and well buried in the soft mud. Her bronze propellers are gone, salvaged some years ago. She is in half and the two parts lie alongside one another. The only connections between them are some cables, perhaps from the salvage of the condensers in 1974.

WARNING HMS *Hazard* lies ½ mile east of the Warner buoy in the centre of the deep water channel leading into the eastern Solent. This is an extremely busy part of the Channel, with ferries, tankers and Navy ships coming and going all the time. The strong tide and poor visibility usually found in the centre of the Channel add to these dangers.

HMS Hazard (Site 104) sank in 1918, following a collision. She now lies in a very busy shipping lane.

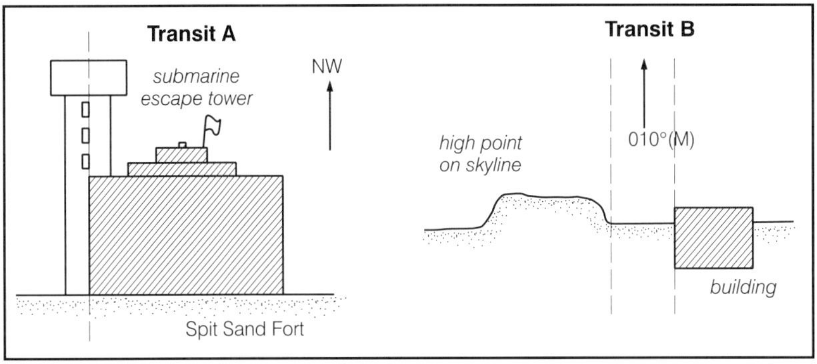

Transit marks for HMS Hazard (Site 104).

105 Collier Bembridge 2½ miles; Portsmouth 4½ miles. 50 43.62N; 01 03.08W. Depth: 28m. This wreck is of a 150ft collier, which sits upright on a bed of grey mud. She is largely intact with bows pointing to the south-east. There is a 1m deep scour around her and she stands 6m proud. Part of the coal cargo can be seen.

106 The Stone Wreck Bembridge 3 miles; Portsmouth 5 miles. 50 43.43N; 01 02.07W. Depth: 20m. This site, 3½ miles south of Langstone Harbour entrance, is a bit of a mystery. To the diver the wreck at first appears as a rocky outcrop, but closer inspection shows that the rocks are large ballast stones of a regular shape. On further examination, some wooden timbers can be seen protruding from beneath the stones.

The wreck lies north-west and south-east and is of a ship about 50ft long and 15ft beam, standing at a maximum of 2m. There is a ½m scour around the outline of the hull. This is an old wreck, possibly a sailing barge. Divers have recovered a wooden pulley and a bronze fireplace.

WARNING The site lies in the centre of the deep water channel leading into the eastern Solent, so take care.

107 Concrete Cylinder Bembridge 2 miles; Portsmouth 4 miles. 50 43.45N; 01 04.30W. Depth: 10m. This obstruction is a cylindrical concrete structure about 100ft long and 8ft in diameter, standing nearly 2m proud on a bottom of fine sand and mud. The obstruction is a petrol barge built for the Allied invasion of France. Each barge carried some 200 tons of petrol and 200 barges were built. The concrete proved highly resistant to petrol and aviation spirit in particular. The reason this one did reach the other side of the Channel is not recorded.

108 Sausages Bembridge 1½ miles; Portsmouth 3½ miles. 50 43.93N; 01 05.32W. Depth: 10m. There are a large number of wartime concrete and steel obstructions on the Warner Shoal, which covers a large area from the eastern side of Ryde Sands round to St Helen's Roads, marked to the north by the Warner buoy and No Man's Land Fort.

The obstructions are of two kinds. During World War Two a submarine defence system was deployed between the Isle of Wight and the Southsea shore to prevent German submarines from attacking warships anchored at Spithead. This system used big concrete cylinders with a diameter of over 7ft. They varied in length from 36 to 150ft. Because they were linked together end to end, they quickly earned the nickname "sausages". After the war many of the cylinders were sunk and they can be found scattered around the Warner Shoal.

The second kind of obstruction on the Shoal is the bombardons. These floating breakwaters were part of the Mulberry Harbours built for the Normandy landings in 1944. These bombardons broke the waves – even in winds of over Force 6 – and enabled small boats to work unloading supplies as soon as they were in place on the coast of France. Made of ¼in mild steel, with watertight buoyancy compartments, the breakwaters were moored in several fathoms of water to give sufficient depth for Liberty ships to anchor behind them. Two miles of bombardon breakwater was used in the actual D-Day operations. Those on the Warner Shoal presumably broke away during towing to France. More information about the bombardons can be found in the companion volume *Dive Sussex*.

The larger sections of both kinds of wreckage – all a favourite haunt of crabs and lobsters – can be found in the following positions: at 50 43.93N; 01 05.32W, at 50 43.65N; 01 04.63W, at 50 43.45N; 01 04.30W and at 50 43.33N; 01 05.40W.

109 Obstruction Bembridge 1 mile; Portsmouth 5 miles. 50 43.22N; 01 04.57W. Depth: 9m. This is a small pontoon in three sections about 12ft square and bolted together to make a structure some 40ft by 10ft by 12ft. It was probably another D-Day construction. There is another one on its side and slightly smaller about ½ mile to the west.

110 Obstruction Bembridge 2 miles; Portsmouth 5 miles. 50 43.03N; 01 02.80W. Depth:16m. This obstruction was first reported in 1968 and is believed to be a large load of spoil dumped in rough weather. The position is 1½ miles north-east of St Helen's Fort and the obstruction stands 1 to 2m proud of the sea bed, with a length of around 60ft. When dived in the late 1990s the site was confirmed as consisting of a mound of mud and clay. There is no sign of any wreckage and no magnetometer reading was obtained.

111 UB-21 Bembridge 3½ miles; Portsmouth 4½ miles. 50 44.23N; 01 01.52W. Depth: 5m. The *UB-21*, a veteran German submarine of World War One, came to an inglorious end when on her way to the breakers in 1920. She sank while under tow 3 miles south of Eastney Point.

UB-21 was one of the smaller U-boats, 292 tons in weight and 118ft long, with a crew of two officers and 21 men. She had two bow tubes and carried four torpedoes and an 8cm gun on her casing. She was launched in 1916 and was one of 176 U-boats that were surrendered at the end of the war. At one period of her long service the *UB-21* was commanded by the burly, jovial Kapitänleutnant Ernst Hashagen, who survived the war. He was rated as an "ace" in the scoring table of the U-boat commands, having sunk over 130,000 tons of shipping during his North Sea and Channel missions in *UB-21* and his later boat *U-62*.

It was while he was in command of *UB-21* that Ernst Hashagen took a leading part in one of the strangest incidents of the submarine war. He described it like this:

> There was the little steamer Fritzoe. We met her in the North Sea and sent a shot from the gun of UB-21 ripping over her bow. She hove-to and I signalled the captain to bring over his papers. He came, but I needed only one look at his battered lifeboats to know that his crew could never make it to the nearest land. The question was, what to do with the ship now that I had her? The expression on the captain's face told me he was wondering the same thing. I had an idea.
>
> "Look here," I turned to him. "You may take your choice of having your ship sunk here or of taking her to Cuxhaven on your own as a war prize. Which shall it be?" You never saw such a look of relief on the face of a man. Without hesitation he agreed to take the Fritzoe to Germany.
>
> "But how do I know you will do as you say?" I asked him. "I can't follow you all the time. I must watch out for British patrol boats. There is nothing to prevent you from trying to give me the slip. Then I would have to shoot a torpedo at you. No, perhaps I had better sink you right here."
>
> The captain turned a bit pale, but stood his ground. "I am a man of my word," he said with fine dignity. We parted and I lost sight of the steamer. I never really expected to see it again. Four days later when I reached Cuxhaven, there was the Fritzoe waiting for us. That Britisher knew how to play cricket. All honour to him. His word was his bond!

The *UB-21* was depth charged many times in her active wartime career and always managed to escape, but demolition teams in 1921 and salvage work in 1970, when she was sold to a Portsmouth firm, more than succeeded. She is now very broken and dispersed. The wreck is in two sections and much flattened so that only a few isolated plates stick up some 2m off the bottom.

112 The Broad Arrow Wreck Bembridge 6 miles; Portsmouth 4½ miles. 50 46.28N; 00 59.87W. Depth: 3m. The remains of a steel wreck located by divers in 1985 are in shallow water about ¼ mile off the beach at Hayling Island just to the east of the East Winner Sand. The wreck is compact and very low, and is well covered in silt. No sign of any machinery has been found but an engine room repeater was discovered marked with the Royal Navy's broad arrow, which would indicate a naval vessel of some sort. From the size and type of fittings seen on the wreck it would seem that the ship's original size would have been about 100ft long.

113 Church Rocks Bembridge 6 miles; Portsmouth 5 miles. 50 45.60N; 00 59.23W. Depth: 3m. This small rocky outcrop was thought to be insignificant until Alexander McKee and Maurice Harknett discovered the reason for the name. Their finds of ancient stonework has confirmed the belief of historians that this is the site of a priory church and village submerged in the 14th century. The rocks, which are usually well covered in kelp, are a mark for local spear fishermen, and a good site for shellfish.

114 Caduceus Bembridge 6 miles; Portsmouth 6 miles. 50 45.85N; 00 57.97W. Depth: 3m. The 418-ton barque *Caduceus* was built of wood in Sunderland in 1857 and measured 124 ft by 27ft by 17ft. At the time of her loss she was being used as a sailing collier by her owners, J. Bolt of South Shields, and was bound from Newcastle to Italy with coal and general goods.

The *Caduceus* was driven ashore and wrecked on 23 October, 1881, approximately ¾ mile to the west of Chichester Bar. She was seen by the crews on the Nab and Warner Light Vessels, and both fired distress rockets. The signals were answered by the Bembridge lifeboat. When it arrived the *Caduceus* was hard ashore with seas breaking over her. Only the stump of the mizzen mast was still standing and Captain Scarle and his crew had lashed themselves to it. It took 14 hours for the Bembridge lifeboat to rescue all the men and get them safely to shore.

Some parts of the *Caduceus* could be seen at low water in the 1950s, but she was not dived until 1970. The divers identified the wreck by finding part of her bell, which was dated 1857. Little is left of the ship now. One of the highest parts is a galvanised iron tank that stands about ½m off the sea bed. The keel and some bronze bolts can be seen, together with timbers still in good condition.

115 HM Submarine A1 Bembridge 2 miles; Portsmouth 3½ miles. 50 44.52N; 00 55.19W. Depth: 14m. The *A1* was the first British designed and built submarine. She is designated as a protected wreck and all diving is banned within a radius of 100m of the position given.

The *A1* was 100ft long and weighed 165 tons. She was laid down on 19 February, 1902, in the Vickers and Maxim yard at Barrow-in-Furness and was launched on 9 July the same year. She cost £41,000. She was to become Britain's first submarine disaster. In March 1904 the *A1* and some Holland class submarines were taking part in manoeuvres that included mock attacks on various Navy ships. *A1* was commanded by Lieutenant Loftus Mansergh. He had lined up his submarine for an attack on the cruiser *Juno* and was unaware that the liner *Berwick Castle* was steaming out to sea on her way from Southampton to Hamburg. The captain of the *Berwick Castle* saw something ahead of him in the water. He rang for full astern and put the helm hard to starboard, but it was too late and he struck the submarine a shattering blow that sent her to the sea bed. Even then, the officers on the liner thought that they had hit a practice torpedo and not a partially submerged submarine.

The sunken submarine was soon located by a steady stream of air bubbles arising from her, but several initial attempts at raising her failed. One month later she was eventually lifted and her crew of 11 were buried. The *A1* was put back into service after repairs, but little more was heard of her by the outside world until August 1910, when a huge explosion took place on board the submarine as she was alongside at Portsmouth. Seven men were badly hurt. One man, the coxswain, was actually blown out through the conning tower and landed in the sea. The explosion was caused by an accumulation of petrol gas.

In August 1911, the *A1* was towed out of Portsmouth to be used as a gunnery target. Her position when sunk was given as ½ mile south-west of No Man's Land Fort but the towing ship failed to pinpoint this position. The submarine was found after being snagged by trawlerman Willie Pledger of Selsey and then dived by Chichester sub-aqua club. She lies north-west to south-east and stands 3.5m proud. There is a noticeable scour around the site.

HM Submarine A1 (Site 115) was the first all-British submarine. She sank after being used as a gunnery target in 1911.

The protection of the *A1* is an unusual collaboration between the Ministry of Defence (MoD), the Department for Culture, Media and Sport (DCMS) and Isle of Wight underwater archaeologist Martin Woodward. After diving the submarine, and finding that she was being damaged by divers, Martin Woodward bought her from the MoD, and then applied for her protection by the DCMS. Plans to raise the first Royal Navy submarine and put her on display are well advanced.

116 Shallom Bembridge 6 miles; Portsmouth 4½ miles. 50 47.00N; 00 59.70W. Depth: 10m. This is the remains of a 20ft cabin cruiser, which sank on 24 May, 1983, after striking a submerged object. She is now very broken.

117 The Net Wreck Bembridge 2½ miles; Portsmouth 5½ miles. 50 42.93N; 01 01.97W. Depth: 15m. This wreck, name unknown, has been trawled into so often that it is sometimes difficult to see the ship for the nets. The wreck was first dived in 1980 when divers found a small vessel about 30ft long in the position about 2 miles north-east of St Helen's Fort. They also reported more wreckage scattered over the sea bed with the largest item a box-like structure standing 1½m proud. This might be another unifloat (see Site **55**).

There must be even more wreckage buried under the mud. A magnetometer survey of the site produces strong anomalies, but on diving only bits of girders are to be found. There are even more remains farther to the west and local divers believe that this comes from a much bigger vessel that was dispersed many years ago. All the wreckage is good for shellfish.

118 Big Box Bembridge 3 miles; Portsmouth 5 miles. 50 43.00N; 01 01.80W. Depth: 14m. This unusual piece of wreckage is ¾ mile north-west of the Nab East buoy. It is a large box section, about the size of a large car. It stands almost 2m high and is very strongly built. It lies in a north-east and south-west direction on the side of a bank and is probably more of the D-Day debris in this area.

119 Capable Bembridge 3 miles; Portsmouth 6 miles. 50 42.77N; 01 00.77W. Depth: 14m. The motor vessel *Capable* was a small coaster of 216 tons, which for many years sailed between the south coast ports east and west of the Isle of Wight.

The MV Capable (Site 119) hit a mine off Bembridge in 1940 and sank just to the south of the Nab East buoy.

The *Capable* nearly became a wreck on 3 March, 1930, when she ran into thick fog shortly after leaving Poole harbour. At 10.30pm she ran aground on the infamous Atherfield Ledges. Luckily the coastguard lookout had seen her plight: a stout rope was rigged and all members of the crew were able to scramble to safety. News of the stranding soon spread and the two lifeboats from Brook and Yarmouth were launched. The Brook lifeboat eventually found the *Capable*, but only after the crew had already left. The Yarmouth lifeboat only just reached Brook Ledge before running aground herself. She was there for several days before a party of troops was able to refloat her.

Although badly damaged, the *Capable* was refloated and towed to Cowes where she was repaired. She finally became a permanent wreck on 5 June, 1940, when she hit a mine off Bembridge while bringing a cargo of stone from Alderney to Portsmouth. The *Capable* sank just to the south of the Nab East buoy. She had a crew of five and two Territorial Army gunners on board; all were lost.

The site today is well broken up, mainly a mass of steel plates and ribs. An anchor can be seen within the wreckage. On one dive in the late 1990s three navigation lamps were found well jammed under some plates. One was eventually rescued but the other two are still there.

The bearing from the Horse Sand Fort is 131 degrees, 2.8 miles, and from St Helen's Fort 80 degrees, 2.72 miles.

120 German Tug Bembridge 4 miles; Portsmouth 6½ miles. 50 42.78N; 00 59.55W. Depth: 23m. This ship was first found in 1957 and her real name is

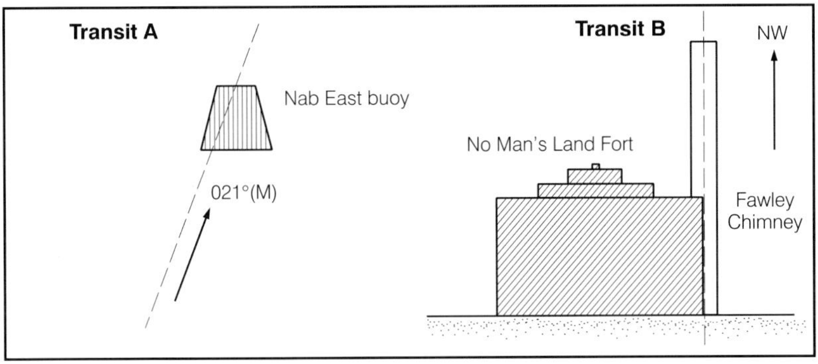

Transit marks for the Capable (Site 119).

unknown, but veteran local diver Maurice Harknett called her the "German Tug" after studying the remains very carefully. Although the wreck is broken and mostly split open, the bows are complete. The two boilers are well proud and the steel propeller remains in place. It is an interesting fin from the bow, where the anchors are still in their hawses, to the stern, which is deep in the mud.

There is plenty of coal amid the wreckage and a big winch and a large rope roller, some 6ft long, give strength to the identification of the tug. Some bottles have been recovered from the wreck. One had the date of February 1922 moulded into the glass. There is a great deal of broken German pottery in the wreckage. This is a good dive as the visibility is often surprisingly clear with over 10m not uncommon. Three bronze dolphins, which might have held a compass bowl, have been recovered from the wreck.

WARNING The wreck lies on the edge of the deep water channel for ships heading into the eastern Solent and is only 400yds north-west of the Nab End buoy, so take care.

121 Lobster Pockets Bembridge 2½ miles; Portsmouth 5½ miles. 50 42.83N; 01 01.25W. Depth: 14m. This unknown small wreck is about 60ft long, standing 1m proud and lying almost east–west. She appears to be upside down, with her iron keel lying across the top. Twin iron propellers remain. Only the outline of the sides of the wreck can be seen from the wood sticking up some 2ft from the mud, in the shape of a ship. This is an excellent site for lobsters and, looking down on the wreck from above, the lobsters look as though they are in pockets made by the internal bulkheads of the old ship.

122 German E-Boat Bembridge 6 miles; Portsmouth 8 miles. 50 42.75N; 00 56.40W. Depth: 15m. This site is the remains of a German E-boat that sank during World War Two after being holed 4 miles south of Eastoke Point. The site was surveyed in 1951 and the wreck was dispersed the same year.

Today the remains of the wreck lie in a crater and very little of her sticks above the rim. The wreck is very flat – the maximum height of isolated parts is only 1m at best. Nothing is clearly recognisable, but the site is still worth investigating. The surrounding sea bed is fairly flat and mainly sand and shingle. A small gun was recovered in 1972.

123 HMS Velox Bembridge 3 miles; Portsmouth 7½ miles. 50 41.52N; 01 02.08W. Depth: 13m. The *Velox*, a British destroyer, was one of the first three Royal Navy ships to be fitted with steam turbines at the beginning of the 20th century. These revolutionary new engines, the invention of Sir Charles Algernon Parsons, were to change the whole face of naval warfare. Suddenly it was possible for ships to reach undreamed of speeds and also to maintain reliability. The Navy raced to fit them into their latest ships.

The first ship to be given the new engine was HMS *Viper*. Her 10,000hp engines propelled her through the sea at the astounding speed of over 36 knots. The *Viper* was 210ft long, but was only 21ft wide and drew 12½ft. Despite this, she mounted one 12-pounder gun, five 6-pounder guns and two torpedo tubes. The new engines worked by a jet of steam being directed onto angled blades on a drum connected, directly or through gearing, to the propeller shaft. The power-to-weight ratio, compared with the old steam-reciprocating engines, was so favourable that all the navies of the world started to adopt the system. The *Viper* was the first of the Snake class. At that time she was the fastest vessel afloat – but her shallow draught tended to make her ride on bow and stern waves with her midships almost suspended out of the water, so her stability in sharp turns was questionable. The *Viper* did not last long. She ran onto the Renonquet Reef off Alderney during manoeuvres with the Fleet on 3 August, 1901.

The next Snake class vessel to be built was HMS *Cobra*. She too could do over 36 knots and her draught was only 7ft. Before being completely ready for service with the Navy she needed some adjustments during sea trials. For that reason there were 25 men, including the manager of Parsons Marine Steam Turbine Company,

The destroyer HMS Velox (Site 123) sank in 1915 after hitting a mine.

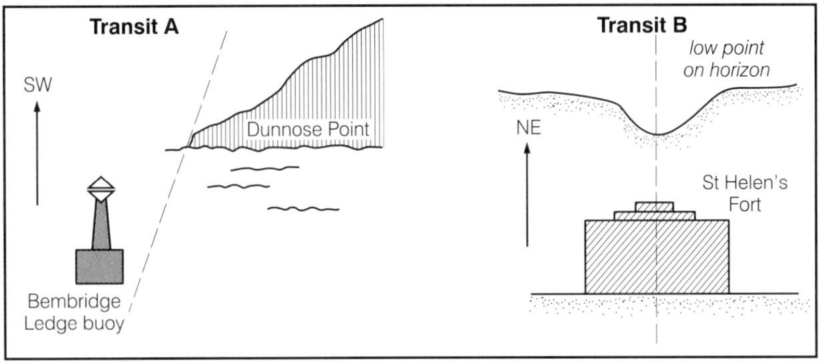

Transit marks for HMS Velox (Site 123).

aboard when the *Cobra* left Newcastle in the evening of Tuesday, 17 September, 1901. The Navy crew of 54 men was already on board. At 4am the next day the ship ran into a full gale and the mid-section was heard creaking under the strain of only being supported at bow and stern; in addition, she rolled heavily. At 7.30am she simply broke in two. Only 12 men survived.

There was a great public outcry – some thought the Snake names unlucky and the steam turbines too powerful, for surely here was evidence that they tore ships in two! The Admiralty officers, to their credit, took little notice and continued to believe in the steam turbine engines. But they did think it wise to change the name of the third Snake class boat from *Python* to *Velox*.

HMS *Velox* was launched in 1902 and completed in February 1904, and she kept her name, that of a C class destroyer, throughout her Navy service. She was a 420-ton ship, 210ft long, with a beam of 21ft and a draught of 9ft. She had her 12-pounder gun just forward of the bridge, two 6-pounders on each side and one aft, and two 18in torpedo tubes. The turbines drove four propeller shafts, each fitted with two propellers, but this arrangement was later modified to only one propeller per shaft.

The *Velox* was vastly important to the Navy. She served her time with no problems of any note and demonstrated that steam turbines were not too powerful and were reliable. She was still proving that on 25 October, 1915, when she hit a mine laid by a German UC class submarine of the Flanders flotilla near the Nab Tower. The *Velox* finally sank 1½ miles east of Bembridge Lifeboat Station.

In 1970, the wreck was bought and dispersed by a salvage company. Today the *Velox* is still an interesting dive. Her propeller shafts remain, as do parts of her turbines, but none of the hull shows above the muddy sea bed. As the wreckage is so widely scattered, it is worth exploring away from the main site and many small items can still be found.

124 Mooring Block Bembridge 3 miles; Portsmouth 7½ miles. 50 41.50N; 01 02.32W. Depth: 12m. This site has very little of interest – it is merely a 2m square concrete mooring block with two large steel rings set into the sides. It is one of several mooring blocks used by the salvage vessel working the site of HMS

Velox. This is the largest of such moorings and is some distance from the main wreckage.

125 Obstruction Bembridge 2½ miles; Portsmouth 8 miles. 50 41.28N; 01 01.73W. Depth: 11m. A small obstruction was located in this position 1½ miles east of Bembridge Lifeboat Station in 1979. It is about 5ft long, lies north-east to south-west, and stands a maximum of 1m off the bottom. It is probably more D-Day debris.

126 Wreck, name unknown Bembridge 2½ miles; Portsmouth 7½ miles. 50 41.02N; 01 01.53W. Depth: 12m. There is a small wreck in this position 1½ miles east of Forelands, about 30ft long and standing 1m high. It looks like a barge, lies east–west and is well broken.

127 Bow of the Campeador V Bembridge 3½ miles; Portsmouth 7 miles. 50 41.35N; 01 00.10W. Depth: 13m. This wreck, 2½ miles east of Bembridge Lifeboat Station, was something of a mystery for many years. She was first located in 1945 and dived by Navy divers who reported finding a small steel craft about 40ft long with a 12ft beam and wooden decking in places. The ship was badly damaged and the divers saw what appeared to be a drifter-type winch forward and roller fairleads towards the stern. Lying just clear of the wreck was a small gun and mounting, and an anchor with a 4ft shank.

Subsequent surveys of the area failed to find any trace of the wreck and it was not until 1979 that an obstruction was spotted during a sonar sweep. Diving on the site since then has showed that the wreck is largely collapsed – and it appeared to be the bow section of a vessel lying on her starboard side. Within the wreck were three portholes on a length of steel plate, still well bolted on although only one was complete. Also well buried was what looked like a large brass shell case. A large,

HMS Campeador V struck a mine in 1940. See Sites 127 and 139.

badly damaged navigation lamp was recovered and this and the other items all seemed too large to have been fitted on a small 40ft craft. There was no sign of the gun and anchor found in 1945.

Further diving and investigation of the site has now shown that this is the bow section of the anti-submarine yacht HMS *Campeador V*. The 211-ton *Campeador V* was built of steel by Philip and Son of Dartmouth for Vernon MacAndrew, also of Dartmouth. (Vernon MacAndrew was a wealthy man and a highly successful yachtsman – at Cowes Week in 1938 he raced his 12m yacht *Trivia* so well that he won 21 prizes, including the King's Cup.)

Campeador V was 128ft long with a 20ft beam and a draught of 8ft. She was the first motor yacht to be driven by two 16-cylinder Gleniffer V-type diesels. MacAndrew and his two close friends, John Muir and Charles Turner (all in their sixties) took her on many long voyages. At the outbreak of war on 3 September, 1939, MacAndrew offered the *Campeador V* to the Admiralty and she was commissioned on 18 September and attached to the Auxiliary Patrol Service. Though her command was given to Commander C.H. Davey, there was no replacing her veteran crew. MacAndrew, Muir and Turner all became Temporary Lieutenants in the Royal Navy Volunteer Reserve.

The winter of 1939–40 was one of the most severe for generations, but out of the first 95 days of the war HM *Campeador V* was at sea for 84 of them. In March 1940 she had a few weeks' respite when she was taken into Southampton for refitting her engines and mounting a gun on her foredeck. Early in May she was back on patrol. At 9am on 22 June, 1940, the *Campeador V* struck a mine, which exploded amidships blowing her in half. The bow section sank immediately, the stern was only just afloat. There were only two survivors: the ship's engineer and a leading seaman. The four officers and sixteen ratings were killed. Later the stern section was towed into shallow water off Bembridge Ledge and abandoned (Site **139**).

128 Sir Jasper Bembridge 5½ miles; Portsmouth 8½ miles. 50 42.20N; 00 57.00W. Depth: 13m. A victim of Solent racing, this J-24 class yacht capsized and sank while overtaking another yacht on 1 November, 1981, near the Nab No. 3 buoy. The position is approximate and diving information is required.

129 Obstruction Bembridge 5½ miles; Portsmouth 8½ miles. 50 41.60N; 00 56.70W. Depth: 11m. This was a very small obstruction on the edge of the dredged Nab Channel and it has not been relocated by divers for some time. This probably means that the obstruction has been destroyed or covered by dredging operations.

130 Wreck, name unknown Bembridge 6 miles; Portsmouth 9½ miles. 50 40.25N; 00 56.60W. Depth: 15m. This wreck was first located 600yds to the north-east of the Nab Tower in 1969. Later divers reported finding an old wooden steamship. The hull was mostly broken up and covered only a small area. The highest point was the boiler, which stands about 3m off the bottom of sand and broken shells. A large, four-bladed propeller is still there, made of steel with a diameter of approximately 1ft. The wreck lies north-east and south-west with its bows to the north-east. A dish recovered from the site had the inscription "made expressly for the United States Lines" on it.

131 Nab Tower Bembridge 6 miles; Portsmouth 9 miles. 50 40.00N; 00 57.00W. Depth: 20m. The tower is at the southern end of the eastern approach to Spithead and Portsmouth and stands 28m high. It has been responsible for guiding ships into the deep water channel since it was set in place on 12 September, 1920.

The story of the Nab starts in 1917, when attacks on British and Allied merchant shipping by the U-boats of the Flanders flotilla based at Bruges reached such a rate that Britain faced starvation. The German U-boats would slip out of Zeebrugge, usually at night, running the gauntlet of the mines and nets with which the Admiralty tried to close the Dover Straits, and prey on shipping in the Channel. Something more was obviously needed – and a hastily convened committee of scientists and sailors finally came up with the idea that they thought could provide the ultimate in anti-submarine operations. Six enormous towers were to be built and sunk in position across the Straits of Dover. These forts would be the supports for huge steel nets reaching from sea bed to surface and, once in position, no U-boat would pass.

Work began at once on two of the towers at Southwick, near Shoreham in Sussex. Each tower was to be 40ft in diameter, with latticed steelwork surrounding the 28m high cylindrical steel tower. This was to be set upon a huge concrete base, designed like a honeycomb for flooding and sinking "in water of 20 fathoms". The base was roughly shaped, with pointed bows and stern for easy towing. Some 3,000 civilian workmen were brought to Southwick, chosen for its huge supplies of shingle for the concrete, and work began under a strict veil of secrecy. Despite this, as the towers grew they became known in the Navy as the "Southwick Monsters" or "The Wedding Cake Ships". The work was supervised by the Royal Engineers, but only one tower had been completed when the war ended in November 1918 and the other tower – half-finished – was broken up and scrapped.

The great tower stayed on shore until Trinity House decided to replace the old Nab Lightship. Then on 12 September, 1920 – a day chosen because the sea was flat and calm – two aged paddle-steamer tugs towed the huge structure to a position near the Nab Light Vessel. As the base was opened to the sea, the tower performed exactly as planned and settled almost gently to the sea bed.

The Nab Tower is 4½ miles east of Bembridge and 6 miles south of Chichester Harbour entrance and was operated as a staffed offshore lighthouse from the time of its sinking until the early 1980s. It used to be staffed by three keepers who were relieved every month, but now it is automated and the tower and its helicopter landing pad are serviced and monitored from East Cowes. The height of the light is 27m. It has an intensity of 100,000 candela, group flashes white every 10 seconds, and can be seen 19 miles away. In fog there are two blasts every 30 seconds. Over the years the tower has developed a slight list of two degrees and has moved 2ft since 1920.

Diving the Nab is interesting. The concrete base has three steps. Each step is 5m high and 2m wide. These steps drop to the sand and shingle sea bed at 20m. The base is a favourite haunt of crabs and lobsters. Diving can be carried out at anytime as a lee from the tide can be found at some point around the base. A rocky ridge at a depth of 13m, with much life, lies 600yds north-east of the Tower.

WARNING Divers should be alert to the fact that the Nab Channel, which is over 400yds wide, starts about 1 mile north-north-east of the Nab Tower and extends 1½ miles north-north-west from that point. It is dredged to a depth of 13m and is intended for heavily laden inward bound tankers. All other boats should keep clear of the channel.

132 Stern of the Bettann Bembridge 5 miles; Portsmouth 9 miles. 50 40.28N; 01 00.95W. Depth: 13m. In January 1967 the Danish coaster *Bettann*, under the command of Captain Petersen, was on a voyage from Cornwall to Germany with a cargo of china clay valued at £35,000. The 500-ton ship started to leak badly while heading up the English Channel and when the electric bilge pumps failed, the crew of five men and one woman began bailing with buckets. Some 24 hours after the leak started the destroyer HMS *Agincourt* took the *Bettann* in tow. She was finally anchored in shallow water in St Helen's Roads. The Bembridge lifeboat was standing by and as the water began to rise over the hatches the crew abandoned ship. Shortly afterwards, she rolled over and sank. Attempts to raise the wreck failed and eventually the *Bettann* was cut into two sections. These sections were then raised and towed out to deep water to be sunk again for good. The stern section, however, never made it to the deep water and sank while being towed 2½ miles west of the Nab Tower on 4 December, 1968.

The stern section is small, only about 45ft long, and stands a maximum of 5m off the sand and gravel sea bed. A couple of portholes were recovered by local divers shortly after the *Bettann* sank, but little of interest has shown since then. Angling boats often visit this site and many lose their anchors, so this is a site for anchor collectors!

See Site **177** for details of the loss and current position of the bow section of the *Bettann*.

133 Wreck, name unknown Bembridge 2½ miles; Portsmouth 7½ miles. 50 40.13N; 01 02.83W. Depth: 13m. This obstruction is located in the centre of the Princessa Shoal. It is reported to stand 1½m high and is limited in extent, possibly a small boat. This site is 1½ miles east of Culver Cliff. Diving information is required.

134 France Aimée Bembridge 2½ miles; Portsmouth 7½ miles. 50 40.08N; 01 03.27W. Depth: 13m. After a collision with the Royal Navy patrol boat HMS *P-35*,

Transit marks for the France Aimée (Site 134).

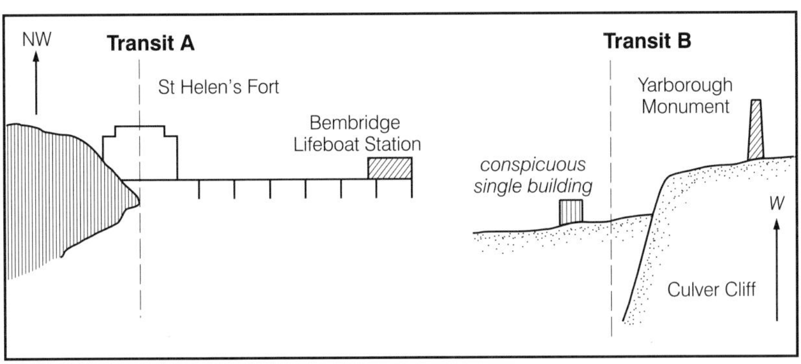

this French collier of 699 tons at first lay on the sea bed on the northern edge of a large hole. Many years later, she rolled into it.

The *France Aimée* was built in 1901 by the Irvine Shipbuilding Company and was owned at the time of the collision by the Société d'Importation du Nord et de l'Est. She was 190ft long with a beam of 28ft and built of steel with a single deck. HMS *P-35* weighed 613 tons, was 230ft long, and carried a 4in gun and two torpedo tubes. She was built by Caird in January 1917 and survived the collision with *France Aimée*. After repairs, the *P-35* carried on in service with the Navy until she was broken up in Plymouth in January 1923.

The collision between *France Aimée* and *P-35* took place on 3 April, 1918, in appalling weather and very low visibility. When the *France Aimée* sank she was on the western edge of the Princessa Shoal, about 400yds to the east of the Princessa Shoal buoy. When first dived in 1964 the ship was heavily covered with big mussels and weed, and tilted to port on the edge of a large hole or dip in the sea bed. By 1972 she had rolled over into the middle of the hole and was then completely on her port side. Today divers will find *France Aimée* with her stern intact, her port side all silted up and her starboard side collapsed, leaving the boiler clear and the highest

Bembridge Ledge is rated a good place to dive.

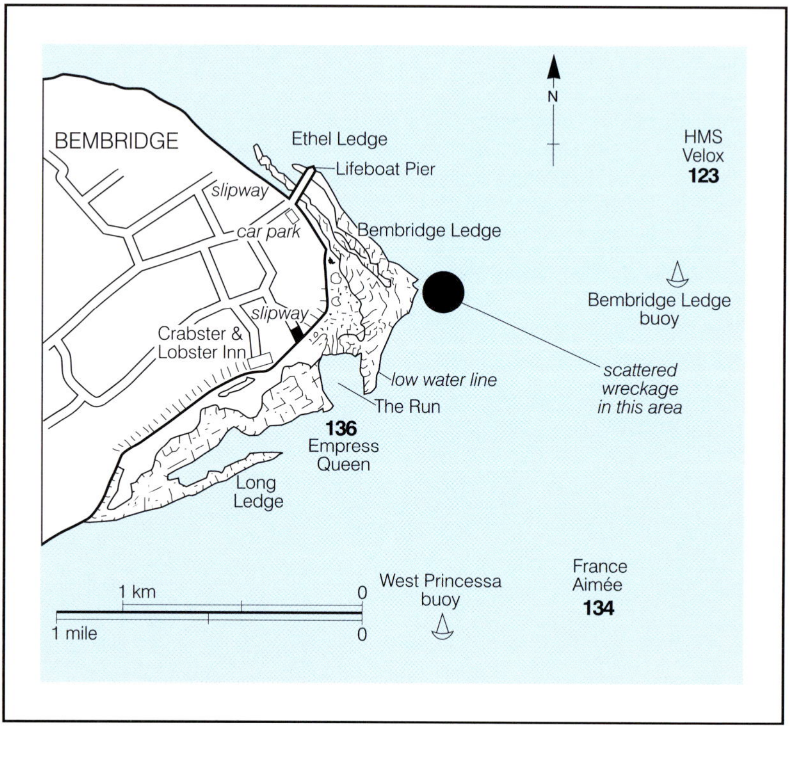

point at 3m. The bows are almost buried, but intact, with one anchor still neatly stowed. Many piles of coal, her cargo, lie on the sea bed around the site. There is a 3m scour around some of the wreckage. A porthole has been raised from the site.

135 Bembridge Ledge Bembridge Ledge is a favourite area for diving. Crabs and lobsters abound among the large slabs of rock that stretch out from the shore as far as the Bembridge Ledge buoy, which is almost 1 mile offshore. At low water the rocks are dry for more than ¼ mile offshore. Many ships, including a submarine, have spent some time aground on the ledges after trying to cut the corner too close. Luckily most of them escaped with little damage. The paddle steamer *Empress Queen* (Site **136**) did not and parts of her can be seen at low tide.

Owing to the large number of crabs and lobsters found on the ledges, there is also a huge number of pots laid here. Great care must be taken to avoid them. The deeper part of the ledges – out towards the Ledge buoy – are a good area for drift diving. There always seem to be many anchors caught up in the rocky slabs. This is because the ledge is also a favourite place for local angling. The depths near to the buoy are around 15m.

Several old ships have been lost in the area and one never knows what one might discover. For example, Isle of Wight diver Dougie Saunders found the remains of one wreck quite by accident: "I was drift diving, and came across a

The paddle steamer Empress Queen ran aground on Bembridge Ledge in 1916 (Site 136).

fair-sized propshaft complete with prop, as well as an old steam boiler and bits and pieces."

One part of the ledge known as "The Run" is popular for snorkelling. This is a shallow channel that meanders between the rocks. The water is usually very clear and there is an abundant marine life. On Long Ledge there are two big lagoons or rock pools full of crystal clear water near Foreland.

136 Empress Queen Bembridge 2 miles; Portsmouth 7½ miles. 50 40.60N; 01 04.00W. Depth: 3m. The *Empress Queen* was a 1,995-ton paddle steamer built in 1897 by the Fairfield Shipbuilding and Engineering Co. She was one of the most powerful paddlers of the period with engines producing some 10,000hp. For many years she was owned and operated by the Isle of Man Ferry Company. During World War One she was employed as a troop carrier and on 3 February, 1916, she ran aground on the rocks of the Bembridge Ledge with over 100 men on board. The Bembridge lifeboat, the *Queen Victoria*, was launched and was soon able to reach the stricken steamer and promptly began to take off the troops and crew. Two full boatloads were safely landed ashore, but on the third trip out, the lifeboat herself was driven onto the rocks. She suffered some damage but was still able to continue the rescue. In all 110 men, a cat and a dog were saved. The coxswain, John Holbrook, was awarded the RNLI silver medal for the rescue.

The *Empress Queen* ended her days on the Bembridge Ledge gradually breaking up over the years. Most of the remains are well smashed and scattered around the rocks. At low water parts of the wreck can be seen sticking out of the sea and she is still a danger to small craft navigating close in.

137 Bow of HMS P.12 Bembridge 3 miles; Portsmouth 8 miles. 50 40.25N; 01 05.50W. Depth: 2m. Part of the bow section of this fast World War One patrol boat is sometimes uncovered when there is a storm. HMS *P.12* was cut clean in half in a collision on 4 November, 1918. The stern section (Site **158**) is a more interesting dive.

138 LCT 529 Bembridge 1 mile; Portsmouth 6 miles. 50 41.75N; 01 04.85W. Depth: 6m. This 200-ton tank landing craft sank a mile from the Nab Tower, but was raised and dumped in the present position. This is a Mk IV landing craft with a length of 187ft and a beam of 39ft. She drew only 4ft.

139 Stern of the Campeador V Bembridge 1 mile; Portsmouth 6 miles. 50 41.88N; 01 04.98W. Depth: 5m. This 213-ton anti-submarine yacht was mined on 22 June, 1940, some 2 miles north-west of the Nab Tower. Her stern was beached in this position and is much broken in very shallow water. Her bow is dived (Site **127**).

140 Torpedo and Tube 50 46.51N; 01 09.94W. Depth: 8m. An obstruction was reported in this position in 1990. Divers found a 21in diameter metal cylinder with an inner cylinder. It protrudes upright from the sea bed to a height of 2.3m. It is badly corroded. There is a recessed brass plate on one side and a steel plate on the other. There is also some sort of release lever flush with the outer skin, which would suggested that this was a deck-mounted torpedo tube.

141 Blackburn Botha Bembridge 5 miles; Portsmouth 3 miles. 50 45.62N; 01 09.32W. Depth: 22m. This might be the wreck of a Blackburn Botha aircraft that was reported lost on 24 February, 1940. The Botha, No. L6111, crashed into the sea while on a minelaying practice flight from the Royal Naval Air Station at Lee-on-the-Solent.

This high-wing twin-engined Botha was powered by two Bristol Perseus air-cooled engines, which gave her a top speed of some 240mph and, though originally developed as a general reconnaissance and torpedo bomber for service with Coastal Command, it seemed to have ended up being mostly used for training. The aeroplane carried a crew of three, had a wingspan of 59ft and was 51ft long. The wreckage is very broken and scattered over a large area.

142 Wreck, name unknown Bembridge 5 miles; Portsmouth 3 miles. 50 45.61N; 01 09.05W. Depth: 21m. An obstruction, probably a wreck, was first noted in this position by the Trinity House vessel *Hebe* in November 1933, but surveys in 1934 and 1980 failed to find it. However, in 1990 a wreck was found in this position. It is fairly small, about 36ft long with a beam of 12ft and appears to be partially buried, with some parts standing 1m proud. Diving information is needed.

143 Wreck, name unknown Bembridge 3 miles; Portsmouth 4 miles. 50 45.05N; 01 08.06W. Depth: 8m. Divers are not sure exactly what this is. It appears to be a shaped structure, possibly of concrete, with some large metal bolts sticking out of it. It stands about 2m high and is leaning at an angle. It might be the keel of a boat (or part of one) but this type of concrete construction, with strengthening bars running through it, was much used in building Mulberry units.

144 Glen Bembridge 3 miles; Portsmouth 2½ miles. 50 44.96N; 01 06.50W. Depth: 28m. The fishing vessel *Glen* caught fire and sank in the eastern Solent on

A Blackburn Botha was reported lost in February 1940 while on a training flight from Lee-on-the-Solent. Wreckage found at Site 141 could be its remains.

10 July, 1981. The wreck was located by sonar in 1990 and the trace shows that the dimensions are right – 36ft long with a beam of 6ft, standing almost 3m proud of the sea bed. The identification is tentative and diving information is needed.

145 Wreck, name unknown Bembridge 3 miles; Portsmouth 3 miles. 50 44.52N; 01 05.36W. Depth: 27m. Another wreck that needs diving. This one is about 66ft long and stands 1m proud. There are two smaller pieces close to the south-west of the main wreckage.

WARNING The wreck lies a little over 400yds to the north-east of No Man's Land Fort, and thus in the deep water channel, so take great care when diving here.

146 Wreck, name unknown Bembridge 2½ miles; Portsmouth 3 miles. 50 44.43N; 01 05.95W. Depth: 23m. This wreck was located in 1990, but little diving information is available. The 50ft wreck is on the side of a steep sand bank, lying along the tide. She stands nearly 3m proud with the shallowest part at the eastern end. The site is some 400yds to the west of No Man's Land Fort and is clear of the main shipping channel.

147 Torpedo Recovery Boat Bembridge 3 miles; Portsmouth 4 miles. 50 43.71N; 01 02.64W. Depth: 20m. A wooden torpedo search-and-recovery boat sank in this position while being towed into Portsmouth Harbour on 30 May, 1970, but the wreck was not located until 1990. The boat is 32ft long with a beam of 9ft and is nearly 3m proud, lying in an east–west direction. Diving is needed to confirm her identity.

148 Flag Theofano Bembridge 4 miles; Portsmouth 6 miles. 50 43.03N; 00 59.46W. Depth: 20m. The *Flag Theofano* was built of steel in 1970 and had formerly been called, in turn, the *Victoria*, the *Boston Express* and the *Rabat*. She was 91ft by 16ft by 8ft. This 2,818-ton Greek motor vessel was carrying 4,000 tons of bulk cement to Southampton from Le Lavandou via Le Havre on 29 January, 1990. While approaching the entrance to the eastern Solent, in appalling weather, the ship capsized with the loss of all crew. The disaster was only discovered when a lifeboat and some bodies were washed ashore. It is believed that the *Flag Theofano* was trying to anchor off St Helen's Road in Force 10 winds and huge seas when she fouled a Channel buoy with her anchor. This caused the ship to heel over and her cargo shifted so far that she capsized.

The wreck was eventually located ¼ mile to the west of the Dean Tail buoy, lying on her port side with her bows to the south-west. It was planned to raise her, but by the time salvage plans were put into operation in August 1990, the ship's superstructure had started to collapse and the ship had rolled almost completely upside down. The cargo of cement had hardened, creating another difficulty. Another attempt to salvage the wreck was made the following year, but it failed, and the wreck was abandoned. It is now marked by four cardinal buoys and the Dean Tail buoy has been removed.

149 Concrete Cylinder Bembridge 4 miles; Portsmouth 8 miles. 50 40.20N; 01 00.07W. Depth: 12m. This obstruction was first found in 1989 and when dived turned out to be a concrete cylinder about 40ft long, standing 1m off the sand and

The paddle steamer Portsdown (Site 150) hit a mine in 1941 during the short crossing from Portsmouth to Ryde.

shingle sea bed. It lies north-west to south-east and has a shallow tidal scour around it. This is probably another cylinder from the World War Two boom defence system of the eastern Solent.

150 Portsdown Bembridge 5 miles; Portsmouth 1 mile. 50 46.55N; 01 06.25W. Depth: 8m. This paddle steamer was built in 1928 for the Southern Railway Company by the Caledonian Shipbuilding Company of Dundee and cost £32,400. The 342-ton ship was 190ft by 25ft by 9ft, and was powered by a two-cylinder compound steam engine and two boilers that gave some 159hp to drive the two paddle wheels.

The *Portsdown* left Portsmouth Harbour Railway Station Pier at 4am on 20 September, 1941, to cross to Ryde Pierhead on the Isle of Wight. Captain Chandler and his 10 crew had about 37 passengers on board, most of whom were servicemen. Once clear of the harbour, the *Portsdown* turned to starboard to cross Spit Sand. Almost immediately there was a huge explosion that split the ferry in two. The smaller bow section turned upside down and sank. Fortunately the stern section stayed upright in the shallow water and it was from this that the survivors were rescued. Captain Chandler, seven of the crew, and 15 passengers drowned. The *Portsdown* was recorded as mined, probably by a magnetic mine dropped by a German aircraft.

Although the stern section of the *Portsdown* was salvaged the bows are still on the sea bed. The wreckage is starting to break up and much is now buried. Diving this site needs great care as there is nearly always a steady stream of boat traffic in and out of Portsmouth Harbour.

The deck gun of UB-81.

AREA 5:

Culver Cliff to St Catherine's Point

This section runs south from 50 40.00N to the edge of Admiralty Chart No. 2045. The area is bounded in the east by 00 56.00W and runs west to 01 17.00W. This means that it takes in much of the best of Isle of Wight diving, which means boat diving. This area is holidaymaker territory on land, and in summer visiting divers should make allowances for slow traffic between resorts.

The tides here are less complicated than elsewhere, but just as strong. The flood tide runs to the east in the area south of St Catherine's Point and slowly turns to the north-east following the shape of the coastline. The strongest streams run south of St Catherine's Point and between St Catherine's Point and Dunnose Point. Off St Catherine's Point the flood tide can reach a speed of 4½ knots and on the ebb can reach 4 knots. The strength of these streams reduces the farther you go out from the shore. Slack water periods occur at about 1 hour before and 5 to 6 hours after high water at Portsmouth. Inshore of Sandown Bay the streams turn earlier, with the ebb turning between 2 and 3 hours before high water at Portsmouth.

Launch sites

YAVERLAND This launch site is off Yaverland Road and the B3395. There is a good concrete ramp beside the Yaverland Sailing and Boating Club. The ramp is fairly steep and runs at an angle to the sandy beach. Vehicle launch is possible. There is a large car park nearby.

SANDOWN A large ramp runs on to the sandy beach at the end of the Esplanade. Approach by Pier Street, off the High Street. Parking nearby is limited.

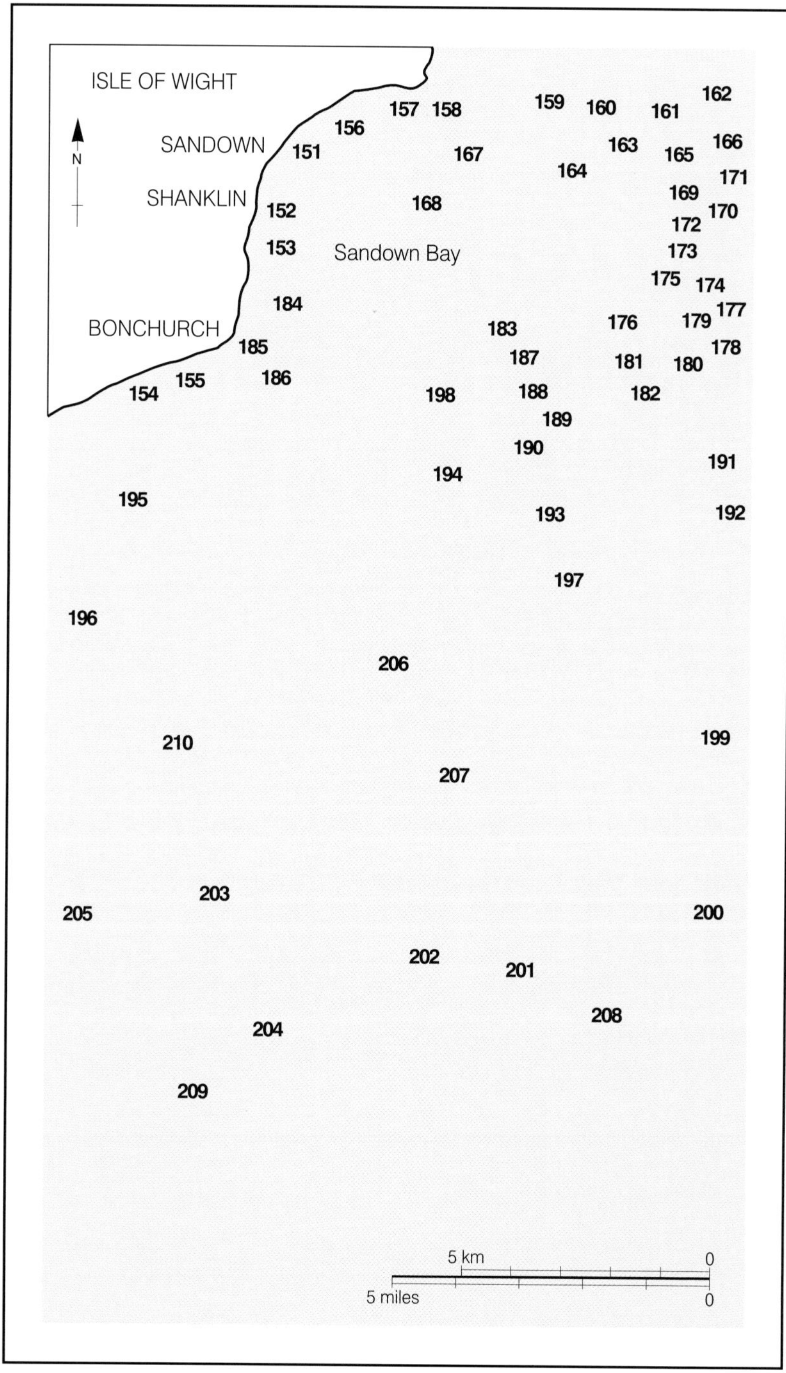
ISLE OF WIGHT
N
SANDOWN
SHANKLIN
BONCHURCH
Sandown Bay
151
152
153
154
155
156
157
158
159
160
161
162
163
164
165
166
167
168
169
170
171
172
173
174
175
176
177
178
179
180
181
182
183
184
185
186
187
188
189
190
191
192
193
194
195
196
197
198
199
200
201
202
203
204
205
206
207
208
209
210
5 km
0
5 miles
0

SHANKLIN There is a large ramp at the southern end of the Esplanade on to the sandy beach, with a car park close by. Known as the Palestine Slipway, it is Council-run and there is a charge, which includes parking space for a boat trailer but not a car.

Shore diving sites

151 Sandown This is a popular resort lying in the centre of Sandown Bay. The 400yd pier, which runs south-east from the shore, is very popular with visitors and divers. Access is straightforward from the beach, but trying to park close by can be a problem in the busy tourist season. The sea bed is mostly sand, but there are a few rocky gullies towards the pier head. Maximum depth is about 7m at high water.

152 Shanklin Another very popular resort town, lying 1¾ miles north of Dunnose. Its once busy pier used to be a much visited dive site, but following severe storm damage some years ago it was demolished. The area is still dived and much of the old pier remains can be found scattered around the sea bed, providing homes for crabs and lobsters.

The former Shanklin Pier can be found at position 50 37.75N; 01 10.25W. To locate this from the beach, travel towards the southern end of Shanklin Esplanade. Almost immediately in front of the distinctive Shanklin lift shaft the footpath rises upwards and outwards over the beach; this locates the original entrance to the pier. The remains of the pier stretch out from here in an approximately south-easterly direction for a distance of some 400m. There is a car park in front of the Shanklin lift shaft.

The sea bed is mostly sand, but a short way out there are rock gullies to explore. Towards the eastern limit of the remains of the pier the depth reaches around 7m at high water.

153 The Moorings This is a small outcrop of rocks, just to the south of the head of the now demolished pier. The name comes from the fact that the area provides a good holding ground for small boat anchors. The area is shallow, with a maximum depth of 7m, but interesting, for all sorts of items have been found by local divers, including an all-brass antique outboard. Crabs and lobsters can also be seen.

154 Ventnor This seaside resort has a population of some 7,000 in winter, but this more than doubles in the busy summer season. It lies in a sheltered position under St Boniface Down, which is the highest point on the Isle of Wight at 236m. Ventnor Pier was another popular dive site for many years, but a serious fire caused great damage to it in 1986 and it was eventually demolished. The site still provides interesting diving. Access off the sandy beach is straightforward and once in the

Opposite: Dive sites in Area 5, Culver Cliff to St Catherine's Point. This area is covered by Admiralty Chart 2045 (Outer Approaches to the Solent); Ordnance Survey Landranger Map 196.

One of the three public slipways at Shanklin. The 'Palestine' slipway at the southern end of the seafront (used by Shanklin SAC).

water the sand soon gives way to good rocky gullies. Some of these are more than 2m deep and inhabited by shellfish.

Just to the east of the remains of the pier head is a rock called The Bean, which dries over 2m at low water springs. There are obstructions around the rock as well as assorted wreckage. The Spyglass Inn on the Esplanade is popular among divers. Apart from the obvious attractions there are pictures of local wrecks and artifacts recovered from them. Car parking is difficult in the summer months, but there is a good-sized car park at the southern end of the Esplanade.

155 Chancellor 50 35.50N; 01 12.25W. Depth: 10m. Built in 1853 by Denny of Dumbarton, this 70-ton two-funnelled paddle steamer was 170ft long with a beam of 17ft and draught of 7ft. She was powered by two steam-diagonal engines of 80hp and ran between Glasgow and Arrochar for the Scottish Loch Long and Loch Lomond Company for nearly 10 years. The *Chancellor* was bought by the Stokes Bay Company in 1863 when the railway had been extended to Stokes Bay and Gosport, and with the addition of the paddle steamer had created a new route to the Isle of Wight. It is said that Queen Victoria favoured this route because it was the shortest and she was not much in favour of sea voyages.

However, the *Chancellor* was not to see much of Queen Victoria. On her second trip of the new route, on 3 July, 1863, she was moored alongside Ventnor Pier when the tide ebbed so much that a rock pierced her hull. As the tide rose again it flooded the forward part of the paddle steamer. She slewed round broadside to the

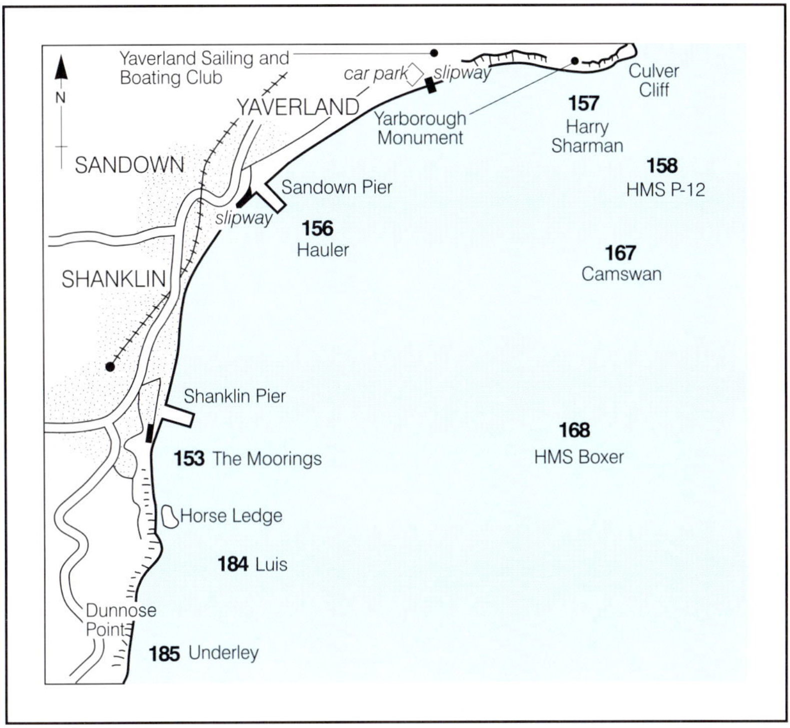

Sandown and Shanklin.

beach on the northern side of the pier, broke her back, and then split in two – she was declared a total loss. Today the remains of the paddle steamer are scattered around the area but she can still be a good rummage dive.

Boat diving sites

156 Hauler Bembridge 5½ miles; Portsmouth 10½ miles. 50 38.90N; 01 08.55W. Depth: 14m. The *Hauler* was a 100ft crane barge used by harbour contractors for piling and dredging operations. She had no propulsion of her own. On 18 September, 1973, she was being towed across Sandown Bay when the tow parted. Before it could be reconnected, she had taken on a lot of water and started sinking, finally going to the bottom ½ mile to the east of Sandown Pier. Until September 1975 the site was marked with a wreck buoy, but then a certain amount of salvage was carried out. Finally, in October 1976, the barge was dispersed with explosives.

Today this wreck is very flat and the highest part, some hull plates, stands no more than 1½m off the sea bed, which is mainly mud with a covering of fine sand. Among the wreckage are yards of rusting wire hawsers and parts of winches. There is no evidence of the actual crane and this may lie some distance from the main wreckage. Either side of the wreck are several large wooden piles approximately 12in square, probably being carried on the barge. The wreck lies east–west.

About 50yds to the north-east of the site is a good-sized rocky outcrop that stands several metres off the bottom. This is often picked up on echo sounders and mistaken for the wreck of the *Hauler*.

Above: The Chancellor (Site 155). Below: The Harry Sharman (Site 157).

157 Harry Sharman Bembridge 3½ miles; Portsmouth 8½ miles. 50 39.80N; 01 06.23W. Depth: 5m. In November 1970 a collision between the 42,000-ton crude-oil carrier *Pacific Glory* and the 46,000-ton *Allegro* left the former crippled and burning at the stern. The old steam tug *Harry Sharman* was sent out to assist with oil pollution control. During this work the tug broke down and ended up stranding at the base of Culver Cliff immediately below the Yarborough Monument. Attempts to salvage the *Harry Sharman* were unsuccessful and the tug was left to the elements. She is easy to find especially at low water when parts of the boiler stick above the surface.

Care is needed as much of the wreck is only just below the surface and could easily be hit by a small boat. Most of the superstructure and the decking have collapsed. The hull is still recognisable and the steel propeller is in place. This is a good shallow or second dive. Small boats can be launched from the beach at Yaverland, 1 mile away.

158 Stern of HMS P.12 Bembridge 3½ miles; Portsmouth 8½ miles. 50 39.40N; 01 05.00W. Depth: 22m. The *P.12* was part of the Portsmouth escort force during World War One. These patrol boats were intended primarily to help relieve destroyers of escort duty, and to be effective submarine hunters. Some 45 patrol boats were built under an emergency programme from 1915 to 1917 and they proved very successful. The 613-ton boats – 244ft long with a beam of 23ft and a draught of 7ft – were powered by twin steam turbines providing 3,500hp, which gave a top speed of 20 knots. The *P.12* was built by J.S. White of Cowes, Isle of Wight and launched on 4 December, 1915. She went into service in February 1916.

On 4 November, 1918, the *P.12* was on patrol off the Isle of Wight when she was in collision with another vessel, which cut her in two. The larger stern section sank in the above position, ½ mile to the south east of Culver Cliff. The bow section was

The patrol boat HMS P.12 sank in 1918 after a collision (Sites 137 and 158). Above: Under way. Right: A metal deck plate recovered in 1985.

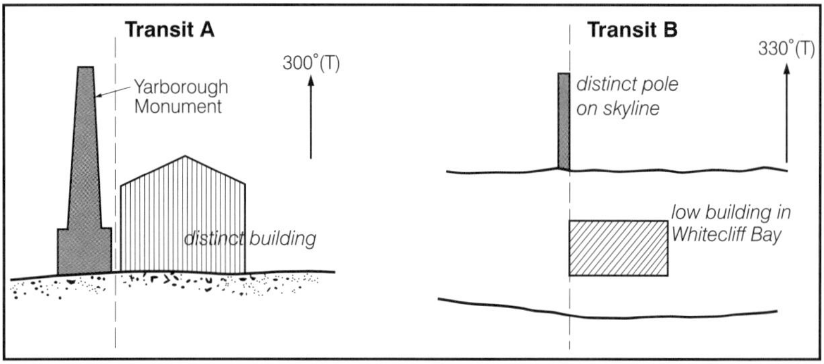

Transit marks for HMS P.12.

eventually beached in Whitecliff Bay. *The Times* of 7 November, 1918 reported one man missing, believed drowned in the collision. The stern section was discovered in 1985 by a small team of divers led by Martin Pritchard.

The wreck is an interesting dive. The stern sank onto a fairly firm sea bed and sits upright. It is reasonably intact and the sharply cut-down counter and larger rudder are quite plain. On the stern deck are many old and now harmless depth charges still in their racks. Farther forward the depth charge-throwing arms are cocked back and loaded waiting for a U-boat to appear. Finning farther forward takes one to the large turbines.

First dives here were a wreck diver's dream. Portholes were lying at regular spaces having fallen out of the rotting steel hull. Around the engines row after row of steam gauges with their needles still set at their working pressure were found, along with many other interesting artifacts. The wreckage is long and narrow and lies across the tide in a north-west and south-east direction, with the stern to the north-west. Part of the bow section (Site **137**) is sometimes uncovered on the beach at 50 40.25N; 01 05.50W.

159 Obstruction Bembridge 3 miles; Portsmouth 8 miles. 50 39.83N; 01 02.22W. Depth: 13m. An obstruction is in this position on the south-eastern edge of the Princessa Shoal, 2 miles east of Culver Cliff. It is very small and stands only ½m high. No other information is available.

160 New Venture 50 39.30N; 01 01.70W. Depth: 20m. The *New Venture* was a 42ft fishing boat, which sank on 31 December, 1978 in this approximate position, 3 miles east of Yarborough Monument. Diving information is required.

161 Wreck, name unknown Bembridge 5 miles; Portsmouth 9½ miles. 50 39.27N; 00 59.05W. Depth: 21m. This unknown wreck lies 4 miles to the east of Culver Cliffs. The wreckage may be only part of a ship as the site is fairly small. The site was dived in 1964 and the divers described the wreck as around 80ft long and 25ft wide. She was a steel-hulled vessel of double-bottom construction. There was considerable wreckage extending some 40yds from the main section. Subsequent dives have showed that the steelwork is of fairly light construction and that the largest part of the wreck is some form of steel tank, which is also the highest part, standing 1½m high.

A dinner plate recovered from the site has an inscription including the words "Southampton Masonic ... Co". The site is of small extent and is not easy to locate. Most of the scattered wreckage now appears to be buried into the sand and gravel sea bed. There is no sign of any engines, which could mean that a part of the ship is missing, but it is more likely that this is a fuel or water barge that was being towed across the Channel during Operation Neptune in June 1944.

162 Obstruction Bembridge 5½ miles; Portsmouth 10 miles. 50 39.98N; 00 57.47W. Depth: 15m. A small obstruction was located ¼ mile south-west of the Nab Tower during a 1978 survey. No further information is available.

163 Wreck, name unknown Bembridge 4 miles; Portsmouth 9 miles. 50 39.20N; 01 01.17W. Depth: 20m. This wreck was first located in the early 1970s and was at first believed to be the British collier *Stanwold*, but that wreck has been identified and located in Sussex waters at 50 38.00N; 00 20.03W. This ship is 3 miles east of Culver Cliff and was first dived in 1978. The divers reported finding a very broken and generally flat wreck, with isolated peaks of around 2m. The bows were to the east-north-east and the stern to the south-west, complete with iron propeller.

Dived again in 1986, the wreck was confirmed as flat with plates and ribs standing only inches off the sea bed. One larger section was seen, approximately 5m square and standing 2m off the bottom, probably part of the bow. Very little was recognisable and the stern was not seen. On later dives, bottles and jars found here were of British origin. Plenty of coal lying around would indicate that this was a steamship, and a collier, but no boiler has been seen so far.

164 Estrelita Bembridge 4 miles; Portsmouth 9 miles. 50 38.83N; 01 01.90W. Depth: 25m. This is a 25-ton 50ft wooden MFV and stands 2m proud. She was sunk on 3 August, 1975, and is now very broken.

165 Crab Rocks Bembridge 5 miles; Portsmouth 10 miles. 50 38.55N; 00 59.17W. Depth: 17m. This "wreckage", 2 miles south-west of the Nab Tower, was first located in 1978. It was about 100ft long and 50ft wide standing between 2 and 4m high and lying east–west.

This position has twice been surveyed since then with a proton magnetometer, but no firm contacts were picked up. The only real contact was on the echo sounder, which did pick up an obstruction of similar proportions, but this appeared to be a rocky outcrop. Diving on the site confirmed the presence of a rocky outcrop. This is now called "Crab Rocks" locally as it is a good spot for edible crabs. Divers have found some small brass fittings among the rocks but nothing to justify calling this a wreck site.

166 Wreck, name unknown Bembridge 5 miles; Portsmouth 10 miles. 50 38.65N; 00 58.40W. Depth: 18m. This site was first located 1¾ miles south-west of the Nab Tower in 1974, and was believed to have been a small fishing boat. The site has since been dived by Portsmouth diver Mike Walsh who found a most unusual “wreck”. It is a large box section made up of several compartments. It is about 40ft long and 12ft wide, and stands 2m high. There is a bulkhead between each compartment and a large hole through each compartment in the same position.

The wreckage lies in an east–west direction and is part of the harbour sections being towed to France on D-Day.

167 Camswan Bembridge 5 miles; Portsmouth 10 miles. 50 38.70N; 01 05.38W. Depth: 18m. The 3,426-ton British steamship *Camswan* was built of steel with corrugated sides by the Blyth Shipbuilding Company in 1917. She measured 335ft by 51ft by 23ft and was fitted with a triple expansion steam engine of 298hp.

At the time of her loss she was owned by the Osborne Steamship Company of Blyth. On 19 October, 1917, on her maiden voyage from Blyth to Naples with a cargo of coal, the *Camswan* was in collision with another British steamship, the *Polbrai*, 8 miles south-west of St Catherine’s Point. The *Camswan* was badly damaged but managed to make it into the shallow waters of Sandown Bay before sinking 1½ miles south-east of Culver Cliff. All the crew were saved.

Much of the wreck was dispersed with explosives during the 1920s, but this is a large site with plenty to explore. The average height of the wreckage is 3 to 4m. The ship’s sternpost stands defiantly about 4m high, with her large steel propeller behind it. Some parts of the wreck are completely flat, but this is still a good rummage dive, as local diver John Nuttall will testify. In 1989 Nuttall found one of the ship’s smaller bells in a newly collapsed section of the wreck. It was engraved “S.S. CAMSWAN 1917”. Shortly afterwards, Martin Woodward found the ship’s telegraph.

168 HMS Boxer Bembridge 5 miles; Portsmouth 10 miles. 50 37.77N; 01 06.37W. Depth: 20m. HMS *Boxer* was one of Britain’s earliest destroyers. One of three identical ships, she was the first of the “A” class torpedo boat destroyers. The other two ships were HMS *Ardent* and HMS *Bruiser*. HMS *Boxer* was laid down in February 1894 and finally completed in June 1895 by Thornycroft at their Chiswick yard, at a cost of £35,780. The destroyer was 200ft long with a beam of 19ft; during her 3-hour trial she achieved a top speed of over 29 knots. HMS *Boxer* carried a crew of 55 and was armed with one 12-pounder and five 6-pounder guns and two 14in torpedo tubes. Her triple expansion engines drove two shafts and produced some 4,000hp, giving her an average top speed of 27 knots. For fuel she carried 60 tons of coal.

At the time of her loss, the 260-ton *Boxer* was Britain’s oldest serving destroyer, but maybe her luck was starting to run out. On 6 February, 1918, she was in collision with HMS *Decoy*, then 2 days later on 8 February she collided with the ambulance transport ship *St Patrick* 1½ miles south-east of Dunnose Point, a little after 7pm. The *Boxer* was badly damaged, with one man killed. She started sinking and finally disappeared in the centre of Sandown Bay at 12.15am on 9 February, 1918.

The site lies 2½ miles out from the beach at Sandown. It was first dived in the early 1970s by the Deo Volente Club, who tried unsuccessfully to purchase the wreck. During 1972 a salvage company raised the condensers and propellers. In the following years the *Boxer* became a popular dive for members of the Shanklin Underwater Club. They recovered many interesting items, including some rum jars.

Above: The destroyer HMS Boxer (Site 168) sank in Sandown Bay in 1918.
Below: Transit marks for finding her.

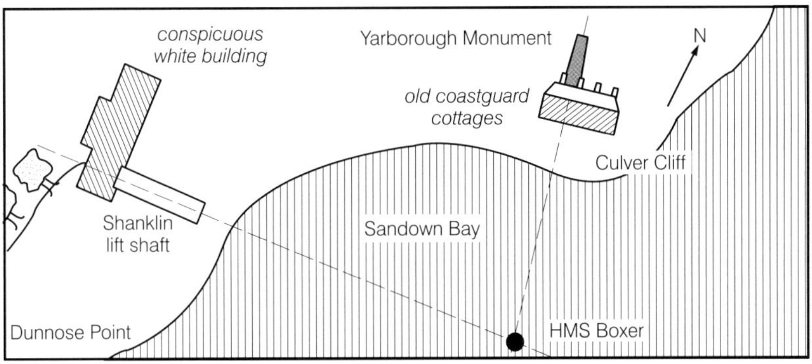

One local diver, Dougie Saunders, was lucky – his jar was still full and well corked. Today the wreck has largely disappeared and very little of the hull remains. Only the boilers stand some 3m off the mud and sand sea bed, but bits and pieces can still be found by those willing to dig into the mud.

169 Wreck, name unknown Bembridge 5½ miles; Portsmouth 10 miles. 50 38.12N; 00 59.53W. Depth: 20m. A small double obstruction is located in this position 2½ miles south-west of the Nab Tower. It is reported to be only 0.6m high. No diving information is available.

170 Elford Bembridge 6 miles; Portsmouth 11½ miles. 50 38.13N; 00 58.48W. Depth: 24m. The 1,739-ton steamer *Elford* ran into a mine laid by a U-boat 2 miles south of the Nab Light Vessel on 18 May, 1917. All the crew managed to take to the boats safely before she sank. The wreck was believed to have broken up some years ago and so the *Elford* was deleted from the charts. In fact, much of the ship remains though most of the hull has rusted away. The *Elford* is well broken now but her boiler, engine and steering quadrant still stand some 5 to 6m proud. Within the wreck, still recognisable as a ship, are many railway wheels and bogies, which were part of her cargo. The bow points to the west. The stern section is lying over some 40 degrees on the starboard side. The *Elford* is difficult to locate as she lies amid an isolated area of rocks that stand almost as proud as she does.

171 Steel Barge Bembridge 7 miles; Portsmouth 11 miles. 50 38.53N; 00 56.35W. Depth: 20m. This steel barge is 2 miles south of the Nab Tower. She is around 60ft long, lies east–west, and stands 3m high. The barge is motorised as two engines and drives have been seen. The wreck is fairly intact and sits upright. The hold is completely filled with a large cylindrical container.

This wreck is very similar to the one at Site **161** and was probably another fuel or water barge heading for the Normandy beaches in 1944.

172 The Hump Bembridge 6 miles, Portsmouth 11½ miles. 50 38.00N; 00 58.73W. Depth: 20m. A large mound giving a strong magnetic anomaly is located in this position 2 miles south-west of the Nab Tower. The site has been dived, but no wreckage was found. Whatever it is appears to be completely buried in the sea bed of sand and shingle.

173 Apley Bembridge 7½ miles; Portsmouth 12 miles. 50 36.98N; 00 56.00W. Depth: 35m. This Royal Navy hired trawler was sunk by a mine on 6 December, 1917, while engaged in sweeping duties. A 250-ton ship, she is now upright 6m proud on the sea bed of shingle. The mine explosion has caused a great deal of damage to the bow and she lies east–west.

174 Barge Bembridge 6½ miles; Portsmouth 11½ miles. 50 37.00N; 00 58.50W. Depth: 28m. A small wreck of barge shape, about 50ft long with a beam of 24ft, lies north–south on the edge of a steep slope, from which she stands 5m proud.

175 Wreck, name unknown Bembridge 5½ miles; Portsmouth 10 miles. 50 38.52N; 00 59.00W. Depth: 18m. Guarded on the north by a rocky ridge 100yds from the actual wreck site, this is a tricky wreck to find. It appears to be only 30ft long, but it is impossible to tell this accurately from sonar details as the wreck lies on the slope of a steep bank. Diving information is required.

176 Pontoons Bembridge 6½ miles; Portsmouth 11½ miles. 50 36.37N; 01 00.92W. Depth: 25m. This site consists of two large steel pontoons. Each one measures about 145ft by 32ft. They are 10yds apart, joined together by some sort of steel mesh, and lie east–west with a maximum height of 3m. These are two of the many harbour and bridge sections that were designed to be towed across the Channel to Normandy during Operation Neptune in June 1944.

177 Bow of the Bettann Bembridge 8 miles; Portsmouth 13 miles. 50 36.13N; 00 57.33W. Depth: 40m. This wreck is the bow section of the Danish motor vessel *Bettann*, which sank off St Helens on 19 January, 1967 (see Site **132** for details of the loss and current position of the stern section). The bow section was towed out to the deep-water spoil ground 6 miles south-east of Culver Cliff and sunk.

The site was dived in 1976 and the divers reported finding the bow half of a fairly modern ship, about 25m long and standing 8m high. There was a diesel engine mounted on the foredeck. The hold appeared to be full of clay. This would certainly tie in with the *Bettann* as she was carrying a cargo of china clay at the time of her loss. The wreck lies across the tide in a north-east and south-west direction.

178 Wreck, name unknown Bembridge 8 miles; Portsmouth 13 miles. 50 36.03N; 00 56.47W. Depth: 43m. This site is of a very small wreck. She is 25ft long and stands less than 2m off the bottom, which is mainly sand. It may be that this is a small fishing boat or a part of a wreck, but is more likely to be discarded debris of some sort as this spot is right in the centre of the deep-water spoil ground 6 miles south-east of Culver Cliff.

179 Cuba Bembridge 8 miles; Portsmouth 12 miles. 50 36.00N; 00 58.58W. Depth: 32m. This is the largest wreck in the area. The *Cuba* was a very big kill for Kapitänleutnant Ernst Cordes on 6 April, 1945, so big that it brought about his own destruction and that of his submarine *U-1195*.

The *Cuba* was built as a two-funnel passenger liner for the French Compagnie Générale Transatlantique by Swan Hunter and Wigham Richardson of Newcastle in 1923. She was 476ft long with a beam of 62ft and her 10,300hp engines could push her 11,420 tons along at 15½ knots. The ship was designed by the French company for the West Indies and Central America route. The *Cuba*'s peacetime cruising career came to an abrupt end after she left Martinique on 24 October, 1940, bound for Casablanca. She was intercepted by a British warship on 31 October. After that she sailed under the British flag and was used sometimes as a troopship. She was managed for the Ministry of War Transport by Cunard White Star.

The *Cuba* was acting as a trooper when heading home to Southampton from Le Havre with 223 troops and crew aboard, plus 29 gunners for her many guns, as part of Convoy VWP 16 on 6 April, 1945. This convoy had six destroyers as escorts, but

The two-funnel pasenger liner Cuba (Site 179) sunk by a torpedo fired from U-1195 .

when Ernst Cordes saw the *Cuba* through his periscope he could not let her pass. At 4.13am he hit her with a single torpedo, which killed only one member of the crew but did the necessary damage to sink the ship. As *U-1195* turned away, the *Cuba* began to settle slowly and stayed upright to the end. This enabled all aboard to be taken off before she went under.

The destroyers were after Cordes from the moment the torpedo struck and they hunted the *U-1195* down – see Site **192**.

The *Cuba* has been heavily salvaged and was dispersed by the Royal Navy in 1959. The majority of the ship is well broken, but some parts of the wreckage still stand 14m proud. This is a fascinating dive with wreckage all around. Some areas are quite recognisable though much of it seems to be piles of steel plate and great girders. It is a very large site and needs several dives to see most of it. The *Cuba* was a luxury liner in her day and passengers had more than 200 portholes to look out of on their voyages. Many of them are still hidden among the wreckage, which has a scour nearly 2m deep on the north-east side. The wreckage lies north-east to south-west on a sea bed of mud, shingle and sand, which is deeply rippled. Visibility is usually poor from dumping on the nearby spoil ground. The two 10-ton propellers have been salvaged.

180 Wreck, name unknown Bembridge 8 miles; Portsmouth 12½ miles. 50 35.70N; 00 58.53W. Depth: 30m. This wreck is difficult to spot on the ordinary echo-sounder, because the sea bed consists of rocky ridges with sand valleys, but the 42ft "unknown" wreck definitely exists. Well broken, she is lying east–west and standing 4m proud in an area of particularly steep ridging.

181 Piper Aeroplane Bembridge 6½ miles; Portsmouth 11½ miles. 50 35.97N; 01 00.67W. Depth: 30m. This Piper light aircraft (G-ARLS) ditched into the sea 4½ miles south-west of the Nab Tower on 31 July, 1975, after losing power in both engines. The pilot escaped with minor injuries. The area was surveyed a month later and an obstruction standing some 2m off the sea bed was located. A local fisherman is said to have got his pot lines hooked into an aeroplane in this area and managed to winch the whole thing off the bottom before it broke away. If it was the Piper then it may well be in a new position nearby.

182 Spoil Ground Wreck Bembridge 8 miles; Portsmouth 13 miles. 50 35.85N; 00 59.40W. Depth: 35m. Whether this is a wreck it is difficult to say. It has never been dived and was located by magnetometer only. Whatever it is sits in the middle of spoil ground where salvage divers say there are bits of metal, large and small, all over the place. As a result of the doubt over the wreck's existence, the Admiralty do not chart it.

183 Camberwell Bembridge 7½ miles; Portsmouth 12½ miles. 50 35.70N; 01 03.67W. Depth: 30m. This wreck is one of a cluster of World War One sinkings approximately 5½ miles east of Ventnor on the Isle of Wight. There has been confusion about the identities of some of these ships for a long time, but it now seems most likely that the wreck in the above position is that of the British steamer *Camberwell*. The 4,078-ton *Camberwell* was built of steel in 1903 by J.L. Thompson and Sons of Sunderland for the Well Line. She was 368ft long with a beam of 50ft

The cargo steamer Camberwell (Site 183) sank after hitting a mine in 1917, with the loss of seven of her crew.

and a draught of 19ft. Her 10 knot top speed came from three-cylinder triple-expansion engines with three boilers producing 409hp.

The steamer left Middlesbrough for London in early May 1917 and took on 5,000 tons of general cargo bound for Colombo, Madras (now Chennai) and Calcutta. At 6am on 18 May the *Camberwell* was warned by a patrol vessel near the Owers that there were mines nearby and that she should keep farther out to sea. Though her master Frederick Adamson did not know it, by 7.10am the *Camberwell* had entered a German minefield laid by the submarine *UC-36*. Five minutes later a huge explosion rocked the ship, blowing off the hatch covers and letting so much water in through a hole in her side that she almost immediately started listing to starboard. Of the crew of 65, seven were British, the remainer mostly Indian (of whom seven died in the mine explosion). The survivors took to the boats and were soon picked up by patrol vessels.

Today the wreck is an interesting and popular dive. The ship is well broken up midships, and is heeled over to starboard. She lies north–south with bows to the south on a sea bed of sand and shingle. The bows and stern are fairly intact and the 4.7in quick-firing gun is still in place on the stern. Much of the cargo, which consisted of a wide variety of goods including wine, olive oil, cement and fertiliser, can be seen in the wreckage. More unusual items recovered are Indian 10-rupee notes and pre-paid postcards intended for the use of British troops stationed in India.

The ship and cargo are owned by Offshore Marine Services of Bembridge.

184 Luis Bembridge 7 miles; Portsmouth 12 miles. 50 36.45N; 01 09.92W. Depth: 17m. This site is the wreck of the British merchant steamship *Luis*. She was built in 1916 of steel by W. Gray and Company of West Hartlepool and measured 380ft by 53ft by 24ft. At the time of her loss she was owned by C. Nielson and Sons.

The 4,284-ton *Luis* had left Halifax in Nova Scotia, bound for St Helen's Roads with a cargo of flour, oats, timber and many tons of 18lb artillery shells destined for the battlefields of France. In the evening of 12 April, 1918, while rounding St Catherine's Point as the thirteenth in a 20-ship convoy, the *Luis* was torpedoed by the German submarine *UC-71*. Oberleutnant Marzecha attacked the convoy from a

This photograph taken on board the salvage vessel shows a pile of shells recovered from the Luis (Site 184). Two divers can be seen at top right.

surface position, despite its strong escort. He fired two torpedoes in quick succession at the *Luis*; the engine room and bunkers on the port side took the hits. Despite the jets of scalding steam in the engine room and his own terrible burns, the second engineer, Robert Coulson, managed to carry another injured man up the ladder to safety. Both men died later, as did two other seamen. Coulson was posthumously awarded the Albert Medal for his bravery. Captain P.W. Woodruff was able to coax his sinking ship in towards the shallow water of Sandown Bay where the *Luis* finally sank ¼ mile offshore opposite Luccombe Chine.

For many years her masts, funnel and bridge were clearly visible sticking out of the water. When they finally collapsed in 1921 the Navy decided that the wreck should be dispersed, as she was a danger to other ships. Dispersal blasting operations were completed in 1923. The *Luis* was forgotten until the early 1970s when a salvage team located the wreck and began hauling up the many tons of shells. People on the beach were entranced to see the crewmen on the salvage vessel breaking the shells from their boxes and then smashing them across the ship's bollards to separate the heads from the brass cases.

Transit marks for the Luis (Site 184).

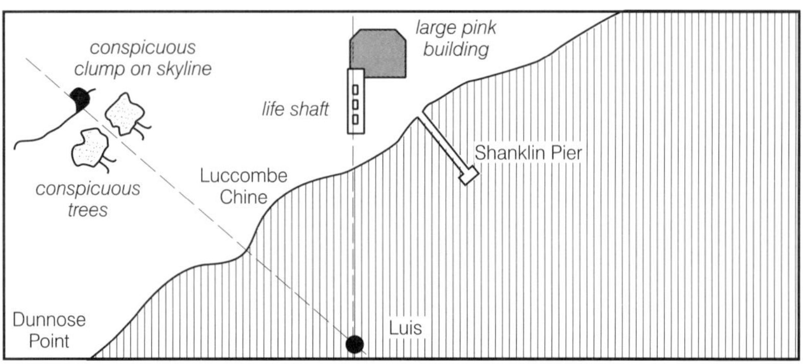

Today the *Luis* is a popular dive site. There is plenty to explore. The wreck is well broken up, but the two huge boilers and parts of the stern stand some 3 to 4m off the sea bed. On the north side of the boilers it is still possible to find the odd shell case and the intricate brass shell heads that the salvage men left behind. Scattered all around the site are quantities of small, round lead shot from the anti-personnel filling of the large shells.

The tidal stream runs quite hard, especially on the ebb. Slack water times on the *Luis* are 3 to 2½ hours before high water at Portsmouth and 5 hours after. Small boats can be launched from Shanklin beach, which is only 1 mile from the site.

185 Underley Bembridge 8 miles; Portsmouth 13½ miles. 50 36.00N; 01 11.00W. Depth: 3m. The *Underley* was 225ft long with a beam of 37ft and 1,292 tons in weight. She was heading for Melbourne, Australia, in September 1871 with a cargo of machinery, gunpowder and cotton worth some £30,000. In addition she carried 30 emigrating passengers. Although it was calm on the night of 25 September, 1871, this fine, fully rigged sailing ship ran onto rocks just off the stretch of coast between Bonchurch and Luccombe. It was expected that she would be quickly towed off after she went ashore, but a fresh wind sprang up from the south-east and impaled the ship on the rocks. The passengers and crew were taken ashore and the *Underley* was abandoned – at the time, the largest sailing ship to become a total loss.

Today the ship is almost totally broken up, but it is possible to find parts of the wreck scattered around the rocks; larger bits have become buried in the sand. The site is worth visiting after a strong south-easterly gale as this can remove large quantities of sand from the site and expose many new parts of the wreck.

WARNING Although the site is very close to the shore, the tide can run quickly here and rummagers should take care not to be caught unawares.

186 Wreck, name unknown 50 35.33N; 01 10.15W. Depth: 50m. An unknown obstruction was reported in this position in 1980. At one time this was believed to be the wreck of the *Polo* – see Site **187**. Diving information is required.

187 Polo Bembridge 7 miles; Portsmouth 12 miles. 50 35.62N; 01 04.12W. Depth: 30m. The 2,915-ton *Polo*, 300ft long with a beam of 45ft, was built in 1913 by Earles of Hull and described as a liner, which did not refer to her size but to the fact that she carried passengers as well as cargo on regular routes. On 12 February, 1918 the *Polo* was carrying 3,200 tons of general cargo and coal from Hull for Malta and Alexandria when Oberleutnant Johann Lohs torpedoed her from *UB-57* at 10.45pm, from periscope depth, as she came down the Channel. The torpedo hit her in the port side just forward of the bridge, opening up a huge hole in her No. 2 hold. The *Polo* listed rapidly to port, so severely that only the port lifeboat and the jolly boat could be launched. Three men were lost in the sinking, which was all over in 8 minutes. Though the cargo manifest makes no mention of any munitions, Lohs had no doubt about what he thought the *Polo* really carried. He wrote in his log: "In Admiralty service with a cargo of mines for the Mediterranean".

Today the wreck lies heeled over to her port side. The stern is the highest part standing some 7 to 8m off the sand and shingle sea bed. Her steering quadrant shows clear. Forward of the boilers much of the ship is broken and flattened; the masts are off to the port side. There is a lot of coal on the site, but no sign of any mines. The wreck has been positively identified by the bell.

188 Wreck, name unknown Bembridge 7 miles; Portsmouth 12 miles. 50 35.08N; 01 02.60W. Depth: 30m. This unknown wreck was first located in 1983 by sonar, but was not dived until 1986. It is a steel wreck, around 60ft long and broken in two midships. The bow is totally upside down. The stern lies on its port side and there is a three-bladed steel propeller of about 6ft diameter partially buried in the bottom. Alongside the wreck are two steel masts. This gives the impression that the wreck is of an old trawler. There is an abundance of marine life on this site, including giant crabs. The wreck stands a maximum of 3m off the shingle and sand sea bed.

189 Kurland Bembridge 8 miles; Portsmouth 13 miles. 50 34.73N; 01 03.33W. Depth: 35m The *Kurland* is one of a cluster of World War One wrecks, which include the *Polo* (Site **187**) and the *Camberwell* (Site **183**). It has been difficult to obtain positive identification of some of these wrecks, but this one is most likely to be the *Kurland*, which was not the victim of any U-boat but of a collision.

Built in 1888 by J.L. Thompson and Sons of Sunderland for the Tyzack and Branfoot Steam Shipping Company, also of Sunderland, this 2,022-ton ship was originally named *William Branfoot*. Measuring 283ft by 36ft by 17ft, she was powered by a triple-expansion steam engine with a single boiler giving 211hp. The *William Branfoot* was later sold to the Belgian Ocean shipping company and renamed *Kurland*.

Soon after the start of World War One the *Kurland* was armed with a 75mm gun on her stern. This gun was used early in December 1917 when the ship was attacked by a German U-boat east of the English Channel as she headed for Calais from New York with a cargo of rifles and ammunition, bricks, horseshoes, wheels, tyres and other war supplies for the Belgian government. The captain, Georges Nyland, managed to shake off the U-boat and continued on his journey.

At 5am on 13 December, as she was clearing the southernmost point of the Isle of Wight, the *Kurland* was rammed amidships by the 860-ton British steamer *Deventia*. The *Kurland* was badly damaged and fast began taking in water. The *Deventia* went full astern and freed herself, but then, much to Georges Nyland's surprise, steamed off into the night, either unaware of the serious damage done or choosing to ignore it. The *Kurland* sank a few minutes later, but most of her crew of 25 survived.

Today the wreck lies with the stern to the south-east and the bows to the north-west. She stands 7m proud. Although badly broken amidships, the stern and bows are reasonably intact and are tilted slightly upwards from the stone and shingle sea bed. The ship had four holds and it is possible to see some of the cargo, particularly the bricks, boxes of rifles, wheels and tyres.

190 Leon Bembridge 8 miles; Portsmouth 13 miles. 50 34.47N; 01 03.57W. Depth: 35m. This is another member of the group of World War One wrecks lying about 5½ miles east of Ventnor. It is certainly the remains of an armed merchantman of the 1914–18 period. Items recovered from the wreckage suggest that this was a French vessel and strengthen the view of many divers that this is *Leon*, although positive identification is needed. The wreck is 600yds to the south-west of the *Kurland* (Site **189**).

The 2,451-ton *Leon* was built in 1895 by W. Pickersgill and Sons of Sunderland and launched as the *Acacia*. The ship was 295ft long with a beam of 42ft. She drew 17ft and was equipped with a three-cylinder triple-expansion engine with two boilers giving 220hp. Well before the war the *Acacia* was sold to the French Compagnie des Vapeurs of Nantes. One of the Admiralty's wartime weekly reports from coastal stations clearly states that the *Leon* was carrying 2,250 tons of coal and 600 tons of coke consigned to Tunis. There seems little sign of this quantity of coal in the wreckage. All other reports say that the *Leon* was carrying coal and general government supplies from Hull, and was bound for Malta and Alexandria. There is a suggestion that the unknown wreck (Site **200**) could be the *Leon*, but diving has yet to confirm or deny this.

If there is doubt that this is the *Leon*, there can be no doubt that Captain Louis Orchambeau was almost asking to be sunk. He was sailing down the Channel as dawn was breaking on 7 January, 1918, with all his navigation lights on and without making any attempt to zigzag. Oberleutnant Johann Lohs, captain of the mine-laying U-boat *UC-75* could not let the opportunity pass. Ignoring the fact that the *Leon* was clearly armed with two big 90mm cannons, the U-boat surfaced to make his torpedo shot all the easier. By now it was dawn, the weather was moderate with an overcast sky, and visibility was about 1 mile. The *Leon* came on across the submarine's bow at a steady 7 knots, steering a course west by north magnetic. Although Captain Orchambeau and a lookout were on the bridge, and another lookout was on the forecastle, incredibly, none of them saw *UC-75*. At 5am Lohs' torpedo struck the *Leon* in the starboard side and blew a great hole into the second hold. *UC-75* had submerged as soon as the torpedo had been fired and the crew of the *Leon* were convinced that they had struck a mine. They continued to believe that until metal fragments picked up from the deck were later examined by the Commanding Officer of HM Mining School and identified as pieces of a German torpedo. (Lohs had no doubt that he had hit the *Leon* and lingered, watching through his periscope until she sank 75 minutes after the torpedo struck. He then turned for home and re-entered Zeebrugge on 8 January, 1918.)

On board the *Leon* there was panic among some of the 34 crew. Four ignored the master's orders and rushed to launch one of the small lifeboats. They made the mistake of lowering it into the water before the ship had lost way, and as it hit the water it capsized. The four men were never seen again. If Lohs had feared that the *Leon*'s wireless would bring depth-charging patrol boats down on him, he need not have worried. Captain Orchambeau quickly found that the explosion had put his radio completely out of action. He waited for a while until it was clear that the *Leon* was sinking under them and then ordered "abandon ship". This time all of the rest of the crew got into the lifeboats without difficulty and were able to sit in the boats and watch their ship plunge to the sea bed. Eventually the survivors of the *Leon* were picked up by a patrol boat and landed safely on the Isle of Wight.

This ship stands upright, some 7m proud. At 30m, the stern is reasonably intact with a large iron propeller in place, and there is a gun on the stern deck, from which 75mm shell cases have been recovered. The ship's holds are open and parts of a varied cargo can be seen in them. Most conspicuous are boxes of .303 rifles but, unfortunately, once on the surface the steel barrels and breeches disintegrate. Between the holds the top of one of the boilers is clear. The bow area is much broken and slightly deeper at 35m.

191 Tenace Bembridge 9½ miles; Portsmouth 15 miles. 50 34.60N; 00 56.05W. Depth: 30m. The 23-ton yacht *Tenace* sank in this position, 5½ miles south of the Nab Tower, after being in collision with the Japanese motor vessel *Heian Maru* on 14 July, 1967. The position was surveyed in 1977, but since then no evidence of the wreck has been found and it is believed to have broken up completely.

192 U-1195 Bembridge 11 miles; Portsmouth 16 miles. 50 33.17N; 00 56.09W. Depth: 30m. Kapitänleutnant Ernst Cordes and 17 of his crew of 34 were killed on 6 April, 1945, after his attack on Convoy No. VWP 16 as it headed for Southampton across Sandown Bay towards the Solent. The convoy had six escorts and two of them turned back to hunt Cordes after he torpedoed the troopship *Cuba* (Site **179**).

Cordes ran to the south-east and the deeper water, but the escorts were quickly on his trail. So he sat his Mk VII U-boat just off the sea bed and shut down all machinery. The ruse did not work. The hunters – the Canadian frigate HMCS *Monnow* and the destroyer HMS *Watchman* – were soon overhead. A Hedgehog depth charge from HMS *Watchman* landed forward of the control tower of the 871-ton, 220ft submarine and blew a hole in the hull. As the submarine flooded she plunged into the sea bed at 30m and lay over 40 degrees to starboard. There were then only 19 men alive in the boat – eight in the control room and eleven near the aft escape hatch. The group in the control room made a straightforward and successful escape, but the angle at which the U-boat was lying made the escape trunking for the aft group lie almost level and meant a scramble along it to the hatch. The crew flooded the compartment almost to the top to equalise the pressure. There were not enough Drager escape sets to go round and chlorine gas began to choke the men. The chief warrant officer aboard took control, but the first man he sent into the trunking panicked and drowned inside. It took three men to pull his body back out of the way. The remainder of the crew also began to panic, but the warrant officer grabbed each one in turn and pushed him up the trunking, and out. The warrant officer was the last to leave; Cordes was not among the survivors.

It was a swift end to a long career as a U-boat captain for Ernst Cordes. He first appears in records as a U-boat commander in 1940 when he lost *U-560* in a collision in the Baltic. His best day was probably 5 July, 1944, when from *U-763* he sent a torpedo with a pre-set gyro and a zigzag course right into the side of the 1,499-ton Norwegian steamer *Ringen* at precisely 4.03pm. The *Ringen* was an old ship – built in 1917 with her home port Oslo – but was being used in Convoy ETC 26 on the eastern feeder route to supply the Allied armies in Normandy. She sank swiftly. On his command debut Cordes was not satisfied with just one ship, however. That same day, at 9.45pm, he damaged another steamer of 4,000 tons with an acoustic homing torpedo called a "Gnat". Three minutes later another of his torpedoes exploded on a 3,000-ton steamer. At 10pm he claimed another strike. Cordes was active again on 11 July, 1944, still in command of *U-763*, when he claimed to have sunk another destroyer with a Gnat torpedo, but there is no record of any British warship being sunk on that date. Certainly Cordes made an attack and reported hearing a Gnat end-of-run detonation after 9 minutes, 28 seconds: he may well have confused this with a hit. Cordes next appears in German records – and goes straight into many a diver's logbook – when, on 21 March, 1945, now commanding *U-1195*, he sank the much-dived Liberty ship *James Eagan Layne* off Plymouth (see the companion volume *Dive South Cornwall*). It was on that same mission, though now much farther up the Channel, that Cordes sank the *Cuba* on 6

April, and brought destruction on himself. Although an approximate position was known for *U-1195* ever since her sinking, it was not until 1975 that a salvage company finally identified the exact spot.

Today, the submarine – which is a war grave and should be dived accordingly – lies on her starboard side at an angle of 45 degrees. She is on a slight sand and shingle slope, with bows to the north-east and down the slope. There is very severe damage – probably from the depth charge – just forward of the conning tower. The stern is high and both steel propellers are still there and well clear of the bottom. The wreck – 200ft long with a beam of 20ft and a depth of 16ft – stands some 4m proud of the sea bed. The highest point is the top of the periscope in which the optical lens can still be seen. The deck gun is missing. The damaged area in front of the conning tower has a big hole in it. Though the bulkhead is still intact, the watertight door is missing and it is possible to see straight into the control room through the yard-wide opening. This part is heavily silted, so much so that the lower parts of the periscopes continue into the silt. The torpedo tubes are still in place and are of steel. The pressure hull is rotting and holes are appearing in it; through one of these it is possible to see one of the large air tanks. The visibility around the wreck is usually good, as a result of light being reflected upwards off the pale-coloured sand and shingle of the bottom.

193 Wreck, name unknown Bembridge 9 miles; Portsmouth 14 miles. 50 33.25N; 01 03.62W. Depth: 31m. Unidentified remains were first located here in 1918 and it is likely that this is a World War One wreck. She lies 5 miles east of Ventnor. The wreck was first dived by salvage divers in 1975 and they reported finding an old coaster, standing some 5m proud of the sand and gravel sea bed. The wreck has often been dived since then, but the remains are now very broken and mostly unrecognisable. The bows are fairly intact, and a large anchor with masses of chain was mixed up within the wreckage. The wreck appears well salvaged, as there are many old hawsers, old tyres and 45-gallon drums spread around the site.

194 Wreck, name unknown Bembridge 9 miles; Portsmouth 14 miles. 50 34.17N; 01 05.83W. Depth: 20m. An unknown ship was reported sunk in this approximate position 3½ miles east of Dunnose Point in May 1918, when two masts were seen sticking out of the water.

195 Isleworth Bembridge 12 miles; Portsmouth 17 miles. 50 35.62N; 01 13.77W. Depth: 51m. On the south-west corner of the old explosives dumping ground of St Catherine's Deep is the wreck of the *Isleworth*, a 2,871-ton steamer laden with 4,200 tons of iron ore from Bilbao for Middlesbrough. The *Isleworth*, 320ft long with a beam of 46ft, was hit 3 miles off Ventnor. She was torpedoed at 1.30pm on 30 April, 1918, by the *UC-17*, which was commanded by Oberleutnant Erich Stephan. Though the captain, the third mate and two gunners for the 12-pounder gun on her stern survived, 29 of the crew died in the sinking.

The British steamer was no stranger to submarines. Built in 1896, the *Isleworth* had been in operation for the Britain Steamship Company throughout the war. The previous September she had been chased by a U-boat on the surface to the north of Scotland, and had escaped only because of the foul weather and onset of darkness. On 20 January, 1918, a torpedo narrowly missed her in the Bristol

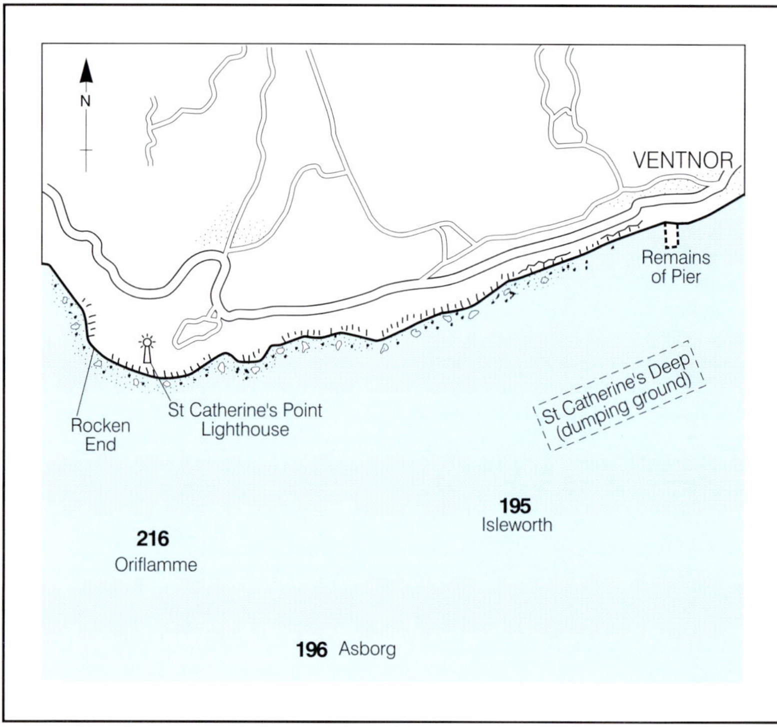

St Catherine's Point.

Channel. Four months later, the torpedo struck the *Isleworth* on the starboard side and the steamer sank within seconds.

Today the wreck is upright, but her depth has tended to restrict diving here. She is collapsing amidships around the area of torpedo damage, though the bow and stern are largely intact.

196 Asborg Bembridge 14 miles; Portsmouth 19 miles. 50 31.50N; 01 15.90W. Depth: 20m. The *Asborg*, a 2,750-ton boat built in 1896 by Short Brothers, was owned by a Norwegian company at the time of her sinking and was travelling from the Tyne to Livorno in Italy. She was 320ft long with a beam of 43ft.

Oberleutnant Johann Lohs in *UC-75* noted the *Asborg* in his log as "a steamer travelling alone with steelplate and coal". He was right: she was carrying 450 tons of steel plates and 3,350 tons of coal. Presumably Lohs got this information from questioning the crew in their lifeboats, because they were all saved after he put a torpedo into *Asborg*'s port side at 3am on 3 January, 1918.

Today the wreck is upright, broken, but 8m proud. The engine room is wide open as a result of the torpedo blast. She lies east–west on a sand and gravel sea bed.

197 Wapello Bembridge 11 miles; Portsmouth 16 miles. 50 31.92N; 01 02.87W. Depth: 30m. The 5,576-ton *Wapello* was built in 1912 by Armstrong Whitworth of Newcastle as the *Clio*, but when owned by the Tank Storage and Carriage Company of London was renamed. She was 396ft long with a beam of 50ft and powered by a four-cylinder quadruple expansion engine with three boilers, which gave her 505hp.

The *Walpello* was heading for Thameshaven from Philadelphia with a full cargo of benzine and had called at Falmouth to pick up an escort for her run up the Channel. As a big ship with a valuable cargo she was given two armed trawlers as escorts. On 15 June, 1917, as she steamed past the southernmost point of the Isle of Wight at 9 knots, she was spotted by Oberleutnant Reinhold Salzwedel in *UC-71*. At 9pm Salzwedel sent a torpedo into the *Walpello*'s starboard side and it blew a huge hole in the bunkers. Two of the crew of 46 died in the explosion. Though the ship sank swiftly, the remainder of the crew, including the master, Captain D. MacDonald, were taken off by the escort trawlers *Caliph* and *Lord Stanhope*.

This was not the first encounter of the *Wapello* with a submarine. She had only recently been attacked on a voyage over the same route – on 21 April, 1917 when off the coast of south-west Ireland – but on that occasion the submarine had surfaced and used a gun. The *Wapello* had replied with her 12-pounder and the submarine had given up the chase. This time the *Walpello* had no chance to get her gun into action and Salzwedel, whose orders had specifically included "around the Isle of Wight" as part of his patrol area, had added another ship to his already impressive list of kills. However, his luck was soon to run out. Only a few months later he was lost nearby in *UB-81* (Site **199**).

The *Wapello* lies on her starboard side across the tide with her stern to the north-west. The big iron propeller is still in place. She is split open amidships, probably because of the torpedo damage. The ship is still well defined and stands some 10m proud from the gravel sea bed. This is a big wreck and it takes several dives to see all round it.

The Walpello (Site 197) was torpedoed by the submarine UC-71.

The merchant steamship Highland Brigade (Site 198) was torpedoed by the submarine UC-71 in 1918 and sank 3½ miles east of Dunnose Point.

198 Highland Brigade Bembridge 8 miles; Portsmouth 13 miles. 50 34.83N; 01 05.17W. Depth: 30m. The *Highland Brigade* was a large merchant steamship of 5,669 tons, 385ft long with a beam of 50ft, and was built in Glasgow in 1901. She was torpedoed by Oberleutnant Marzecha in *UC-71* on 7 April, 1918, south-east of St Catherine's Point. The stricken ship managed to limp on to a point 3½ miles to the east of Dunnose Point where she finally sank. All the crew were saved.

A large part of the *Highland Brigade*'s cargo was tin ingots. In the early 1950s this was a valuable commodity and a certain amount was salvaged during 1953. Later, in 1964, salvage operations were started by Risdon Beazley who worked this site on and off until 1970. The wreck now belongs to Martin Woodward.

The hull of the wreck is still fairly intact and is heeled over to port; the bows were flattened to enable the salvors to reach the cargo. The central superstructure and bridge appear to be missing or have collapsed into the hull. The wreck lies east–west, with the bows to the east. The highest part is the stern, which stands some 10m off the sea bed. Part of the cargo was telephone equipment and much of this sort of material has been found, including candlestick telephones. The binnacle has been recovered, having been caught in the grapnel of a dive boat.

199 UB-81 Bembridge 14 miles; Portsmouth 19 miles. 50 29.37N; 00 58.20W. Depth: 28m. The first mission of this 650-ton, 182ft U-boat was her last. *UB-81* was brand new when she left Zeebrugge on 28 November, 1917. In command of the boat was an old hand at submarine warfare – Reinhold Salzwedel – who ranked 11th in the table of record sinkings of all U-boat captains, having sunk 150,000 tons of Allied shipping in 12 missions with the Flanders flotilla. Salzwedel had been decorated many times and was the holder of the prestigious *Pour le Mérite*, Germany's highest war decoration of that time and commonly known as the "Blue Max".

The mission on which *UB-81* set out on that November night was to be Salzwedel's thirteenth. It did not seem to be unlucky at the start and, carrying 10 torpedoes for her four bow and one stern tubes, *UB-81* slid through the Dover defences without being detected, even though she made the run close in at the Folkestone end of the Barrage and over the mine-strewn nets. Salzwedel wasted

The UB-81 now lies on the sea bed 14 miles south-east of the Isle of Wight (Site 199). Above: a rare photograph of her. Right: Shell cases, the bridge telegraph and other items recovered from the wreck.

no time in getting into action and before midnight on 30 November was attacking a convoy some 12 miles off Beachy Head. He had no success, however, and moved farther down Channel. Here he sank a ship he called the "Molesan". She was the armed merchantman *Molesey* of 3,218 tons. The *Molesey* stayed afloat long enough for the crew to take to the boats. This dive is described in the companion volume *Dive Sussex*.

UB-81 moved on to the west and into a violent storm. The ride on the surface for all 34 men in the U-boat became so uncomfortable that Salzwedel took her to 20m for a smoother run. At 5.45pm on 2 December, when the submarine was 2 miles south of the Owers Light Vessel, a tremendous explosion suddenly threw her sideways. The lights went out and water spurted into the stern compartment. The U-boat sank swiftly and settled heavily on the sea bed at 30m. With the added depth the inflow of water increased rapidly and the only action the crew could take was to slam the watertight hatch and seal off the rear compartment entirely. Despite the battering the explosion had given the boat, not one of the crew was injured. A swift check of the rest of the submarine showed that apart from the stern, she was undamaged.

What Salzwedel hit must have been a British mine, for the Navy was now well aware of the fondness of German U-boat commanders for the area around lightships and laid fields accordingly. However, it might have been a German mine laid by another U-boat of the UC class from the Zeebrugge base. It made no difference whose mine had done the damage, for no matter how hard Salzwedel and his engineers tried there seemed no way that *UB-81* would surface. The water in the flooded stern compartment was pinning the U-boat to the sea bed. Salzwedel knew that he could not waste any more precious compressed air in trying to get some buoyancy into his stern tanks. It was clear that the explosion had ruptured them. The boat was lost, so now Salzwedel tried to save his crew.

By pumping all his remaining air into the bow tanks, he hoped that he could raise the bow high enough to get the seaward end of the bow torpedo tubes out of the water and then at least the slimmer members of the crew could get out. All torpedoes were pushed to the stern. Torpedoes from loaded bow tubes were withdrawn awkwardly, for the boat's bows were already lifting as the air hissed into the forward tanks. Then most of the crew were ordered as far aft as possible. Finally the bow would rise no more. Cautiously, the inside end of the highest bow tube opened. Cold night air rushed into the submarine. They had done it! The first man out of the polished tube was the engineer Denker, and he saw how close they had been, and still were, to disaster. The mouth of the tube was a bare 18in above the sea surface, and every moment a wave threatened to break right into it. Quickly, Denker reached down and hoisted Leutnant Freudendahl up onto the slippery slope of the submarine's bow. Freudendahl was Salzwedel's second-in-command and was to be in charge of the party on the exterior of the submarine. One by one crew members were hauled up – from two tubes now – until there were seven men on the outside. Then Freudendahl called a halt fearing that any more weight would push the mouth of the tubes under the sea. The sea was becoming violent and each swell seemed to hover over the tube openings on the sides, though the rest of the bow stopped the sea from plunging straight in. It was icy cold out on the casing, and there was no sign of a ship. All was dark, except for the warning flashes from the lightship.

On Salzwedel's orders flare pistols loaded with star shells were discharged into the air and SOS signals flashed by means of a lamp handed up through one of the tubes; but nothing happened, and the men crouched in the cold for hours while their crewmates remained motionless in the stern, straining their ears to catch any of the muffled exchanges between Salzwedel and Freudendahl. Suddenly there was a shout from outside. No one needed telling that an English ship had found them; the noise of engines drummed through the hull. English voices shouted across the water. More engine noises came close as more boats arrived. Outside Freudendahl saw his men transferred to the first English Naval patrol boat to find them. He was last across, but before he left he could hear the *UB-81* crew queueing to come up. Freudendahl was speculating about the difficulty that some of the fatter, larger crew members were going to have in the narrow torpedo tubes and wondering whether it would be possible to get them out through the conning tower hatch, which was now not all that far under, when the question became superfluous. HMS *P.12* (Site **158**), one of the British patrol boats, crashed into her when trying to get in close to the stricken submarine. The patrol boat's bow bit deep into the U-boat's hull. There was a screaming hiss of compressed air escaping and within seconds *UB-81* was gone in a swirl of black water. A moment later great gouts of air burst through the surface in two places from the open torpedo tubes and then there were only the waves hurrying along in the searchlights' beams. There were no more survivors, and it seems likely that Reinhold Salzwedel, the other young lieutenant aboard, and 25 crewmen died very quickly, as they would hardly have had the time or the strength to shut the bow tube doors against the December sea.

After the sinking there were British reports that said that only two crewmen escaped through the torpedo tubes, and that a British patrol boat, seeing a vague form emerge in the darkness, turned a full speed to ram. The two Germans clinging to the bow waved and shouted, but the patrol boat did not stop. It crashed into the hull and sank the U-boat. The reason for this story is not clear. Perhaps it was part of the propaganda war that was waged at the time – a story to play on the nerves of the rest of the Flanders flotilla. Certainly the names of all the eight survivors are given by German sources and they claimed it was an accident that caused the British boat to ram the stricken submarine. It is hardly likely that they would say this if the sinking had been deliberate.

How long the *UB-81* lay on the sea bed in that position where she sank no one can know. If there was enough air left in the undamaged bow tank it may be that the tides pushed her around almost at once. Certainly, when the Navy looked for her in 1961 she was gone. Then in 1970 the submarine was found at 50 27.00N; 00 51.00W – 12 miles from the place where she sank. In 1974 the *UB-81* was discovered again, upright on a flat sand and shingle sea bed some 14 miles south-east of the Isle of Wight. The diver who found her while working for a salvage firm noted that the only real damage, even though slight, appeared to be to her bow. When dived in 1989, however, the *UB-81* was found broken in two just aft of the conning tower, which is split in two. The highest point is the gun, barrel pointing to the surface, with ready-use ammunition for the gun all around. The main hatch is open to the control room. Parts of the gun and bridge telegraph have been recovered.

200 Wreck, name unknown Bembridge 16 miles; Portsmouth 21 miles. 50 26.70N; 00 57.65W. Depth: 33m. This unknown wreck 15 miles south-east of St Catherine's Point was first located in 1958 during a survey by HMS *Dalrymple*. The wreck sits upright and lies east–west. She is nearly 400ft long and is fairly intact except for considerable damage to the bows and mid-section. Her large steel propeller is still in place. The holds have evidence of cargo, which seems to have been mainly bricks, glass and steel tubes. The wreck stands well off the sea bed, up to 9m clear. There is a hint that this may be the *Leon* (see Site **190**), but so far diving has not confirmed this.

201 Gerarda Bembridge 13 miles; Portsmouth 17 miles. 50 30.83N; 00 55.90W. Depth: 30m. Positively identified in 1989 by her bell, this 1,673-ton iron steamer, 257ft long with a beam of 34ft, sailed on her maiden voyage from Shields for Genoa on 21 October, 1882, with a cargo of coal. In the early hours of 24 October, in stormy weather, the steamer collided with the Glasgow barque *Benares*, which was bound for London from Calcutta. The *Benares*' bows were badly damaged, but the *Gerarda* was hit more seriously and started sinking. Fourteen of the crew were rescued; eight men and Captain D. Johnston died.

Today the *Gerarda* is broken in two. Most recognisable is the stern, which is upside down and 6m proud. A four-bladed steel propeller of 12ft diameter is still in place. The port side is fairly intact, but the starboard is breaking up, showing the boiler and engine room. Both anchors lie off the wreck, together with winches and chains.

202 Fallodon Bembridge 17 miles; Portsmouth 23 miles. 50 26.00N; 01 06.00W. Depth: 30m. Built by Bartram and Sons in 1903 for the London and Northern Steamship Company, the *Fallodon* was 339ft long with a beam of 48ft. The steamship was on her way from Le Havre, bound for Glasgow in ballast on 28

Deadeye from the rigging of the steamer Gerarda (Site 201), which sank after a collision in 1882.

December, 1917, when she was torpedoed. "Five torpedoes, five kills," exulted Oberleutnant Steindorff in his log in *UC-71* after seeing the 3,011-ton *Fallodon* sink. Certainly Steindorff had made his Christmas mission from 22 to 30 December a sad one for the Allies, with 15,658 tons of shipping sunk. The *Fallodon* sank about 12 miles off St Catherine's Point with the loss of one of the crew. Diving information is needed.

203 Wreck, name unknown Bembridge 17 miles; Portsmouth 23 miles. 50 27.00N; 01 11.70W. Depth: 36m. An unknown ship was reported as having sunk in this approximate position 8½ miles south-east of St Catherine's Point. No sign of any wreck has so far been found.

204 Wreck, name unknown Bembridge 19 miles; Portsmouth 24 miles. 50 25.00N; 01 10.00W. Depth: 35m. An unknown ship was reported sunk in this position by the steamship *Blydendyks*, whose crew saw a mast awash here in 1924, 11 miles south-east of St Catherine's Point. The area was surveyed later, but no sign of a wreck was found.

205 HMS Swordfish The first of the S-class submarines was laid down at Chatham Dockyard on 1 December, 1930 and was launched by Lady Tyrwhitt on 10 November, 1931. The *Swordfish* had an overall length of 202ft and a beam of 24ft. When surfaced, she had a draught of 11ft forward and 13ft aft. The standard displacement of the submarine was 640 tons and her engines produced 1550bhp, and the electric motors 1,300hp. The submarine's performance was good: on the surface she had a top speed of 14 knots and a cruising speed of 9 knots, at which

The 202ft submarine HMS Swordfish (Site 205) was lost in 1940.

she had a range of 3,800 miles; submerged, her top speed was 10 knots but at this speed her endurance was only 1 hour. At 2 knots the *Swordfish* could stay down for 36 hours, with a maximum operating depth of 300ft. She was well armed, with six 21in torpedo tubes in the bow, and also a 3in gun and a.303 Lewis gun.

HMS *Swordfish* left Portsmouth for her 12th patrol on 7 November, 1940, under the command of Lieutenant Michael Langley. Her destination was the French coast near Ushant, where she was to relieve the submarine *Usk*. But then she disappeared. For many years it was believed that she had been lost somewhere near Ushant, probably falling prey to a German destroyer.

In 1983, Isle of Wight diver Martin Woodward found the remains of the *Swordfish*, south of St Catherine's Point in 50m. It appeared to have hit a mine, probably shortly after diving. The hull is broken into two sections. The bow from the gun forward lies on its port side and the stern sits upright. The bridge telegraphs were found still set at "slow ahead". The aft escape hatch was found open, so it is possible some of the crew were able to make an escape from the doomed boat, but none survived. The position of the wreck, which is a war grave, has not been disclosed.

206 World War Two Barge Bembridge 8 miles; Portsmouth 13 miles. 50 34.53N; 01 03.60W. Depth: 34m. This motorised barge was found by chance 300yds north-west of the *Leon* (Site **190**) and looks like a D-Day casualty. The barge sits upright on a sea bed of sand and mud and is almost complete. She is around 65ft long with a beam of 20ft. Twin diesel engines and twin 2ft diameter propellers can be seen. The wreck is about 3m proud at the stern and the hold is empty.

207 Gripfast Bembridge 10 miles; Portsmouth 15 miles. 50 33.55N; 01 09.90W. Depth: 23m. The steamship *Gripfast* was built in 1883 by Hall Russell and Company of Aberdeen and was fitted with a two-cylinder compound steam engine with one boiler giving 180hp. She was 200ft long with a beam of 28ft. On 13 November, 1893, the 825-ton ship was heading for London from Swansea with a cargo of coal. As the *Gripfast* was clearing the Isle of Wight a huge explosion took place somewhere towards the bows. Almost immediately she began shipping water and settling by the head. The sound of the explosion was heard several miles away in Ventnor, and longshoremen launched their boats to go to the rescue.

Aboard *Gripfast* two of the crew had been killed in the explosion. The remainder, including Captain George Stephen, took to the ship's boats. Thirty minutes later the *Gripfast* went down. At the time, the steamer was believed to have sunk in deep water, but she had settled on to a shallow bank of sand and shingle that lies on the south-eastern side of St Catherine's Deep. There the *Gripfast* remains, well broken, with only the boiler and parts of her engine standing 4m proud. Much of the plating is now scattered around the site, probably because of the fierce tidal streams that run through this area.

208 U-90 Bembridge 12 miles; Portsmouth 17 miles. 50 31.33N; 01 01.16W. Depth: 30m. This 998-ton 215ft U-boat, built in 1917, joined the German III High Sea Fleet flotilla on 10 September, 1917. The U-boat had four commanders during her service sinking 35 ships, which totalled 104,509 tons. The *U-90* survived the war and was handed over to Britain after surrendering. Unlike many other surrendered U-boats, she was not kept as a gunnery target, but was despatched to the breaker's yard. While under tow to be broken up the *U-90* began taking on water when 11 miles south-east of St Catherine's Point. Attempts to keep her afloat failed and she ended up on the bottom of the English Channel.

209 Coastal Motor Boat Bembridge 15 miles; Portsmouth 20 miles. 50 27.16N; 01 08.28W. Depth: 30m. It is difficult to identify this wreck more positively as she is upside down, but the boat is certainly 65ft long with a steel hull of riveted construction. Twin drive shafts with 2ft diameter propellers stick out of the rotting hull. Through holes it is possible to see the superstructure, which has portholes fitted. It is tempting to call this a motor torpedo boat, but it would be safer just to put her into the years of World War Two. The wreck lies 3m proud.

210 Faith 50 27.30N; 01 06.60W. Bembridge 15 miles; Portsmouth 20 miles. Depth: 36m. The 564-ton sailing-steamer *Faith* was built in 1852 by John Laird of Birkenhead for the African Steamship Company. She was 196ft long with a beam of 26ft and a draught of 16ft. In addition to masts and sails the *Faith* was fitted with a small steam engine producing 110hp to drive a single propeller. The steamer made her maiden voyage from London on 27 January, 1853, to the African port of Fernando Poo (now Bioko in Equatorial Guinea). On her return the *Faith*'s captain wrote a glowing report about her performance.

The *Faith* was used as a troopship during the Crimean War, and was returned to her owners in September 1855. She was then sold to the Turkish Government. Three months later – on 30 December, 1855 – the *Faith* was on her way from London to Constantinople with general cargo when she foundered some 10 miles off St Catherine's Point. The exact cause of her loss is unknown, but it was later reported that the steamer went down head first within 30 minutes of the "disaster" (whatever that was) being discovered. One member of the crew was lost, but Captain Young and the others escaped in the ship's boat.

The first dive on the wreck was in poor visibility and little could be seen except the collapsing boiler and the small engine. Later dives were in better conditions and much more could be seen – including two bronze cannon in the forepart. Bottles of wine and spirits, portholes and the ship's bell were recovered and salvage work is

Martin Pritchard with bottled fruit from the wreck of the steamer Faith, which sank in 1855 (Site 210).

continuing. The wreck lies in a south-west to north-east line with the bows to the south-west. The hull plating has largely rusted away or collapsed leaving the boiler as the highest point, 3m off the sandy sea bed. Within the bow area are the ship's two anchors and chain and close by is a spare two-bladed iron propeller, looking more like an aeroplane's than a ship's propeller. The boiler is collapsing so much that it looks like a pile of brass tubes. Aft of the engine is the shaft with the propeller still on it, though the top of the upper blade has broken off. Lying close by is the rudder. The masts are off the port side.

The lighthouse at St Catherine's Point.

AREA 6:

St Catherine's Point to Freshwater Bay

This section runs from 01 17.00W to link up with Area 1 at 01 33.00W. To the south, it reaches to the foot of Admiralty Chart No. 2045.

The whole of the south-west coast of the Isle of Wight – where many ships have been lost under the steep cliffs – is included in this section. In the places where there were no towering cliffs for the old-time sailor to become embayed, there were dangerous reefs stretching out up to 1½ miles offshore. These ship-rippers run along the front of the cliffs all the way from St Catherine's Point to Hanover Point. The only real break in the cliffs comes at Freshwater Gate, mid-way between Hanover Point and the Needles.

This part of the coast contains shipwreck after shipwreck. A 17th century astrolabe was found by Martin Woodward in 15m off St Catherine's Point in 1986 and divers with treasure in mind should remember the name Chale Bay, between Atherfield Point and Blackgang Chine. It is in those 2 miles of Chale Bay that "Armada" coins have been washed ashore. ("Armada" in this context means pieces of eight.) No one has yet located the shipwreck from which they have come, but the whole of this piece of coast is difficult to explore. All diving must be boat diving and there is no shelter from strong southerly or south-westerly winds. Many wreck sites are close to the shore, which means coming in among the same reefs that have destroyed so many ships. The tides, too, have helped with the wrecking of those ships. For example, the flood tide in the area has a tendency to set in towards the Brook and Atherfield Ledges, especially when there are strong westerly winds. It is said that over a thousand ships lie around the coasts of the Isle of Wight, and many of those are here, along the short stretch of coastline from Atherfield Point across Chale Bay, and on to the most southerly tip of the Isle of Wight at St Catherine's Point – some 3 miles in all. It is one of the largest ship graveyards in the world and divers come across scattered wreckage almost everywhere.

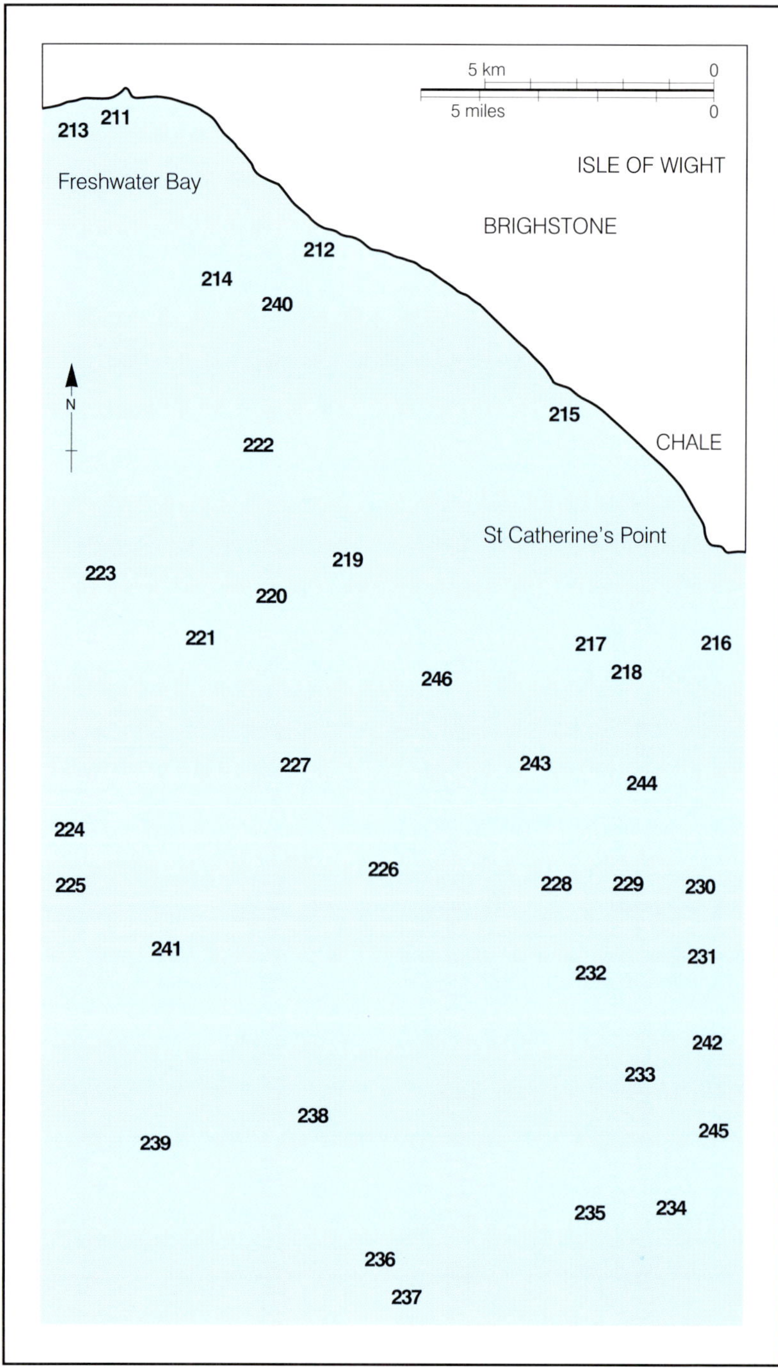
5 km
0
5 miles
0
ISLE OF WIGHT
213
211
Freshwater Bay
BRIGHSTONE
212
214
240
N
215
CHALE
222
St Catherine's Point
219
223
220
221
217
216
218
246
227
243
244
224
226
225
228
229
230
241
231
232
242
233
238
239
245
235
234
236
237

One of the first recorded wrecks in this area was the *St Mary of Bayonne*. This small French ship was carrying a cargo of 147 barrels of white wine, which was intended for delivery in Picardy. So strong were the winds that she was blown north and finally ran ashore in Chale Bay on 22 April, 1313. As might be expected, the news of the wreck spread fast and the locals were soon on the spot buying or grabbing the wine from the crew. Even the Lord of Chale, Walter De Godeton, was there stealing barrels. We know that because there is a record of the court in which he was arraigned and heavily fined.

It was the wreck of another ship many years later – at Blackgang Chine – that led to the erection of St Catherine's Lighthouse. On 11 October, 1836, the *Clarendon*, a three-master of 345 tons, returning from the West Indies with a crew of 16 and 10 passengers, was driven on shore by mountainous seas that smashed the whole ship to pieces in just four waves. Local fishermen, led by John Wheeler, worked heroically to rescue three of the crew, but all the rest were lost. The sight of the broken and mangled bodies recovered from the surf and laid out along the beach – there were two little girls among the victims – caused such a local uproar and public outcry that work on the lighthouse began the very next year. It was completed in 1840.

ST CATHERINE'S LIGHTHOUSE A small light was first set up at St Catherine's Point in about 1323 by Walter de Godeton – the same Sir Walter who was earlier fined for looting a wreck. He erected a chapel, appointed a priest to say masses for the Godeton family, and added to the priest's duties the showing of lights to warn ships away from the dangerous coast. This continued until about 1530, when the endowment was swallowed up in the Reformation.

The present light was completed and the light first shown in March 1840. The lighthouse is near to the site of Sir Walter's chapel at Niton Undercliffe, 5 miles from Ventnor. The first tower was too high and often became covered in fog, so in 1875 the light was lowered by 43ft by taking out a section of 20ft from the upper section and another 23ft out of the middle tier. The tower is now 26m high and the main light, giving one flash every 5 seconds, is 42m above high water. It has a power of 5.2 million candela and is visible up to 30 miles away. A fixed red subsidiary light is displayed from a window 7m below the main light and shows westward over the Atherfield Ledges. This can be seen for 16 miles. The fog signal house used to be near the cliff edge, but erosion caused such serious cracks that in 1932 the signal was moved to a lower tower, annexed to the front of the lighthouse. It gives a 3-second blast every 45 seconds. The small tower was built as a replica of the main structure. Locals call them "the Cow and the Calf".

Tides are strong. In the western part of the area the flood tide reaches around 2 knots on springs and this gradually increases as the tide approaches St Catherine's Point, where the speed can reach 4½ knots. Similarly, in the western area inshore of the 20m line, the flood tide may be about 1 knot, but it increases as it approaches

Opposite: Dive sites in Area 6, St Catherine's Point to Freshwater Bay. This area is covered by Admiralty Chart 2045 (Outer Approaches to the Solent); Ordnance Survey Landranger Map 196.

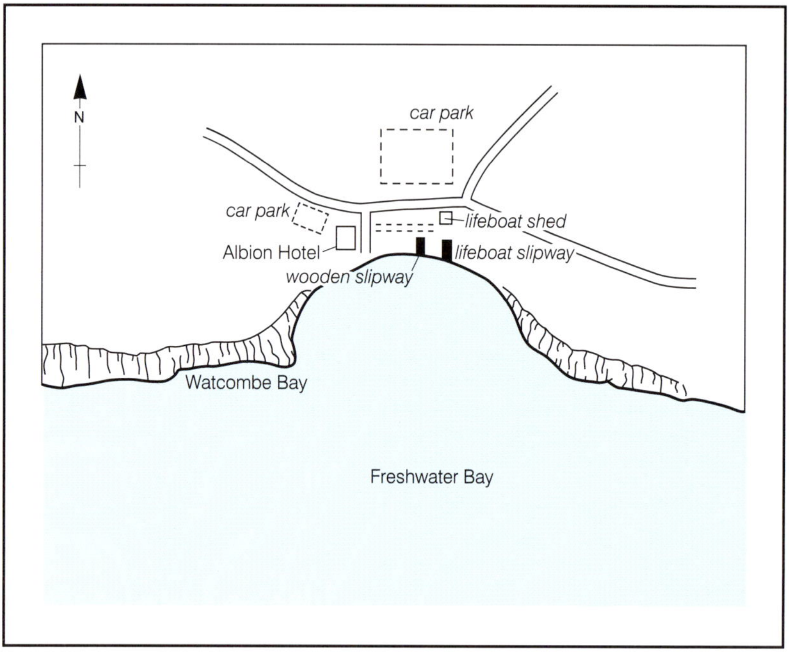

Freshwater Bay.

St Catherine's Point. The ebb works the opposite way. Off St Catherine's Point it can reach 4 knots, but it gradually reduces as it travels west, and once again the tides are less strong inshore of the 20m line. Slack water occurs at 1 hour before and 5 hours after high water at Portsmouth.

Launch sites

BROOK POINT This is suitable only for small inflatables (see Brook Ledges, Site **212**).

FRESHWATER BAY Freshwater Bay should not be confused with the town of Freshwater, which is well inland. At Freshwater Bay there are two slipways, one wooden and one of concrete, built to allow the launching of the Freshwater inshore rescue boat across the shingle beach. Permission can sometimes be obtained to use the rescue boat slipway to launch small boats. There is a large car park across the road from the beach. A small café and the Albion Hotel are close by.

Above:* *The two slipways at Freshwater Bay. The one in the foreground is made of wood; the other is concrete and is used for the inshore rescue boat.

Below:* *The beach at Brook Bay.

Shore diving sites

211 Freshwater Bay There is easy access for the diver to the water here, but the diving is not particularly interesting. The floor of the bay is mainly sand and shingle, with a maximum depth of 6m. There are areas of rock around the seaward edges of the bay that carry a large amount of seaweed. Divers should keep clear of the area of the lifeboat launch slip and, though there is practically no tidal movement in the bay, there can be an uncomfortable swell rolling onto the beach. Several small boats moor in Freshwater Bay during the summer months. SMBs should be used.

Parts of the 185-ton steam tug *Carbon* can be seen at low tide – at 50 39.20N; 01 28.10W – in the shallows of the eastern end of Compton Bay. Formerly known as the *John Hollway*, the tug was bought by the Royal Navy in 1900. She was 72ft long with a beam of 17ft. At the end of her long naval career, the *Carbon* was under tow south of the Isle of Wight in heavy weather on 10 November, 1947. Early in the morning, the tow parted and the tug was lost in the darkness. She was found aground and full of water. An attempt to refloat her failed and the *Carbon* was abandoned as a total wreck. Storm seas soon demolished her wooden superstructure.

212 Brook Ledges The Brook Ledges cover some 2 miles of the south-west coastline. There is a car park at Brook Point and a pathway down to the beach. The path is gated immediately above the beach but it is possible to lift small inflatable boats over the gate and launch off the beach.

This area has numerous wrecks, which have been documented from the earliest recorded days of shipping. The whole area seems to be littered with bits and pieces of ships and divers have picked up all manner of fittings, including a ship's sextant and sounding leads. Local diver Dougie Saunders was snorkelling over the western end of the Ledges one evening in shallow water, when he saw a timber hull below him, jammed between some rocks. The shape was clear and there were timbers sticking out of the sand. All around were large copper pins that once held the planks together. This wreck would be worth looking for again when the sand has shifted.

This is a very interesting diving area. The water is shallow with a maximum depth of 10m. The visibility is usually good except when an onshore wind stirs up the sand close in.

213 War Knight Yarmouth 8 miles; Lymington 9½ miles. 50 39.90N; 01 31.03W. Depth: 15m. The wreck of the 410ft, 7,951-ton armed steamer *War Knight* lies less than ¼ mile from the centre of Freshwater Bay. On 24 March, 1918, the British ship was homeward bound from Philadelphia, USA. She was part of a large convoy coming up the Channel at night with no lights burning. Keeping station in the darkness was difficult, but the convoy had been warned that there were German submarines about. For some reason the *O.B. Jennings*, an American tanker in the convoy, turned across the *War Knight*'s bows. The *O.B. Jennings*, of 10,300 tons, was fully laden with a cargo of highly inflammable naphtha oil. The collision set off the naptha and both ships were enveloped in flames. Thirty-two men died in the fire, almost the whole of the crews of both vessels. The ships were soon taken in tow by escorting destroyers, even though the *O.B. Jennings* was blazing fiercely. As the

Above: ***This dramatic photograph shows the War Knight (Site 213) ablaze off Freshwater Bay in March 1918. Below: Transit marks for the War Knight.***

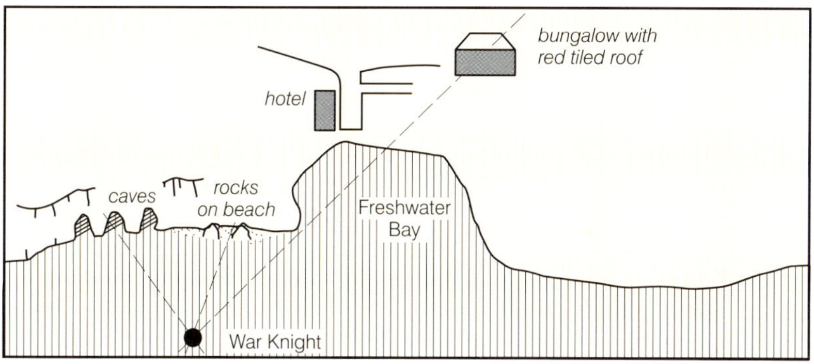

War Knight was towed in, she struck a mine laid by a German U-boat to catch Portsmouth and Southampton shipping, and the steamer's own supplies of ammunition started exploding. The destroyer pulled her as quickly as possible into the nearest shallow water – off Freshwater Bay – and sank her with gunfire in the hope that she could be salvaged later.

The *O.B. Jennings* was towed right round to Sandown Bay and anchored there. She burned fiercely for 4 days before the Navy put a torpedo into her to sink her and put the fire out. The ship was later raised, repaired and joined an outward bound convoy for America, but she was again torpedoed, this time by a German U-boat 100 miles from New York. This time she sank in deep water for good.

The Navy had been right when it had warned the convoy that there were submarines about: there was one very close indeed. Kapitänleutnant Fritz Wassner, a German U-boat ace who had already sunk nearly 100,000 tons of Allied shipping, was more than surprised by the explosion. He had fired no torpedoes. In his log he wrote:

> 24.3. Close to UB-59, a loud detonation with high flames. Oil from a tanker is burning.
>
> We later found out that it was the result of a collision between the English steamer War Knight, 7951 t. with the American steamer O.B. Jennings, 10300 t. The English steamer later ran on to one of the mines laid by UC-17 by the Needles.

When the *War Knight* finally sank, her hull split open and much of the cargo spilled out. Sides of bacon and 28lb slabs of lard soon washed up on the beaches, much to the delight of the locals. The ship was too badly damaged to refloat. Some years later she was heavily salvaged, which has left the wreck very flattened. The only parts standing up are small sections of the hull, the boiler and the bows, which are 3m proud of the sea bed. Piles of anchor chain are hanging out of the chain locker. Although well broken, the *War Knight* makes an interesting dive over a wide area. The sea bed is mainly sand and shingle with some outcrops of rock, particularly one large rock some 100yds to the north of the site. This rock never shows above water. The wreck lies north-north-west to south-south-east and has a ½m scour on one side.

Small boats can be launched from Freshwater Bay and be on the site in minutes. Some divers swim out from the beach at Watcombe Bay, but this can be dangerous, for if the ebb tide catches them there is nothing but sheer cliffs for 3 miles to the west.

214 Juno Yarmouth 10 miles; Lymington 11 miles. 50 38.00N; 01 28.00W. Depth: not known. This position is a very approximate guess. All that is really known of the location of this Dutch frigate of 36 guns is that she was wrecked off Sudmoor Point on 9 or 10 December, 1786, when homeward bound from the East Indies. Reports of the loss of life vary from six to over 100, but the lower figure is probably correct. The *Juno* has not been located by divers, to the authors' knowledge, though there are rumours that some of her cargo has been found.

A gripping account of the loss of the *Juno* was given in *The Times* of 15 December, 1786, which printed a "Letter from Cowes" on that day. It read:

> On the night of the 10th inst. the Juno, Dutch frigate of 36 guns and 250 men, Captain De Wits, from the East Indies to Holland, was drove on shore at Sodmore on the south-west part of the Isle of Wight; four of the men came on shore upon a raft, and in attempting to go off to the ship in a fishing boat, the boat overset and three of the men were drowned, and after that eleven men came ashore, on another raft, who were near 2 hours coming on shore; the ship distant about a mile from the shore.
>
> A reward was offered by R. Bull, Esq, to any person that would get on board her, when a smuggling boat put off, but could not get near the ship; and had it not been for the said smuggling boat the above

> eleven men would not have got to shore as soon as they did. The raft on which they were being checked by the eddy tide. Whether any more of the people are got on shore is not yet known here. Wind south-west blows hard.

There is more information in the log of James Wheeler, a former Navy sailor and local fisherman of Chale Bay. He records some 60 wrecks from 1746 to 1808. Of the *Juno*, he wrote that she struck at 5am on 9 December and ran ashore "at Sudmore Point in a storm at south by east". He adds that she had on board a "great quantity of handkerchiefs, pieces of silk, clothes and money, and other things of great value were lost, and five or six men were drowned". He later added another note: "The wreck was sold for £444." That was a vast sum for those days and one wonders what a Dutch East Indiaman warship of 900 tons would have on board that made her wreckage worth so much.

215 Auguste Yarmouth 4 miles; Lymington 15 miles. 50 37.00N; 01 22.00W. Depth: 8m. The *Auguste*, a three-masted iron-hulled German barque of 1,298 tons left Freemantle, Western Australia, with a cargo of Jarrah wood intended to be made into blocks to pave London's roads. But the wood ended up spread along the beaches of the southern coast of the Isle of Wight, when Captain Ammerman's ship drove onto the eastern side of Atherfield Ledges in a southerly gale and low visibility on 15 February, 1900. The Atherfield lifeboat was launched, but at first was unable to make any headway against the giant seas lashing the beach. It was not until 10 hours later that the gale shifted direction slightly and the lifeboat finally got away. All 18 crew and Captain Ammerman were saved by the lifeboat, but the ship was a total loss.

Today the *Auguste* lies alongside the Ledges and is well split up, but it is possible to swim inside one section where the waterlogged remains of some of the cargo can still be seen.

216 Oriflamme Bembridge 14 miles; Portsmouth 19 miles. 50 33.20N; 01 17.80W. Depth: 33m. Built of steel in 1899 the *Oriflamme* was one of the early steam tankers. During her war service the tanker had a 4.7in gun on the stern of her 336ft hull. The *Oriflamme* was bound for Le Havre from New York and laden with 5,000 tons of benzine when, at 5.45am on 25 November, 1917, she hit a mine 9 miles south of the Nab Light Vessel. She was badly damaged and one of the benzine tanks was broken open. There was no fire until a distress rocket was set off, which ignited the escaping benzine. Even so, tugs managed to tow the 3,764-ton tanker some distance until she finally sank 1 mile south of St Catherine's Point.

The *Oriflamme* now lies on her port side with her bow pointing to the north-east. The highest point is the stern, 8m above the fine sand sea bed. She is very broken and has been swept. There is a rocky ledge about 300yds east of the site with a depth of 25m over it, which can be mistaken for the wreck on an echo-sounder.

217 Tank Landing Craft Yarmouth 16 miles; Lymington 17 miles. 50 33.20N; 01 21.73W. Depth: 41m. This wreck was first found in 1972. Divers report that it lies east–west and is upright 3m proud of the sand and gravel sea bed.

218 Wreck, name unknown Yarmouth 16½ miles; Lymington 17½ miles. 50 33.17N; 01 21.10W. Depth: 55m. This wreck of a small steamer stands upright, some 6m proud on hard sand, with just a slight scour around her. It was at first thought to be the *Molina* – until that ship was positively identified by her bell (Site **221**).

219 Westville Yarmouth 12 miles; Lymington 14 miles. 50 34.30N; 01 26.60W. Depth: 29m. This British steamer of 3,207 tons was torpedoed on New Year's Eve, 1917, when carrying 4,965 tons of coal from Blyth to Blaye, on the Gironde near Bordeaux in France. She was 7 miles west-north-west of St Catherine's Light when the torpedo, fired from *UB-35* by Oberleutnant Kurt Stöter, hit her in the port side.

Captain George Bell had almost certainly brought it on himself. It was a dark night and, according to Admiralty instructions, *Westville* and other ships in the area were blacked out. However, Captain Bell was worried about a ship close on his starboard side and switched on his bow lights to warn her off. Stöter reacted immediately. He fired from the surface using the steel snout of his boat as a foresight for his aim. The hit was a killing one, but the 335ft steamer stayed afloat long enough before capsizing for the crew to take to the boats without loss.

The *Westville* now lies upright with her bows to the north-west. She is well broken, but bow and stern stand 6m proud of the sand and shingle sea bed.

220 HMS Warwick Deeping Yarmouth 13 miles; Lymington 15 miles. 50 34.22N; 01 27.72W. Depth: 36m. This 545-ton anti-submarine trawler was originally intended for peacetime fishing when built by Cochrane Shipbuilders of Selby in 1934 for the Newington Steam Trawler Company of Hull. She was 154ft long with a beam of 26ft. In September 1939 the *Warwick Deeping* was bought by the Admiralty and converted for war with a 4.7in bow gun, depth charge racks and a machine gun on her stern, and submarine detection gear.

In the evening of 11 October, 1940, the *Warwick Deeping*, together with another armed trawler, *L'Istrac*, was patrolling to the south of St Catherine's Point when they were spotted by German E-boats from the 5th Torpedo Boat flotilla based at Cherbourg. Commanding this force of five E-boats – *Falke*, *Greif*, *Kondor*, *Seeadler*

The steamer Westville (Site 219) was torpedoed on 31 December, 1917.

and *Wolfe* – was Korvettenkapitän Henne. Shortly before midnight the Germans opened fire on the trawlers with their deck guns, then followed up with torpedoes. *L'Istrac* was finished off quickly and sank 9 miles south of St Catherine's Point (Site **234**).

Warwick Deeping, despite taking several hits, was luckier. She headed for the Isle of Wight. Two torpedoes were fired at her, but one went underneath her and the other failed to explode. However, water poured into the trawler from the earlier shell bursts and when it rose above the engines the trawler came to a stop and began heeling to port. (The Germans then left the *Warwick Deeping* and headed south. On this same mission they sank two Free French submarine chasers, the *CH7* and the *CH6*.) The 22 crew of the *Warwick Deeping* took to the boats and reached shore without loss. Their ship finally sank some 6 miles west of St Catherine's Point.

Today the wreck lies in an east–west direction with her bows to the east. She is reasonably intact standing some 7m proud. On the stern there are still depth charges in the racks and an iron propeller in place. The 4.7in bow gun is lying on the sea bed alongside the hull. This is a popular wreck dive and visibility can reach up to 15m. Many items recovered from the wreck can be seen in the Shipwreck Centre at Bembridge.

221 Molina Yarmouth is 12 miles; Lymington 13 miles. 50 33.80N; 01 28.90W. Depth: 35m. Built in 1905, this 1,122-ton Norwegian steamer, 229ft long with a 109hp engine, was torpedoed by Oberleutnant Stöter in *UB-35* on the same day that he sank the *Serrana* (Site **12**).

The *Molina* was part of a 10-ship convoy that crossed the Channel from Le Havre. She was in ballast bound for Swansea. At 1.30am on 22 January, 1918, Stöter's torpedo hit the *Molina* in the port stern quarter. Captain Roald Larsen said later that the explosion was so big that it blew off most of the stern. The *Molina* sank in less than 5 minutes, but all aboard took to the boats and reached Portsmouth Harbour without loss.

The ship is upright, though most of the decking has corroded. The engine and bow area and a large anchor winch are still fairly intact. The *Molina* lies with her bows to the north-west and was positively identified by her bell, recovered in 1985. The ship's starboard side is collapsing inward. The stern is flat and her bronze propeller has gone. Much of the hull is fragile and will soon start breaking up. The wreck is 5 to 7m proud in places.

222 Witte Zee Yarmouth 13 miles; Lymington 15 miles. 50 35.83N; 01 28.40W. Depth: 32m. The 328-ton *Witte Zee* was an ocean-going tug belonging to the famous towing and salvage company Smit & Co and was based at Rotterdam. She was built in 1943 and measured 122ft by 25ft by 14ft.

On 23 February, 1964, the 7,300-ton freighter *Brother George* ran ashore on the Brook Ledges while on a voyage from Manchester to her home port, also Rotterdam. Several tugs were soon on the scene hoping for the salvage contract, but the contract was given to the *Witte Zee*. Captain Klein, master of the tug, soon closed in on the freighter with his crew waiting to fire a towing line. Just as they were about to fire the tow line, a particularly large wave rolled up behind the tug and crashed over her stern. She rolled heavily and was sluggish to right herself. Her bow had been holed on the rocks of Brook Ledge and water was rushing in. Captain Klein quickly decided that he should head for the safety of the Solent for repairs.

The Dutch tug Witte Zee (Site 222) sank 4½ miles south of Freshwater Bay in 1964.

However, it soon became apparent that the hull was flooding fast, and help was called. Luckily the other tugs and the Yarmouth lifeboat *Earl and Countess Howe* were close by. The tug *Gatcombe* took off eight of the crew and the tug *Abeille* took the sinking boat in tow. By the time the lifeboat was alongside, the decks of the *Witte Zee* were awash, and the rest of the crew soon abandoned ship. Two hours later the stricken tug disappeared beneath the waves, 4½ miles south of Freshwater Bay.

Plans to salvage her in 1965 never materialised. The wreck now lies north–south, bows to the north and 6 to 7m off the sea bed. There is a shallow scour around the site. The hull is breaking open in places.

223 Wreck, name unknown Yarmouth 11 miles; Lymington 12 miles. 50 33.86N; 01 31.82W. Depth: 40m. This unknown wreck was first located 6 miles south of Freshwater Bay in 1945. It was first dived in April 1965 and the divers' report stated that the wreck was well broken up and appeared to consist of mainly loose girders and ribs. She was approximately 30ft long and stood 5m high. Later dives show that the wreck is at least 150ft long and still stands some 5m high off the sea bed of stone and sand. The high point is the stern of the vessel, which is totally upside down. It is collapsing on one side but the other is still fairly sound. The drive shaft, its tunnel and parts of the ship's machinery can be seen clearly. There is a deep scour of some 2.5m along the side of the wreck. The wreck lies in a north-east to south-west direction.

There are no other clues to the identity of this site. It was suggested that this could be the wreck of the Dutch ship *Ajax*, but another position for the *Ajax* has now been confirmed close by (Site **224**).

224 Ajax Yarmouth 13 miles; Lymington 14 miles. 50 30.50N; 01 32.46W. Depth: 35m. This site was first thought to be that of the destroyer HMS *Acheron*, but salvage teams working in the area during the 1970s were quite definite that this wreck was not a destroyer, but appeared to be a large trawler or small coaster. Despite more diving it was not until 1998 that a bell was recovered proving that this was the Dutch steamer *Ajax*.

The 942-ton *Ajax* was built in 1923 in the yard of Hamburg-Elbe Schiffswerke. She was 220ft by 34ft by 15ft and fitted with a three-cylinder triple-expansion steam engine, with a single boiler producing 126hp. Originally *Ceuts*, she was also called *Elbe* before being named *Ajax*. On 8 August, 1940, the *Ajax*, in ballast and with a crew of 19, was part of a small convoy to Falmouth from Southampton. She joined convoy CW9 as it assembled to the east of the Isle of Wight. As the convoy passed by St Catherine's Point it was attacked by German Stuka dive bombers. The *Ajax* and another ship in the convoy, the *Coquetdale*, were targeted. The *Ajax* was hit by several bombs, killing four of the 19 crew and a naval gunner. She sank within minutes. The *Coquetdale* went down only a short time later (Site **27**).

Today the *Ajax* is on her port side and lies east–west along the tide. There is a deep scour around the northern side of the wreck, which is 6m proud. She is now starting to break up.

225 HM Submarine Upstart Yarmouth 14½ miles; Lymington 16 miles. 50 30.37N; 01 32.75W. Depth: 35m. This site, 9½ miles south of the Needles, is definitely a submarine, and is probably the *Upstart* (previously the *P-65*), a U class submarine of 740 tons and 197ft long. She was sunk as an asdic target on 29 July, 1957. The *Upstart* was located by divers in 1975, who thought she might be the British submarine *A3*, but the *A3* sank on the Princessa Shoal in 1912 (see the companion volume *Dive Dorset*) and was subsequently salvaged.

The *Upstart* is partly buried in the shingle sea bed, and is heeled over to port. She lies east–west with bows to the east. The conning tower is of round construction and is the highest point, standing 8m off the bottom. The tower hatch is open, as is another one on the aft deck. The pressure hull appears to be in good condition. The gun and the two propellers are missing.

The British submarine Upstart (Site 225) was located by divers in 1975.

226 Wreck, name unknown Yarmouth 17 miles; Lymington 18 miles. 50 30.30N; 01 25.95W. Depth: 40m. This "wreck" site was first located in November 1979 by a Trinity House vessel searching for the wreck of the *Pool Fisher*, which sank in the area earlier that month. However, the *Pool Fisher* has been located several miles away (Site **241**). The sea bed in the above position is very rocky and uneven. Depths can vary between 37 and 50m. There are several tall rock pinnacles around the area and one of these pinnacles might indeed constitute this "wreck".

227 HMS Acheron Yarmouth 15 miles; Lymington 18 miles. 50 30.46N; 01 32.60W. Depth: 48m. As 149 men died in the sinking of the *Acheron* in December 1940, the wreck of this British destroyer is undoubtedly a war grave and should be dived accordingly.

The *Acheron* was 323ft long with a beam of 32.2ft and a draught of 12ft. She had been built by Thornycroft in 1930 and with her 34,000hp turbine engines could reach a speed of 35 knots. She carried four 4.7in guns, two 2-pounders, five machine guns and had eight torpedo tubes.

The *Acheron* struck a German mine in the early morning of 17 December. The 1,350-ton destroyer had left Portsmouth for high-speed trials south of the Isle of Wight following a refit. She carried a full complement of 190, and 25 dockyard men were also aboard; her captain was Lieutenant R. J. Wilson. The destroyer was beginning to turn to the east when she exploded. "There was a muffled roar and the darkness was transformed to brilliant light as she erupted into flame," said one survivor. The suddeness of the explosion, which blew her in two, is made clear by the story of stoker Reg Willis who told how he climbed out of an escape hatch: "I saw the bow was missing. I just jumped – there was nothing else to do!" The *Acheron* sank swiftly. Lieutenant Wilson, other officers and 145 ratings were lost. Another two officers and 13 ratings were wounded. The Admiralty announced the loss of the *Acheron* 9 days after her sinking.

The *Acheron* was pinpointed by Martin Woodward in 1984. He found the two sections about ¼ mile apart. They are now mostly buried in sand.

HMS Acheron (Site 227) sank in 1940 with the loss of 149 men.

228 Redesmere Bembridge 20 miles; Portsmouth 25 miles. 50 29.93N; 01 21.45W. Depth: 37m. Built by the Sunderland Shipbuilding Company in 1911, the 2,123-ton *Redesmere* was 290ft long and had a beam of 43ft. The steamer was making 9 knots on her way from Barry to Southampton with a cargo of 3,600 tons of coal at 4am on 28 October, 1917, when she was torpedoed by Oberleutnant Howaldt in *UB-40*. The attack was so sudden that 19 men died and when Captain David Jackson reported the loss to the owners, the Watson Steamship Company, he said that they had been "mined or torpedoed six miles west-south-west of St Catherine's Point". The torpedo struck just aft of the engine room bulkhead in hold No. 3 and sent the *Redesmere* down in 1½ minutes.

The steamer is upright standing 5m proud of the gravel and sand sea bed. She lies north–south. There is a 1m deep scour along her east side.

229 Ashanti Bembridge 17; Portsmouth 22½ miles. 50 30.00N; 01 20.00W. Depth: 40m. Built in 1936 by the Goole Shipbuilding and Repairing Company, the 534-ton *Ashanti*, fitted with a 102hp oil engine, was a British ship belonging to T.E. Evans and Company, but taken over as a supply ship for the Normandy landings of 1944. She was 184ft with a beam of 27ft.

On 10 June, 1944, the *Ashanti* made her way to the Isle of Wight convoy assembly point. The day before the first ships to form part of the Mulberry Harbour at Arromanches had been sunk in position and *Ashanti* was to be one of the first ships to use this artificial harbour and unload vital supplies for the Allied armies pushing inland. Her cargo was vital. She was packed with jerricans of petrol for the tank regiments.

At 3.10am, as she waited for the rest of the convoy in the assembly point 35 miles north of the Mulberry Harbour in France, well south of St Catherine's Point, a German E-boat torpedoed the *Ashanti*. The resulting explosion and flames were seen for miles. No one could survive and the crew of 10 and seven gunners were all lost.

No diving information is available and the position given is approximate.

230 Londonier Bembridge 16 miles; Portsmouth 21 miles. 50 29.97N; 01 19.27W. Depth: 37m. The 279ft *Londonier*, a 1,846-ton Belgian merchantman of the Lloyd Royal Belge line, was built in 1911. She was torpedoed from a surface position by Oberleutnant Marzecha in command of *UC-71* on 13 March, 1918. This was only Marzecha's second mission captaining a U-boat. Twelve of the crew of the Belgian ship were lost.

Today the *Londonier* sits upright on a hard sand bottom from which she is 5m proud. She lies north-east to south-west and is very broken.

231 Crestflower Bembridge 11 miles; Portsmouth 22 miles. 50 29.03N; 01 18.88W. Depth: 35m. Though this site is listed by the Admiralty as that of the 367-ton armed trawler *Crestflower*, there is another uncharted wreck a little over 1 mile away, which is definitely a World War Two armed trawler and might also be the *Crestflower* (see Site **245**).

Whichever is the real *Crestflower*, there is no doubt about what happened to the 150ft ship, which was built in 1930 and used by the Navy, who bought her in August 1939 as a minesweeper. The ship was fitted with a single 12-pounder gun on her bows and was based at Portsmouth. On 21 July, 1940, the *Crestflower* was

The trawler Crestflower (Site 231) photographed shortly after her construction in 1930, alongside the Lord Brentford.

sweeping 6 miles south of St Catherine's Point when she was attacked by German aircraft. Badly damaged and with two of her crew dead, the ship foundered shortly afterwards.

The wreck at the above position has been dived, but in poor visibility. She appears to be lying on her starboard side and is obviously breaking up. Two portholes have been recovered but they gave no clues. The wreck stands 7m proud of the hard sand sea bed.

232 Braat II Bembridge 20 miles; Portsmouth 25 miles. 50 28.83N; 01 21.03W. Depth: 38m. A Norwegian ship of 1,834 tons with a length of 265ft and a beam of 42ft, the *Braat II* was built in 1914 at Fredriksstad. On 7 March, 1918, the ship was in the English Channel heading from Newport for Rouen with a cargo of 2,780 tons of Welsh coal. She was not zigzagging as ordered, because her master, Caspar Solberg, was about to change course and head across the Channel for Rouen.

At 5.30am, Kapitänleutnant Rhein in the surfaced *UB-30* fired a single torpedo from his bow tubes. It struck the *Braat II* below her waterline on the starboard side aft. Captain Solberg ordered the crew to abandon ship almost at once as *Braat II* started to list. The 21 crew landed safely at Portsmouth after being picked up from their boats by a Navy patrol boat. *UB-30* did not survive the war, being rammed and depth charged by armed trawlers off Whitby when commanded by Oberleutnant Stier on 13 August, 1918. There were no survivors.

Divers report that the *Braat II* is upright, with her bows to the east, and stands 6m proud of the gravel sea bed. The holds are still full of coal.

233 Mendi Bembridge 19 miles; Portsmouth 24 miles. 50 27.47N; 01 19.90W. Depth: 40m. Originally listed as the wreck of a lighter, diving revealed something completely different. This is really the wreck of a big steamer sitting on a sea bed of hard sand and all indications are that it is the RMS *Mendi*, which sank on 20 February, 1917, with a huge loss of life.

The *Mendi* was used on the Cape of Good Hope, West Africa and Liverpool run and in February 1917 was carrying some 800 South African labourers to France, where they were to be employed on the construction of gun sites and other defence works behind the front lines. At 5am, with fog adding to the pitch black before dawn, the *Mendi* and her destroyer escort were some 7 miles off St Catherine's Point when the steamer *Darro* sliced into the *Mendi's* starboard side. The *Mendi* sank swiftly without being able to launch her boats – 656 men died, including 31 of the crew.

Today the wreck lies in a north-east to south-west direction and is over 12m proud. She is breaking up. Much of the decking has collapsed and this leaves the large boiler standing above the main wreckage, in which there are many cases of shells and rifle ammunition. Distinctive square portholes can be seen. This is considered a war grave and should be dived accordingly.

234 L'Istrac Bembridge 19; Portsmouth 24 miles. 50 25.90N; 01 19.60W. Depth: 36m. For many years this wreck was listed by the Admiralty as that of the British steamer *Tweed*, but diving on the site in the 1990s has shown that the wreck is actually that of the World War Two anti-submarine patrol vessel *L'Istrac*.

L'Istrac was originally a French auxiliary patrol vessel. She was one of the many ships that sailed across the Channel in 1940 before the French ports fell to the advancing German Army. Together with all the other vessels seeking shelter in Portsmouth, *L'Istrac* was taken over by the Royal Navy. On 11 October, 1940, just

The RMS Mendi (Site 233) sank 7 miles off St Catherine's Point in 1917, following a collision, and now lies in 40m.

before midnight, *L'Istrac* was on patrol south of St Catherine's Point with the armed trawler *Warwick Deeping* when they were attacked by E-boats of the German 5th Torpedo Boat flotilla (see Site **220**). At first the crew of *L'Istrac* believed that the approaching craft were British and turned on her identification lights. The Germans immediately opened fire with their deck guns. Badly damaged and wallowing, *L'Istrac* was finished off by a torpedo from the E-boat *Greif*. The crew of *L'Istrac* were picked up safely at dawn.

Today the wreck is well broken. The highest point is the boiler, standing 3 to 4m proud. Guns and quantities of ammunition can be seen and the asdic binnacle and helm stand are among recoveries.

235 Mulberry Harbour Unit Yarmouth 22 miles; Lymington 23 miles. 50 25.75N; 01 20.70W. Depth: 38m. This site, 9 miles south of St Catherine's Point, is a large section of Mulberry Harbour. It was lost during Operation Neptune, when dozens of these floating harbour sections were towed across the English Channel to the Normandy beaches. This is a steel section around 120ft long, lying in an east–west direction and standing some 7m off the sandy sea bed.

236 Iduna Bembridge 20 miles; Portsmouth 25 miles. 50 25.00N; 01 25.50W. Depth: 36m. This is also the official position of the *South Western*, which joined the *Iduna* 50 years later (Site **237**). First to settle in this position was the three-masted, 860-ton sailing steamship *Iduna*, built in 1868, which sank after a collision while carrying a cargo of coal from North Shields. All 170ft of her landed upright on the hard sand.

Many years later, strong sonar traces were plotted by a dive boat in the area, which were believed to come from the *South Western*. However, when the site was dived, the boilers and engines that stood some 5m high were not those of the *South Western* at all. The wreckage on which the divers found themselves was of a wooden hull about 170ft, lying east–west. Amid the wreckage lay a ship's bell. This bore the name "IDUNA" and confirmed the identity of the wreck.

237 South Western This 674-ton armed British steamer was built in 1874 by J. and W. Dudgeon for the London and South Western Railway Company and was 222ft with a beam of 27ft. She was a victim of Kapitänleutnant Fritz Wassner in *UB-59* on 16 March, 1918, who spotted her in the early dusk, alone and on course for St Malo from Southampton with general cargo. Wassner's first torpedo missed. The *South Western* appeared not to notice and ploughed on into the night. Wassner noted in his log that she was on course for Cherbourg and set off after her. When he found the steamer again it was just before midnight and she was still on the same course, about 9 miles south-west-by-south from St Catherine's Point. Wassner fired again. This time the explosion of the torpedo sent the whole of the forepart of the ship flying up into the air. Nonetheless, the *South Western* floated for 20 minutes before sinking. Twenty-four of the crew died.

The *South Western* is probably very close to the position given, but only more diving will find her.

238 Double Ender Yarmouth 19 miles; Lymington 22 miles. 50 26.97N; 01 26.97W. Depth: 38m. Called the "Double Ender" by salvage divers, this is a double-ended ship of some kind, sitting upright. She has no upperworks and appears to be just a hull, though there is some wreckage close by to the south that may have been some sort of bridge. She is 6m proud of the hard sand sea bed and lies east–west. More diving information is needed for full identification.

239 Espagne Yarmouth 19 miles; Lymington 21 miles. 50 26.50N 23; 01 29.55W. Depth: 37m. The *Espagne*, 236ft with a beam of 36ft, was built in 1909 at the Anversois shipyard at Hoboken in Belgium, and was fitted with a three-cylinder triple-expansion steam engine with two boilers giving 150hp.

On 25 December 1917, this armed steamship of 1,463 tons got no mercy from Oberleutnant Steindorff in *UC-71* – even if it was Christmas Day. Perhaps Steindorff was in a temper: he noted in his log that earlier that morning he had failed to sink the 5,756-ton *Hyacinthus*, despite hitting her with a torpedo, and she had reached harbour "south of the Isle of Wight". The *Espagne* was not so lucky. Steindorff hit her in the port side at 6.30am, when she was off St Catherine's Point. So unexpected was the attack that only three of the crew survived. *UC-71* survived the war only to founder off Heligoland on the way to surrender on 20 February, 1919.

The site is listed by the Admiralty as that of the *Espagne* and the wreck may well be that ship, but there are some things that do not fit. The wreck is only 3m proud and is very broken amid shallow hills of sand and shingle. Much of it is buried in the sand hills. What can be seen are two boilers standing on their ends and at least two railway carriage frames and wheels. We know that the *Espagne* was in ballast bound from Le Havre for Newport, so where did the railway carriages come from? The only wreck in the area that did have carriages listed in her cargo is the *Myrtle Grove*, which was sunk a month earlier, farther to the west (Site **29**).

240 Wreck, name unknown Yarmouth 10 miles; Lymington 12 miles. 50 37.93N; 01 27.17W. Depth: 10m. The remains of this old cargo steamer can be found in this position in shallow water. The ship appears to have grounded stern first onto the Brook Ledges ¾ mile off Sudmore Point. The highest part of the wreck is the boiler, and there are some deck planks still in place. There is a large winch at the south-western end of the wreck.

241 Pool Fisher Yarmouth 19 miles; Lymington 21 miles. 50 27.50N; 01 26.60W. Depth: 39m. The *Pool Fisher* was built in 1959 by NV Scheepswerf Foxhol in the Netherlands for James Fisher and Sons of Barrow-in-Furness. Her building measurements were 218ft 6in by 33ft 6in by 14ft 1in. She was powered by an 830hp diesel engine.

On 6 November, 1979, the 1,028-ton British motor vessel *Pool Fisher* was on passage from Hamburg to Runcorn with 1,250 tons of potash. She was passing south of the Isle of Wight, punching into gale force winds, when she suddenly started to capsize. Before she sank, the crew managed to send a VHF Mayday – "Mayday, this is Pool Fisher. Mayday. We are going over. South west of St Catherine's Point." A request for a more exact position brought only "We are going now ..." A massive sea and air search was launched immediately. Two survivors were found four hours later and plucked from the sea by helicopter. Twelve crewmen and the wife of the chief engineer were lost. An investigation into the loss found that the hatch fixings on No. 1 hold were either insecurely fastened or failed in the bad weather allowing huge amounts of water to enter, causing the capsize.

The MV Pool Fisher (Site 241) capsized in 1979 off St Catherine's Point.

The *Pool Fisher* lies north–south with her stern to the north. Her bows have broken away and stand on end. The rest of the ship is upside down with her superstructure in the sea bed below. The propeller is the highest part, standing 7m proud.

242 Wreck, name unknown Bembridge 16 miles; Portsmouth 21 miles. 50 29.61N; 01 19.00W. Depth: 39m. This old steamship is located 400yds south-east of the wreck of the *Londonier* (Site **230**). The wreck is showing her age and very broken. The single boiler and engine are the highest parts, standing 4m off the shingle sea bed. A broken propeller can be seen at the stern. Two small portholes with steel covers and part of a sextant have been recovered, but give no clue to her identity. She lies north-west to south-east with the bows to the north-west.

243 Daylesford Yarmouth 14 miles; Lymington 15 miles. 50 30.50N; 01 28.20W. Depth: 36m. The *Daylesford* was built in 1882 by R. Thompson and Sons of Sunderland and was owned by the New Lines Steam Ship Company of Leith. She measured 240ft by 34ft by 17ft and was driven by a two-cylinder compound steam engine with two boilers giving 175hp. On 1 April, 1911, the 1,406-ton British steamer was on her way from Blythe to Torre de Mar with a cargo of coal and coke when she collided with the Russian schooner *Puhlin* and sank. Captain John Simpson and his 17 crew are reported as having been saved. (The *Puhlin* lasted a little longer but foundered and is somewhere on the sea bed off the south-west coast of the Isle of Wight.)

The *Daylesford* lies some 7 miles south west of St Catherine's Point and very broken, so much so that much of her is flat on the sea bed. The boilers and engine are the highest points, some 3m proud.

244 Ernest Legouve Yarmouth 15 miles; Lymington 16 miles. 50 31.21N; 01 28.48W. Depth: 44m. This 2,246-ton steel sailing barque was built in 1901 by Atel et Chant of Nantes and was owned by the Société Générale d'Armement. She was 276ft long with a beam of 44ft and a draught of 22ft. On 5 April, 1917, she was torpedoed and sunk while on her way from London to Buenos Aires with a cargo of cement in bags.

The wreck is upright and some 8m proud. The cargo shows as cement boulders.

245 Armed Trawler Bembridge 19 miles; Portsmouth 24 miles. 50 27.76N; 01 18.71W. Depth: 38m. Lying just ¾ mile east of the *Mendi* (Site **233**) ammunition recovered from the site confirms this armed trawler as a victim of World War Two. She is well broken, with the bows collapsed over to the port side. A large gun that was mounted on the foredeck has now fallen clear. The single boiler is the high point of the wreck, 4m proud of the sand and shingle of the sea bed. It is possible that this is the wreck of the armed trawler *Crestflower* (Site **231**).

246 Wreck, name unknown Yarmouth 11 miles; Lymington 12 miles. 50 37.86N; 01 25.98W. Depth: 12m. This is an old steel or iron steamer that was lost on the eastern end of the Brook Ledges. She is broken and scattered over the rocks. The main hull is jammed between two ledges and in it can be seen the collapsing boiler and part of the propeller shaft. There is some lead piping and at least one porthole, which is just out of reach. Wooden rigging deadeyes and a brass letter "S" have been brought up and they may give a clue to this ship's identity. Because of the rocky sea bed, depths over the site vary between 6 and 12m. Location by echo-sounder is difficult.

Haslar Marina, Gosport.

APPENDIX 1:

Dive Services

Dive boats

Boats are listed in order from west to east, and the list includes some boats based outside these waters, which take divers out to wrecks and sites described in this book. *Diver* magazine is the best source of information about other boats that operate in this area.

Poole *Ocean Spirit* (skipper Jim Scott), 12 divers (as day boat), 10 divers (live-aboard), 51ft, all electronic gear, magnetometer, on-board compressor (tel. 0860 683921).

Nat West II (skipper Frank Elston), 12 divers, 9.99m catamaran, all electronic gear, oxygen, magnetometer, crane. Accommodation for 4 on board. Also operates 78ft *Loyal Helper* live-aboard for 12 divers with on-board compressor (tel. 01202 884077 or mobile 0585 951944).

Muircu (Sea Hound) (skipper Jeff Way), 12 divers, 34ft, all electronic, magnetometer, oxygen on board. Also picks up at Swanage Pier (tel. 01202 461718 or mobile 0585 108695).

Lymington *New Dawn Diver* (skipper Richard Rimmer), 12 divers, 40ft, all electronic gear, magnetometer, oxygen on board (tel. 01483 211103).

Yarmouth *Triton* (skipper Stephen Robbins), 6 divers, 6m RIB, electronic gear. Also picks up at Lymington (tel. 01983 529023).

Gosport *Hero* (skipper Steve Collett), 10 divers, 31ft, all electronic gear, magnetometer, oxygen on board (tel. 01329 313382).

The New Dawn Diver operates from Lymington.

Portsmouth *Woodpecker* (skipper Peter Street), 10 divers, 32ft, all electronic gear, magnetometer, oxygen on board. Also picks up at Gosport (tel. 023 9261 3284).

Meridian *Express* (skippers David and Paul Faithfull), 12 divers, 38ft, electronic gear, oxygen on board. Also picks up at Gosport (tel. 023 9261 2743).

Bracklesham Bay *Big Blue II* (skipper Nick Fecher), 12 divers, 7.8m RIB, electronic gear, oxygen on board (tel. 01243 672031).

Air and equipment

New Milton New Dawn Dive Centre, Walkford Farm Offices, Walkford Lane, New Milton, Hants BH25 5NH. Air, Nitrox, servicing, equipment (tel. 01425 616062). Also at 148 Send Road, Send, Woking, Surrey GU23 7EZ (tel. 01483 211103).

Southampton Andark Diving, 256 Bridge Road, Lower Swanwick, Southampton SO13 7FL. Air, Nitrox, servicing, equipment (tel. 01489 581755).

Portsmouth Horsea Island Dive Centre, Port Solent Complex, North Harbour, Portsmouth. Air. Controls civilian diving in lake. Bookings: diver manager Mark Boxall (tel. 01489 480480).

Solent Divers, 122–128 Lake Road, Portsmouth PO1 4HH. Air, servicing, equipment (tel. 023 9281 4924).

Isle of Wight Scuba Techniques, Emsworth Lane, Porchfield, Isle of Wight PO30 4LR. Air, Nitrox, servicing, equipment (tel. 01983 529023).

Diving and Marine (Isle of Wight), The Anchorage, Long Lane, Newport, Isle of Wight PO30 2NQ. Air, equipment, servicing, diving author Martin Pritchard gives advice on dive sites (tel. 01983 525169).

East Wittering Wittering Divers, 12 Oakfield Road, East Wittering, West Sussex PO20 8RP. Air, Nitrox, servicing, equipment (tel. 01243 672031).

Dive clubs

Many clubs welcome visiting divers, who should carry proof of their qualifications if they wish to join dives. The current telephone number for any BSAC branch secretary can be obtained from BSAC headquarters (tel. 0151 350 6200).

The 32ft Woodpecker is based at Portsmouth and takes 10 divers.

BSAC branches in Hampshire

Alton Branch meet at Alton Sports Centre on Tuesdays at 9pm.

Andover Branch meet at Andover Leisure Club on Tuesdays at 9pm.

Basingstoke Branch meet at Lord Wandsworth College, Long Sutton, on Mondays at 7.45pm.

Whitehill SAC, Bordon, meet at Barbados House, Station Road, Bordon on Thursdays at 7pm.

Eastleigh Branch meet at Fleming Park Leisure Centre on Tuesdays at 9pm.

Aldershot Dolphins meet at Farnborough Rugby Club on Tuesdays at 9pm.

Atlantic Diving, Gosport, meet at Rowner Recreation Centre on Wednesdays at 8pm.

Gosport Branch meet at Bridgemary Manor Hotel on Thursdays at 9pm.

F & G Dolphins, Gosport, meet at the RAOB Club, Forton Road on Wednesdays at 7.30pm.

South England Dive Devils, Hook, meet at the Raven Hotel on Sundays at noon.

Calshot Branch meet at the Applemore Sports Centre on Wednesdays at 8pm.

Southsea Branch meet at St Edmund's Pool on Mondays at 8.30pm.

Southdown Divers, Portsmouth, meet at Staunton Park School on Tuesdays at 9pm.

Ringwood SAC meet at the Ringwood Recreation Centre on Thursdays at 9.30pm.

Romsey Branch meet at Stanbridge Earls School on Tuesdays at 8pm.

St Edward's SAC, Romsey, meet at St Edward's School, Sherfield English, on Thursdays at 7.15pm.

Southampton Branch meet at LSU Pool, The Avenue, on Mondays at 7.30pm.

New Forest/Waterside, Southampton, meet at LSU Pool, The Avenue on Wednesdays at 8pm.

BSAC branches on the Isle of Wight

Wight Dolphins, Freshwater, meet at West Wight Swimming Pool on Fridays at 8pm.

Vectis Sea Otters, Newport, meet at Medina Pool on Fridays at 8pm.

SAA clubs

Contact SAA Southern Region representative Jenny Marks (tel. 01202 842663) for meeting places and contact telephone numbers.

Portland Sub-Aqua Club

Abbey Divers

Hamworthy SAC

Caversham Park Aquanauts

Hurn Sub-Aqua Club

Arnewood Divers

Solent Icebreakers SAC

Portland Plungers Diving Club

Port Bredy Divers

707 Divers

Crosfield Sub-Aqua Club

Plessey Radar Sub-Aqua Club

The 78ft Poole based dive boat Loyal Helper can accommodate 12 divers.

The town quay at Lymington.

APPENDIX 2:

The Diver's Code of Conduct

Divers must at all times adhere to the BSAC code of conduct. It is reproduced here with the kind permission of the British Sub-Aqua Club, and has been extracted from the BSAC *Safe Diving Practices* booklet, available from BSAC headquarters.

THE DIVER'S CODE OF CONDUCT

More and more people are taking to the water. Some for recreation; some to earn their living. This code is designed to ensure that divers do not come into conflict with other water users. It is vital that you observe it at all times.

Before leaving home

Contact the nearest British Sub-Aqua Club Branch or the dive operator local to the dive site for their advice. Seek advice from them about the local conditions and regulations.

On the beach, river bank or lakeside

1. Obtain permission, before diving in a harbour or estuary or in private water. Thank those responsible before you leave. Pay harbour dues.

2. Try to avoid overcrowding one site, consider other people on the beach.

3. Park sensibly. Avoid obstructing narrow approach roads. Keep off verges. Pay parking fees and use proper car parks.

4. Don't spread yourselves and your equipment since you may upset other people. Keep launching ramps and slipways clear.

5. Please keep the peace. Don't operate a compressor within earshot of other people – or late at night.

6. Pick up litter. Close gates. Be careful about fires. Avoid any damage to land or crops.

7. Obey special instructions such as National Trust rules, local bye-laws and regulations about camping and caravanning.

8. Remember divers in wetsuits are conspicuous and bad behaviour could ban us from beaches.

In and on the water

1. Mark your dive boats so that your Club can be identified easily. Unmarked boats may become suspect.

2. Ask the harbour-master or local officials where to launch your boat – and do as they say. Tell the Coastguard, or responsible person, where you are going and tell them when you are back.

3. Stay away from buoys, pots, and pot markers. Ask local fishermen where not to dive. Offer to help them recover lost gear.

4. Remember ships have not got brakes, so avoid diving in fairways or areas of heavy surface traffic and observe the "International Regulations for the Prevention of Collisions at Sea".

5. Always fly the diving flag when diving, but not when on the way to, or from, the dive site. Never leave a boat unattended.

6. Do not come in to bathing beaches under power. Use any special approach lanes. Do not disturb any seal or bird colonies with your boats. Watch your wash in crowded anchorages.

7. Whenever possible, divers should use a surface marker buoy.

On conservation

1. Never use a speargun with an aqualung. Never use a speargun in fresh water.

2. Shellfish, such as crabs and lobsters, take several years to grow to maturity; over-collecting in an area soon depletes stocks. Only take mature fish or shellfish and then only what you need for yourself. Never sell your catch or clean it in public or on the beach. Don't display your trophies.

3. Be conservation conscious. Avoid damage to weeds and the sea bed. Do not bring up sea-fans, corals, starfish or sea urchins – in one moment you can destroy years of growth.

4. Take photographs and notes – not specimens. Shoot with a camera not a speargun – spearfishing makes fish shy of divers. Never spearfish wrasse or other inshore species since once an area is depleted of such fish, it may take a long time for them to re-colonise.

On wrecks

1. Do not dive on a designated wreck site. These are indicated on Admiralty Charts and marked by buoys or warning notices on the shore nearby.

2. Do not lift anything which appears to be of historical importance.

3. If you do discover a wreck, do not talk about it. Pinpoint the site, do a rough survey and report it to the BSAC Archaeology Adviser and the Council for Nautical Archaeology who will advise you.

4. If you do not lift anything from the wreck, it is not necessary to report your discovery to the Receiver of Wreck. If you do lift, you must report.

5. If your find is important, you may apply for it to be designated a protected site. Then you can build up a well qualified team with the right credentials and proceed with a systematic survey or excavation under licence without outside interference.

Don't Let Divers Down – Keep To The Diver's Code

RESPECT OUR WRECKS

A "Respect Our Wrecks" code was launched in March 2000 by the British Sub-Aqua Club, PADI, and the Sub-Aqua Association to ensure that the best possible wreck diving practices are observed by recreational divers in the UK. The code states that all wreck divers should:

1 *Respect War Graves.* Many wrecks are also war graves. Treat them with the respect you would give a churchyard.

2 *Respect the Wreck Environment.* Many wrecks make great habitats for marine life. Treat them with the care you would give a coral reef.

3 *Respect the Future.* Explore the wrecks, where allowed, but don't damage or disturb them. Take photographs rather than souvenirs, so that our wrecks remain for future divers to see.

4 *Respect our History.* Many wrecks have an important history and hold clues to our maritime past. If you find anything, report it to the Receiver of Wreck, who will pass on the information to archaeological experts.

5 Respect Yourself. Make sure that you are properly trained for wreck diving.

6 *Respect Your Family and Friends.* Some wrecks contain dangerous cargoes or live munitions. Don't disturb them or bring them ashore.

7 *Respect the Law.* Know and respect maritime laws and avoid a criminal record.

APPENDIX 3:

Shipwreck Register

This is a list of ships lost within the approximate area covered by this book. They are listed by year of loss, name or type of vessel, and the general area of loss where known. Wrecks covered in the main text of the book have the appropriate site number included. Vessels under 50 tons have, in general, not been listed. Ships known to have been salvaged after sinking or stranding have not been included. However, it must be stressed that this is not a definitive list. It is almost certain that some of the vessels listed were subsequently salvaged. Accuracy of dates, names and locations are not guaranteed, they have been sourced from many different references and there is frequently variation in information relating to the same ship. Therefore this list should be used as a starting point for further research and is, of course, not a complete list of all shipwrecks in this area.

1262	Unknown wreck	Southampton
1280	*Just*	Back of the Wight
1301	Unknown wreck from Calais	Compton Bay
1304	*Mariote de Portsmouth*	Back of the Wight
1309	Unknown wreck	River Medina
1313	*Blessed Mary*	Chale Bay
1314	Unknown wreck	Chale Bay
1315	Unknown wreck	Back of the Wight
1320	*St Mary*	Yarmouth
1320	Unknown wreck	Hanover Point
1320	*Ralph de Georges Petition*	Back of the Wight
1335	Foreign ship	Back of the Wight
1336	*Jesus Christ*	Brighstone Bay
1340	*Tarrit*	Back of the Wight
1341	Spanish ship	Back of the Wight
1375	*Maudeleyn*	Back of the Wight
1399	Unknown wreck	Back of the Wight
1409	Unknown wreck	off the Needles
1439	*Grace Dieu*	Hamble River (Area 2)

1447	Carrack	Back of the Wight
1463	*Maudeleyne*	Back of the Wight
1466	*Santa Maria*	Back of the Wight
1501	Unknown wreck	Brighstone Bay
1538	Unknown wreck	Solent
1544	*Conception*	off Dunnose Point
1545	*Mary Rose*	Solent (**77**)
1567	*Santa Lucia*	Yarmouth (**41**)
1587	Unknown wreck	Back of the Wight
1587	*Michealmas*	Back of the Wight
1599	Unknown wreck	Portsmouth
1607	Unknown wreck	Yarmouth
1610	Unknown wreck	Hanover
1627	Unknown wreck	Portsmouth
1627	*Campen*	off the Needles (**16**)
1627	*Vliegende Draeck*	Yarmouth
1628	*Campion*	off Isle of Wight
1631	*Diligence*	Portsmouth
1631	Unknown wreck	Sandown Bay
1634	Unknown wreck	Back of the Wight
1634	Unknown wreck	Back of the Wight
1635	Unknown wreck	Back of the Wight
1636	Unknown wreck	Stokes Bay
1636	*Bonaventure*	Portsmouth
1636	*Rainbow*	Portsmouth
1636	*Bird Phoenix*	Compton Bay
1637	Unknown wreck	Back of the Wight
1650	*Ulysses*	Back of the Wight
1652	Unknown wreck	Portsmouth
1653	Unknown wreck	Back of the Wight
1653	Unknown wreck	Back of the Wight
1654	*Report*	Back of the Wight
1656	*Pelican*	Stokes Bay
1659	Unknown wreck	Back of the Wight

Three of the many silver lion dahler coins recovered from the Dutch East Indiaman Campen (Site 16).

1667	*Teneriffe Merchant*	Cowes Road
1668	Unknown wreck	Lee-on-the-Solent
1668	Unknown wreck	Back of the Wight
1670	Unknown wreck	Hanover Point
1671	Unknown wreck	Back of the Wight
1683	*Hope*	Back of the Wight
1688	*Helderenberg*	Back of the Wight
1689	*Alexander*	Spithead
1690	*St David*	Portsmouth
1691	*St Anthony*	Scratchell's Bay
1692	Unknown wreck	Chichester
1692	*Ruzzee Prize*	St Helen's Roads
1693	*Spy*	Portsmouth
1693	*Mermaid Prize*	Portsmouth
1695	*Shark*	Back of the Wight
1697	Unknown wreck	Cowes
1701	Unknown wreck	Back of the Wight
1701	Dutch vessel	Atherfield Ledges
1701	Dutch vessel	Niton
1703	*Newcastle*	Spithead
1704	Unknown wreck	Back of the Wight
1704	Unknown wreck	Bembridge Ledge
1704	Unknown wreck	Atherfield Ledges
1704	Unknown wreck	Sandown Bay
1704	Unknown wreck	off Dunnose Point
1704	Unknown wreck	Ventnor
1704	Dutch fly-boat	Chilton
1705	*Looe*	Scratchell's Bay
1706	*Nassau*	Bembridge Ledge
1709	*Hind*	Hurst Castle
1711	*Edgar*	Spithead
1741	*La Thereisvicaute*	Cowes
1743	*Maria*	Sandown Bay
1743	*Success*	Sandown Bay
1743	*St Dominic*	Sandown Bay
1744	*Curten*	Ryde
1746	*Tygar*	Back of the Wight
1746	*Loyal Macs*	off Bembridge
1746	Unknown wreck	Colwell Bay
1746	Unknown wreck	Ladder Chine
1747	*Modeste*	Portsmouth
1747	Unknown wreck	Back of the Wight
1747	*Love gally*	off the Needles
1747	*Marshall*	Ryde
1748	*Providence*	Ryde
1749	Unknown wreck	Brighstone Ledge
1749	*Pretty Patsy*	off Bembridge
1749	Unknown wreck	Chilton
1750	*Warren*	Brighstone Bay

1750	*Jonge Hans and Greten*	Brook Bay
1750	*St Johannes*	Atherfield Ledges
1750	*Speedwell*	Atherfield Ledges
1750	*St Laurence*	Back of the Wight
1750	Unknown wreck	off Bembridge
1751	Unknown wreck	Bullplace
1751	*Paul Katharina*	Yarmouth
1751	Galliot	Brook Bay
1752	*Constant James*	Watershoot Bay
1752	*Katherine*	Back of the Wight
1752	Four ships	Bembridge Ledge
1753	*Samuel*	Hurst Castle
1753	Unknown wreck	Southampton
1753	*St George*	Chichester
1753	*Addrainne*	Walpen Chine
1753	Unknown wreck	Ladder Chine
1753	*Friendship*	Back of the Wight
1753	*Swanholm*	Typit Ledge
1753	Unknown wreck	Compton Bay
1753	Unknown wreck	Compton Bay
1753	Unknown wreck	Brighstone Bay
1753	*Jacob*	St Helen's Roads
1753	*Young Green*	Back of the Wight
1753	Unknown wreck	Back of the Wight
1753	*Liefde*	Back of the Wight
1753	*Deakins and Maudsley*	Rocken End
1753	*Assurance*	off the Needles (**15**)
1753	*Dragon*	Atherfield Ledges
1754	*Francis*	Hayling Island
1754	*Diana*	Compton Grange
1754	Unknown wreck	Typit Ledge
1754	*Mary Anne*	Ship Ledge
1754	*Sandwich*	Atherfield Ledges
1754	*Hambro*	Brighstone
1755	*Jubilee*	Brighstone Bay
1755	*St Peter*	Compton Bay
1755	*Ann*	Typit Ledge
1755	Unknown wreck	Watershoot Bay
1755	*Samuel*	Brook Chine
1755	*Anna-Maria*	Back of the Wight
1756	*Attwood*	Typit Ledge
1756	Unidentified ship	Typit Ledge
1756	*Diane*	off Isle of Wight
1757	*Jonge Bonne*	Brighstone Bay
1757	*Seahorse*	Horshoe Bay
1757	*Young Abraham*	Atherfield Ledges
1757	*Prince George*	off the Needles
1757	Galliot	Brighstone
1757	Collier	Ventnor

1758	*Invincible*	Horse Tail Sand (**101**)
1758	*St Martin*	Gilkicker Point
1758	*Morning Star*	Portsmouth
1758	*Cyprus*	Brook Chine
1758	*Faithful*	Yarmouth
1758	A snow	Brook Bay
1758	*Alcyde*	Scratchell's Bay
1759	*St Vincent Ferrier*	Atherfield Ledges
1759	Unknown wreck	Back of the Wight
1759	Dutch ship	Swingwill Ledge
1760	Unknown wreck	Brook Bay
1760	Unknown wreck	Sudmore Point
1760	*Vries van Leuwaarden*	Brook Bay
1760	*Henry*	Warden Ledge
1760	*Bluebell*	Atherfield Ledges
1760	*Elizabeth*	Back of the Wight
1760	*Jonge Arnoldus*	Warden Ledge
1760	French cutter	Sudmore
1760	French vessel	Totland
1760	*Koorn Bears*	Bembridge Ledge
1762	*Vrouw Barbara*	Cowlease Chine
1762	*Two Brothers*	Bembridge Ledge
1763	*Shark*	Portsmouth
1763	*Peter and Ann*	Southsea
1763	*Voortfightighejd*	Cowes
1764	*Aletta*	Gilkicker Point
1764	*Union*	Lymington
1764	*Katherine and Elizabeth*	unknown
1764	*Young Hendrick*	Back of the Wight
1764	*Dutch West Indiaman*	Ryde
1765	*Apthrope*	Scratchell's Bay
1765	*San Miguele*	Watershoot Bay
1766	Unknown wreck	Compton Bay
1766	*Susanna*	Back of the Wight
1766	Unknown wreck	Freshwater Gate
1766	*Jonge Brother Parrenga*	Atherfield Ledges
1766	Dutch galliot	Atherfield Ledges
1767	*James*	Rocken End
1767	*Three Friends*	Knowles
1767	*James*	Hanover
1768	*Tryall*	off Isle of Wight
1769	*Chance*	Christchurch Bay
1769	*Phoenix*	Typit Ledge
1769	*Bergetha and Marie*	Brook Chine
1769	*Twee Gebroders*	Back of the Wight
1769	*Katherine*	St Lawrence
1769	Brig	Atherfield Ledges
1769	Sloop	St Lawrence
1770	*North Star*	Sudmore Point

1770	*King George*	Sudmore Point
1770	Dutch ship	Sudmore
1771	*Liberty*	Christchurch Bay
1771	*Edward*	Atherfield Ledges
1771	*Osterley*	off the Needles
1771	Unknown wreck	Atherfield Ledges
1771	*Calvert*	Back of the Wight
1771	*Edward Althorpe*	Atherfield Ledges
1772	*Carolina*	Shingle Bank
1772	*Endeavour*	Atherfield Ledges
1773	*Conway*	off the Needles
1774	*Morning Star*	Rocken End
1774	*Philadelphia Packet*	off the Needles
1775	*Three Brothers*	Hurst Point
1775	*Union*	Atherfield Ledges
1775	*Middleburgs Hoop*	Typit Ledge
1775	Unknown wreck	Back of the Wight
1775	*Martin*	Freshwater Bay
1776	*Charles Sharp*	Portsmouth
1776	*Britannia*	Back of the Wight
1777	Unknown wreck	Shingle Bank
1777	*Property*	Back of the Wight
1777	*Vrow Dorothea*	Mill Bay
1777	*Ascension*	Ryde
1778	Unknown wreck	Brighstone Bay
1778	Unknown wreck	Freshwater Gate
1778	Unknown wreck	Ship Ledge
1779	*Revenge*	Stokes Bay
1779	*Francis*	Typit Ledge
1779	*St Antonio*	Mixton
1779	*Fothergill*	Freshwater Whitecliff
1779	*Nostra Senora de Conceicao*	Atherfield Ledges
1780	*Surprise*	Hurst Castle
1780	*St Antonio*	Brighstone Bay
1780	*Howe*	Cowlease Chine
1780	*Buen Jesus de Alem*	Warden Ledge
1780	*Helmsley*	Yarmouth
1780	*Incendiary*	off the Needles
1780	*Berion Zues*	Back of the Wight
1781	*Neptune*	Portsmouth
1781	*Rodney*	Southampton
1781	*Hopkins*	Portsmouth
1781	Unknown wreck	Brighstone Bay
1781	*Roberts*	Scratchell's Bay
1782	*Douglas*	Stokes Bay
1782	*Royal George*	Spithead (**80**)
1782	*Catherine and Mary*	Back of the Wight
1782	*Shrewsbury*	Cowes
1782	*Anna Rebecca*	Back of the Wight

1783	Unknown wreck	Bullplace Ledge
1783	Unknown wreck	Barnes High
1783	*Leopold*	Back of the Wight
1783	Unknown wreck	Back of the Wight
1783	*Johanna*	Blackgang
1783	Unknown wreck	Bembridge Ledge
1783	*Fruitful Vine*	Bembridge Ledge
1783	Unknown wreck	Brighstone Bay
1783	*Swan*	Back of the Wight
1784	*Three Friends*	Stokes Bay
1784	*Earl Cornwallis*	Rocken End
1784	*Sunna*	Sandrocks
1784	*Independence*	Mixon
1784	*Friendship*	Mixon
1784	*John and Jane*	Back of the Wight
1784	*Hirsch*	Grange Chine
1784	*President*	West Solent
1784	*Juanna*	St Catherine's Point
1785	*Robert*	Stokes Bay
1785	*Juffrow Anna Louisa*	Brook Bay
1785	*Woohlfaart*	Back of the Wight
1785	*Merchant*	Atherfield Ledges
1785	Unknown wreck	Brook Bay
1785	*Jeune Dragon*	Back of the Wight
1785	*Dorothea Charlotta*	Typit Ledge
1785	Unknown wreck	Sudmore Point
1786	*James*	St Lawrence
1786	*Maria*	Back of the Wight
1786	Unknown wreck	Old Node
1786	*Two Brothers*	Chale Bay
1786	*Juno*	Sudmore Point (**214**)
1789	Unknown wreck	Atherfield Ledges
1790	*William and John*	Chale Bay
1790	*Three Sisters*	St Lawrence
1790	*Kent*	Bembridge Ledge
1790	*Isis*	Back of the Wight
1790	*Good Intent*	Ryde
1791	Unknown wreck	Knowles
1791	*Weymouth*	Rocken End
1791	*Four Friends*	Back of the Wight
1791	Unknown wreck	Sudmoor
1791	*Wohlsaart*	Back of the Wight
1791	Unknown wreck	Atherfield Ledges
1792	Unknown wreck	Grange Chine
1792	*Vrow Classina*	Back of the Wight
1792	*Hoppett*	Cowes
1792	*Ancona*	off Isle of Wight
1792	*Dolphin*	Typit Ledge
1792	*Nancy*	Back of the Wight

1793	Unknown wreck	Stokes Bay
1793	*Three Friends*	Lymington
1793	*Tweed*	Shingle Bank
1793	*Garland*	Walpen Chine
1793	*Vrow Anna Maria*	Back of the Wight
1793	*Harvey*	Chale Bay
1793	*St George*	Atherfield Rocks
1793	*Ann*	Yarmouth
1793	*Friends Increase*	Rocken End
1793	*Countess Hoberton*	off the Needles
1794	*Lark*	Portsmouth
1794	*Impetueux*	Portsmouth
1794	*Hornett*	Portsmouth
1794	*Juno*	St Catherine's Point
1794	Unknown wreck	Sudmore Point
1794	*General Clark*	Brook Bay
1794	*Botton*	Back of the Wight
1794	*Ann*	Yarmouth
1795	*Boyne*	Spithead (**76**)
1795	*Peggy*	Stokes Bay
1795	*Favourite*	Stokes Bay
1795	*Sisters*	Portsmouth
1795	*Von Hemmert*	Chichester
1795	*Countess of Cardigan*	Stokes Bay
1795	*Princess of Wales*	Portsmouth
1795	*Betsy*	Portsmouth
1795	*Blessing*	Shingle Bank
1795	*Commerce*	Portsmouth
1795	*Princess Maria Carolina*	Spithead
1795	*Britannia*	Portsmouth
1795	*Britton*	Portsmouth
1795	*Gloriana*	Portsmouth
1795	Unknown wreck	Southmore
1795	Unknown wreck	Ship Ledge
1795	*Nostra Senora D'Epler*	Back of the Wight
1795	*Alexander*	Back of the Wight
1795	Unknown wreck	Ship Ledge
1795	*Emeraton*	Back of the Wight
1795	*Friends Increase*	Niton
1795	*Nostra Senora D'Etal*	Niton
1796	*Hawk*	Hayling Island
1796	*Thomas Wilson*	Portsmouth
1796	*Lyde*	Shingle Bank
1796	*Greyhound*	Portsmouth
1796	*Mary*	Portsmouth
1796	*Fair American*	Bembridge Ledge
1796	Unknown wreck	Sandown Bay
1797	*Bailies*	Horse Sand
1797	*Jane and Sarah*	Stokes Bay

1797	*Success*	Stokes Bay
1797	*Prince of Piedmont*	Chichester
1797	*Cadiz Packet*	Stokes Bay
1797	*Buena Elenna*	Brook Chine
1798	*Iris*	Portsmouth
1798	*La Siene*	Portsmouth
1798	*Richard and Ann*	Southsea
1798	*Gute Enwarting*	Atherfield Rocks
1798	*Henry Addington*	Bembridge Ledge
1799	*Impregnable*	Hayling Bay (**100**)
1799	*Malvina*	Portsmouth
1799	*Williamson*	Shingle Bank
1799	Unknown wreck	Bembridge Ledge
1799	Unknown wreck	Walpen Heath
1799	*Three Sisters*	Puckaster Cove
1799	*Betsy*	Yarmouth
1799	*Britannia*	Yarmouth
1799	Unknown wreck	Grange Chine
1799	*Deux Amis*	Grange Chine
1799	*Moor*	Back of the Wight
1799	*Dorothea Elizabeth*	Atherfield Rocks
1799	*Guernsey Lilly*	Yarmouth
1799	*Thetis*	Sandown Bay
1800	*Purissima Conception*	Portsmouth
1800	*Industry*	Portsmouth
1800	*Thetis*	Portsmouth
1800	*Incredible*	Horse and Dean Sand
1800	*Hope*	Portsmouth
1800	*Friends*	Portsmouth
1800	*Hunter*	Portsmouth
1800	*Two Friends*	Portsmouth
1800	*Jupiter*	Portsmouth
1800	Unknown wreck	Alum Bay
1800	*Henri et Loutuil*	Back of the Wight
1800	*Therapsy*	Ladder Chine
1801	*Laird*	Portsmouth
1801	*Scout*	Shingle Bank
1801	*Rising Sun*	Portsmouth
1801	Unknown wreck	Shingle Bank
1801	*Assistance*	Shingle Bank
1801	Unknown wreck	Chichester
1801	*Bon Amigos*	Southsea
1801	*Adcona*	Shingle Bank
1801	*Exbury*	off Isle of Wight
1801	Unknown wreck	Atherfield Rocks
1801	*Tartar*	West Cowes
1802	*Providence*	Hurst Castle
1802	*Triton*	Lymington
1802	Unknown wreck	Back of the Wight

1803	*New Draper*	Chichester
1803	Unknown wreck	Chale Rocks
1803	*Abelino*	Back of the Wight
1803	*Aurora van Farrer*	Rocken End
1803	Unknown wreck	Sudmore Point
1803	*Louisa*	Back of the Wight
1803	*Grenada*	Cowes
1803	*Hindostan*	Culver Cliff
1803	*Caton Bleche*	Sandown Bay
1804	*Melcomb*	Shingle Bank
1804	*Three Sisters*	Chichester
1804	*Andalusia*	Back of the Wight
1804	Unknown wreck	Brook Bay
1804	*William and Margaret*	off Isle of Wight
1804	*Venus*	Rocken End
1804	*Hannibal*	Sandown Fort
1805	*Diana*	Portsmouth
1805	*Hero*	Portsmouth
1805	Unknown wreck	Rocken End
1805	Unknown wreck	Brook Chine
1805	*Atlantic*	Back of the Wight
1805	Unknown wreck	Cowes
1806	*Dasher*	Gosport
1806	*Friends*	Portsmouth
1806	*Isabella*	Horse Sand
1806	*Commerce*	Lymington
1806	Unknown wreck	Back of the Wight
1806	*Hope*	Back of the Wight
1807	Unknown wreck	Portsmouth
1807	*Small Bridge*	Portsmouth
1807	*Sarah Ann*	Southsea
1807	*Liguero*	Cowes
1807	*Alliance*	Back of the Wight
1807	*Redbreast*	off the Needles
1807	*Jupiter*	Back of the Wight
1808	Unknown wreck	Spit Sand
1808	Unknown wreck	Stokes Bay
1808	Unknown wreck	Mother Bank
1808	*Ann*	Back of the Wight
1808	*Harlequin*	Yarmouth
1808	*Elizabeth*	Back of the Wight
1808	Unknown wreck	Rocken End
1808	*Hope*	Back of the Wight
1809	*Carmarthen*	Shingle Bank
1809	*Melburn*	Southsea
1809	Unknown wreck	Horse Sand
1809	*Oak*	Southsea
1809	Unknown wreck	Stokes Bay
1809	*Jeshie*	Stokes Bay

1809	*Saturnus*	Portsmouth
1809	*Eclipse*	Stokes Bay
1809	*Melantho*	Stokes Bay
1809	*Hoffnung*	Stokes Bay
1809	*Enterprize*	Stokes Bay
1809	*Union*	Stokes Bay
1809	*Hibernia*	Stokes Bay
1809	*Good Intent*	Christchurch Bay
1809	*Bell*	Portsmouth
1809	*Gold Hunter*	Shingle Bank
1809	*Clarendon*	Portsmouth
1809	*Romulus*	Back of the Wight
1809	*Oak*	Yarmouth Roads
1810	*Mary and Elizabeth*	Shingle Bank
1810	*Friendship*	Southsea
1810	*Rover*	Ryde
1810	*Mary*	off the Needles
1810	*Eagle*	Back of the Wight
1811	*Aurora*	Lymington
1811	*Bird*	Lymington
1811	*Sarah*	Lymington
1811	*Valiant*	Portsmouth
1811	*Hellen*	Portsmouth
1811	*Good Intent*	Portsmouth
1811	*Banknote*	Atherfield Rocks
1811	*Ceres*	White Cliff
1811	*Pomone*	off the Needles (**15**)
1812	Unknown wreck	off Isle of Wight
1812	Unknown wreck	Atherfield Ledges
1812	*Albion*	Atherfield Rocks
1812	*Sportsman*	Back of the Wight
1812	*Trio*	Noman Sand
1813	*Providence*	Southsea
1813	*Queen Charlotte*	Spithead
1813	*Peter*	Stokes Bay
1813	*Good Advice*	Brook Bay
1814	*Ann*	Portsmouth
1814	*Good Intent*	Hurst Castle
1814	*De Good Verwagting*	Chilton Chine
1814	*Salome*	Atherfield Rocks
1814	*Woodman*	Warden Ledge
1814	*Industry*	Ryde
1815	*Antigonus*	Horse Sand
1815	*Queen Charlotte*	off the Needles
1815	*Avance*	Chale Bay
1816	*Caroline*	Portsmouth
1816	*Eleanor*	Shingle Bank
1816	Unknown wreck	Blackgang Chine
1816	*Minerva*	off Isle of Wight

1816	*Mistletoe*	off Dunnose Point
1816	*Fox*	Bembridge Ledge
1817	*Independent*	Portsmouth
1817	*Unity*	Spit Sand
1817	*St Dominick*	off the Needles
1818	*British Tar*	Lymington
1818	*Rambler*	Southampton
1818	*Hemsley*	Spithead
1818	*Kingston*	Southampton
1818	*Speculator*	Back of the Wight
1818	*Somerset*	off Isle of Wight
1818	*Pilgrim*	off the Needles
1818	*Royal Oak*	Grange Chine
1819	*Susan*	Portsmouth
1819	*Jupiter*	Back of the Wight
1819	*William*	Sandown Bay
1819	Unknown wreck	Back of the Wight
1819	*Elise*	Brook Bay
1820	*Julius*	Cowes Roads
1821	*Ann and Susannah*	off the Needles
1821	*Herman*	Niton
1821	*Ales*	Back of the Wight
1823	*Victoire*	Lymington
1823	*Drover*	Southsea
1823	*Eliza*	Hamiltons Bank
1823	*Brilliant*	Warden Ledge
1823	*Le Courier*	Chale Bay
1824	*Carl Johan*	Christchurch Bay
1824	*Fly*	Portsmouth
1824	*Pomona*	off Isle of Wight
1825	*Vine*	Shingle Bank
1825	*Ann*	Hayling Island
1825	*Mary*	off the Needles
1826	*Good Intent*	Hurst Beach
1827	*Diamond*	Portsmouth
1827	*Speculation*	Cowes
1827	*Happy Return*	Back of the Wight
1829	Unknown wreck	Horse and Dean Sand
1829	*Nightingale*	Shingle Bank
1829	*Carn Brea Castle*	Brook Bay
1830	*Friends*	Stokes Bay
1830	*Diana*	Back of the Wight
1830	*Wolf*	Back of the Wight
1830	*Crown*	Brook Chine
1830	*Thomas and Dorothy*	St Helen's Roads
1830	*Research*	Back of the Wight
1830	*Rosine*	Atherfield Ledges
1830	*Cameo*	Back of the Wight
1830	*Moland*	Brook Bay

1831	*Carl*	Back of the Wight
1831	*Neath Trader*	Cowes
1831	*Julie*	Yarmouth
1832	*Bainsbridge*	Atherfield Ledges
1832	*Cressique*	Chale Bay
1832	*Charles II*	Sandown Bay
1833	*Annabella*	Portsmouth
1833	*Two Brothers*	Christchurch Ledge
1833	*Clara*	Back of the Wight
1833	*Blessington*	Freshwater Bay
1833	*Henrye*	Sandown Bay
1833	*Hero*	Sandown Bay
1834	*Ann*	Christchurch Bay
1834	*William Hamilton*	Lymington
1834	*Lark*	Solent
1835	*Providence*	Back of the Wight
1835	*Two Marys*	off Isle of Wight
1835	*Samuel*	off Isle of Wight
1836	*Liberty*	Ryde
1836	*Eliza Pigeon*	off Isle of Wight
1836	*Clarendon*	Blackgang Chine
1836	*Auguste*	Brook Bay
1837	*Jean Marie*	Blackgang Chine
1838	*Enighden*	Chale Bay
1838	*Claire*	Brook Bay
1840	*Edgar*	off Isle of Wight
1841	*Thomas*	Back of the Wight
1841	*Alert*	off Nab Light
1841	*Dibdin*	Black Rock
1841	*Castor*	Back of the Wight
1841	*Mary Ann*	Freshwater Bay
1841	*Dover*	Freshwater Sands
1842	*Kent*	Barton
1842	*Lively*	Bembridge Ledge
1842	*Mary Coxon*	off Isle of Wight
1842	*Edward*	Back of the Wight
1842	*Four Friends*	Warden Ledge
1843	*George 4th*	Hayling Island
1843	*George*	Atherfield Ledges
1845	*Siam*	Compton Bay
1846	*Sphinx*	Chale Bay
1846	*Ann and Elizabeth*	Spithead
1847	*Perdoitus*	Blackgang Chine
1848	*Ann*	Shingle Bank
1848	*Ark*	Ryde
1848	*Llan Rumney*	Atherfield Point
1850	*Dream*	off the Needles (**15**)
1850	*Tale Banre*	Sandown Bay
1851	*Mary Ann*	Hayling Island

1851	*Vivid*	Cowes
1851	*Ocean*	Yarmouth
1852	*Fareham Trader*	Hamiltons Bank
1852	*Amity*	Horse Sand
1852	*Arrow*	Spithead
1852	*Flowers*	Dean Sand
1852	*Sophia*	L'Etan Rock
1852	*Japara*	Compton Bay
1852	*St Barbe*	south of the Needles
1852	*St Joseph*	off St Catherine's Point
1852	*Tjsemboelvert*	off the Needles
1853	*Friends*	Hurst Castle
1853	*Surprise*	Hayling Island
1853	*Asia*	Southampton
1853	*Prince Regent*	Southsea
1853	*Navarino*	Rocken End
1853	*Neptune*	Chale Bay
1853	*Edouard*	off Isle of Wight
1853	*Hibernia*	Ventnor
1855	*Faith*	off St Catherine's (**210**)
1856	*Perseverance*	Boulder Bank
1856	*Maria Gustave*	Shingle Bank
1856	*Cruzier*	Southsea
1856	*George Lord*	Compton Grange
1856	*Cashmere*	Blackgang Chine
1856	*Ocean*	off Isle of Wight
1856	*Mars*	Atherfield Ledges
1856	*Marie Mathilde*	Atherfield Ledges
1857	*Temerario*	Brighstone Bay
1857	*Redport*	Back of the Wight
1858	*Friends*	off Isle of Wight
1858	*Abbey Langdon*	Freshwater
1859	*Ann and Eliza*	Hurst Castle
1859	*Eastern Monarch*	Spithead
1859	*Nimrod*	Sandown Bay
1859	*Lelia*	Rocken End
1859	*Nelus*	off Isle of Wight
1859	*Mirabita*	Brighstone Ledge
1859	*Sentinel*	Brook Bay
1859	*Jane*	Blackgang Chine
1860	*James and William*	Chichester
1860	*Shamrock*	Chichester
1860	*Falcon*	off Dunnose Point
1860	*Ann*	Cliff End
1861	*Thames*	Southsea
1861	*Eclipse*	Chichester
1861	*John Wesley*	Freshwater Cliff
1861	*Victor Emmanuel*	Blackgang Chine
1861	*Hero*	Freshwater Bay

1861	*Corsair*	off Dunnose Point
1861	*Ant*	Sandown Bay
1862	*Cedrine*	Brighstone Ledge
1862	*Ellen Horsfall*	Cowlease Chine
1862	*Lotus*	Ladder Chine
1863	*Ridesdale*	Calshot
1863	*Three Sisters*	Atherfield Ledges
1863	*Chancellor*	Ventnor (**155**)
1863	*Widgeon*	off Nab Light
1863	*Brilliant*	St Catherine's Point
1864	*Lion*	Solent
1864	*Rambler*	Ventnor
1864	*Thetis*	off St Catherine's Point
1865	*Ocean*	East Winner Shoal
1865	*Hope*	Hurst Castle
1865	*Lucy*	Niton
1865	*Jesper*	Bembridge Ledge
1866	*Christina*	Back of the Wight
1866	*Tale Baure*	Sandown Bay
1866	*John Hicks*	off Isle of Wight
1866	*Tennant*	St Helen's Roads
1866	*Sauvegarde*	off Isle of Wight
1867	*Johann*	Rocken End
1867	*Fortuna*	Atherfield Ledges
1868	*Mary Lewis*	off St Catherine's Point
1868	*C.B.*	Atherfield Rocks
1868	*Florence*	Nab Light
1868	*Blonde*	off the Needles
1869	*Magellen*	Totland
1869	*Rio de Janerio*	Back of the Wight
1870	*See Bee*	Highcliff
1870	*Normandy*	south-west of the Needles
1870	*Dongeree-Hotte*	off St Catherine's Point
1871	*Underley*	Luccombe Chine (**185**)
1871	*J.B. Bradley*	Back of the Wight
1871	*Hephzibah*	Hanover Point
1871	*Costa Rica*	off St Catherine's Point
1871	*Catharina*	off Isle of Wight
1871	*Anna*	Grange
1871	*Cassandra*	Brook Bay
1872	*Dacca*	Rocken End
1872	*Valid*	Rocken End
1872	*L'Etoile*	Sudmoor Point
1872	*Lapwing*	off Isle of Wight
1872	*Hope*	Stag Rock
1872	*Malcolm Brown*	Compton
1873	*Woodham*	Chilton Chine
1873	Unknown wreck	off St Catherine's Point
1873	*Quail*	Brighstone Bay

1873	*Sisters*	Atherfield Ledges
1873	*Kanagawa*	off Isle of Wight
1873	*Vallid of Androssan*	St Catherine's Point
1874	*Hermose Habanero*	Sudmoor Point
1875	*Robert*	Cowes Roads
1875	*Meteor*	off Isle of Wight
1875	*Mistletoe*	Stokes Bay
1875	*Pirro*	Sandown Bay
1876	*Glenaray*	Blackgang
1876	*Christina*	off St Catherine's Point
1877	*Cloud*	Puckaster Point
1877	*John Douse*	Luccombe Ledge
1877	*Alpheta*	Bembridge Ledge
1877	*Brothers*	Ryde Roads
1877	*Bastistina*	Warden Ledge
1877	*Champion*	Single Bank
1878	*Pilot Boat No. 5*	off St Catherine's Point
1878	*Leopold Auguste*	off St Catherine's Point
1878	*Manora*	Shanklin
1878	*Charles Emilie*	Brook Ledge
1878	*Ithiel*	Brook Ledge
1878	*St Etienne*	Warden Ledge
1879	*Iron Age*	River Medina
1879	*Mignonette*	Brook Bay
1879	*Newbiggin*	Atherfield Ledges
1879	*Steman*	Blackgang
1879	*Schiehallion*	Rocken End
1879	*Anglo Saxon*	Goose Rock
1879	*Alpheus Marshall*	Atherfield Ledges
1879	*Marie*	off St Catherine's Point
1879	*Belen*	Nab Light
1880	*Donna Zola*	Chale Bay
1880	*Hero*	off Isle of Wight
1880	*Providence*	Ryde Pier
1880	*Blanche*	Nettlestone Point
1880	*Queen Bee*	off St Catherine's Point
1880	*Sea Flower*	Nettlestone Point
1880	*Atlas*	Atherfield Ledges
1880	*Joseph and Mary*	Brook Bay
1881	*Essen*	St Catherine's Point
1881	*Caduceus*	East Solent (**114**)
1881	*Indian Chief*	off Isle of Wight
1881	*Tartar*	Seaview
1881	*Lucknow*	Ryde Sands
1881	*Eclipse*	Ryde
1881	*Gertrude*	Ryde Sands
1881	*Providence*	Warden Ledge
1881	*Tor*	St Helen's Roads
1881	*King Koffer*	Fort Victoria Pier

The bell recovered from the Beau-Monde, which was wrecked off St Catherine's Point in 1883.

1881	*Claremont*	Atherfield Point
1881	*Ida*	off St Catherine's Point
1881	*Devonshire*	off St Catherine's Point
1881	*Fenna*	off the Needles
1881	*Arrow*	Cowes Roads
1881	*Trio*	Ryde
1881	*No. 13*	Ryde
1881	*Alarm*	off the Needles
1882	*William and Eliza*	Milford on Sea
1882	*Heron*	Southsea
1882	*Wheatfield*	Blackgang Chine
1882	*Emma*	How Ledge
1882	*Lady Jane*	Ryde
1882	*Iduna*	off St Catherine's Point (**236**)
1882	*Aleyone*	Ryde
1882	*Gerarda*	off St Catherine's Point (**201**)
1882	*Neva*	Ryde
1882	*Emma*	Seaview
1883	*Tartar*	Chichester
1883	*Elizabeth*	Langstone
1883	*Echo*	Shingle Bank
1883	*Magellan*	Shingle Bank
1883	*Rotterdam*	Spithead
1883	*Pride of the South*	Long Ledge
1883	*Snowdrop*	off Bembridge
1883	*Charles Marie*	Yarmouth
1883	*Jeune Gustave*	Sandown Bay
1883	*Frederick*	off the Needles
1883	*Foam*	Totland Bay
1883	*Georges Henri*	Ladder Chine
1883	*Beau-Monde*	St Catherine's Point
1883	*Jane*	Cowes Roads
1883	*Castle Craig*	Brook Ledge
1884	*William and Eliza*	Hurst Castle

1884	*Southbourne*	Christchurch
1884	*Richard*	Portsmouth
1884	*Simla*	Needles
1884	*Wyre*	off St Catherine's Point
1884	*Indian Empire*	off St Catherine's Point
1884	*Commodore*	Rocken End
1884	*Jaunita*	Cowes Roads
1884	*Etoile-de-la-Mer*	Horseshoe Bay
1885	*Olive Branch*	off St Catherine's Point
1885	*Perserverance*	Sandown Bay
1885	*Flirt*	off Dunnose Point
1885	*Clarinda*	off St Catherine's Point
1886	*Caroline*	Christchurch
1886	*William Thornborrow*	Brook Ledge
1886	*Isabel*	Bembridge Ledge
1886	*Britons Queen*	Bembridge Ledge
1886	*Cormorant*	Whale Chine
1886	*Fleur de Lys*	Cowes Roads
1886	*Mexico*	off Isle of Wight
1887	*Jane*	Solent
1887	*Laura*	Spithead
1887	*Midge*	Lymington
1887	*Lark*	Spithead
1887	*Amalie*	off St Catherine's Point
1887	*Pride of the Sea*	Yellow Ledge
1887	*Flaxmoss*	off St Catherine's Point
1887	*Lioness*	off Bembridge
1887	*Medway*	Yarmouth
1888	*Comet*	Hurst Castle
1888	*Kongsek*	Blackgang
1888	*Friends*	Ryde
1888	*City of Corinth*	off St Catherine's Point
1888	*Sirenia*	Atherfield Ledges
1888	*Smyrna*	south-west of the Needles
1888	*Saxmundham*	off St Catherine's Point
1889	*Thistle*	Milford on Sea
1889	*Rose*	Milford on Sea
1889	Unknown wreck	off the Needles
1889	*Bondevennen*	off St Catherine's Point
1889	*Cleddy*	off St Catherine's Point
1889	*Isle of Cyprus*	off Isle of Wight
1890	*Longest Day*	Eastoke Point
1890	Unknown wreck	Netley
1890	*Mary*	off St Catherine's Point
1890	*Irex*	Scratchell's Bay (**17**)
1890	*Leo*	Woody Bay
1890	*Carboceer*	Ship Ledge
1890	*Cameo*	Ship Ledge
1890	*Dizzy Dunlop*	Atherfield Ledges

1890	*Constance*	off St Catherine's Point
1890	*Mary Johnstone*	off St Catherine's Point
1890	*Tyne*	off Isle of Wight
1891	*Annie Clarke*	Southsea
1891	*Catherine*	Lymington
1891	*Midge*	Old Castle Point
1891	*Jeune Benoni*	Niton
1891	*Henri and Leontine*	Brook Bay
1891	*Marion Ross*	off Bembridge
1892	*Vectis*	Shingle Bank
1892	*Gudrun*	Shingle Bank
1892	Unknown wreck	Portsmouth
1892	*Mosquito*	Southampton
1892	*Comburyy Castle*	Back of the Wight
1892	*Queen of England*	Atherfield Ledges
1892	*Gripfast*	off Dunnose Point (**207**)
1892	*Catan*	off Isle of Wight
1893	*Rachel Harrison*	Pennington Spit
1893	*RTC No. 9*	Stokes Bay (**57**)
1893	*Esmeralda*	Christchurch
1893	*Volzy*	off Ventnor
1893	*Helen Burns*	off St Catherine's Point
1893	*St Helena*	off St Catherine's Point
1893	*Lively*	Totland Bay
1893	*William Cass*	off St Catherine's Point
1894	*George Henry*	Shingle Bank
1894	*Nightingale*	Gilkicker Point
1894	Unknown wreck	Spit Sand Fort
1894	*Camille*	off St Catherine's Point
1894	*C.A.*	off St Catherine's Point
1894	*Volage*	Ryde Sands
1895	*Alpha*	Stokes Bay
1895	*S.B. Hume*	Milford on Sea
1895	*Robert and Sarah*	Portsmouth
1895	*Alfred*	Southampton
1895	*Emily Kate*	Spithead
1895	*Hudibras*	Netley
1895	*Ganymedes*	Shingle Bank
1895	*Joannis Millas*	Chilton Chine
1895	*Hilda*	Back of the Wight
1895	*Noordster*	Brook Point
1895	*Highland Home*	Freshwater Bay
1895	*Spree*	off Isle of Wight
1896	*Francis*	Calshot
1896	*Mastiff*	Ryde Pier
1896	*William and Mary*	Ryde
1896	*Vigilant*	off St Catherine's Point
1897	*General Havelock*	Chichester
1897	*Swift*	Southsea

1897	*Alcester*	Typit Ledge
1897	*Emma*	Springvale
1897	*Freiburg*	off St Catherine's Point
1898	*Celerity*	Calshot
1898	*Pearl*	Southsea
1898	*Swallow*	Southsea
1898	*Ingo*	Shingle Bank
1898	*Ernst*	Shingle Bank
1898	*Ceres*	Shingle Bank
1898	*Ethel Maud*	Christchurch
1898	*Marie Therese*	Christchurch
1898	*Lepanto*	off St Catherine's Point
1898	*Mathilde*	Blackgang Chine
1899	*Arno*	Selsey Bill
1899	*Economy*	Southampton
1899	*Rosalie*	Bembridge Ledge
1899	*Midge*	Ryde Sands
1899	*Moland*	off Brook Point
1899	*Eilian*	off St Catherine's Point
1900	Unknown wreck	Spithead
1900	Unknown wreck	Shingle Bank
1900	*Martin*	Southsea
1900	*Georgina*	Chichester
1900	*Elizabeth*	Netley
1900	*Lucilla*	Egypt Point
1900	*William Gordon*	Back of the Wight
1900	*Auguste*	Atherfield Ledges (**215**)
1900	*Rose Hill*	off St Catherine's Point
1900	*San Sebastian*	off Isle of Wight
1901	*Plover*	Ryde
1901	*Cid*	Cowes
1901	*Slater*	Bonchurch
1902	*St Marcouf*	Lymington
1902	*Princess Royal*	Stanswood Bay
1902	*Beatrice*	Brambles Bank
1902	*Mary Farleigh*	Eastney
1902	*Russie*	Jeremy Rock
1902	*Cambrian Princess*	off St Catherine's Point
1902	*Clyde*	off St Catherine's Point
1902	*Vesta*	off St Catherine's Point
1902	*Fenja*	Freshwater Bay
1903	*Pearl*	Southsea
1903	*Dewdrop*	Browndown Point
1903	*Fairy King*	East Winner Shoal
1903	*Diver*	Christchurch Bay
1903	*Bimbo*	off Bembridge
1903	*Trixie*	Ryde Roads
1903	*Three Sisters*	off Ryde
1903	*Teal*	Yarmouth Roads

A Royal Navy porthole complete with copper drip tray.

1903	*Whisper*	Ryde Sands
1903	*Cuckoo*	Ryde
1903	*Dodo*	Ryde
1903	*Violet*	Ryde
1903	*Eros*	Back of the Wight
1903	*Nesta*	Seaview
1903	*Eira*	Ryde Pier
1903	*Humber*	Back of the Wight
1903	*Solent*	Back of the Wight
1903	*Exe*	Back of the Wight
1904	*Preciosa*	West Solent
1904	*Duncrag*	off St Catherine's Point
1904	*The Saint*	How Bank
1904	*Dolly*	Atherfield Ledges
1905	*Lancer*	Southsea
1905	*Ino*	Ryde
1905	*Gloire de Marie*	off Dunnose Point
1905	*St Monan*	Atherfield Ledges
1905	*Satyr*	Ship Ledge
1905	*Albatross*	Newtown
1906	*Hopewell*	Shingle Bank
1906	*Red Witch*	Stokes Bay
1906	*Ellen and Sarah*	Shingle Bank
1906	*Firefly*	off St Catherine's Point
1906	*Rutte*	off St Catherine's Point
1906	*Dolores*	off St Catherine's Point
1906	*Anita*	off Isle of Wight
1906	*Briton*	Chilton
1907	*Eros*	Solent
1907	*Sandown*	off Bembridge

1907	*Berlin*	off Isle of Wight
1907	*Reindeer*	off Isle of Wight
1908	*J.W.V.*	Southampton
1908	*Margory*	Calshot
1908	*Pilgrim*	Portsmouth
1908	*Tiger*	off St Catherine's Point
1908	*Hopedale*	off St Catherine's Point
1908	*Ceylon*	off St Catherine's Point
1908	*Cayo Soto*	off Isle of Wight
1909	*Gwendoline*	River Test
1909	*Bertha*	Lymington
1909	*Peter*	Gilkicker Point
1909	*Gerhard*	off St Catherine's Point
1909	*Mint*	Foreland Ledge
1909	*Blink Bonny*	No Man's Land Fort
1909	*Orange Blossom*	Sandown Bay
1909	*William and Mary*	Chilton Chine
1909	*Oscarborg*	off St Catherine's Point
1909	*Olive Leaf*	Sconce Point
1910	*Giraffe*	Calshot
1910	*Britannia*	Chichester
1910	*Spalpeen*	Bramble Bank
1910	*Two Sisters*	River Itchen
1910	*Zulu*	Portsmouth
1910	*Nemrod*	Ladder Chine
1910	*Rene*	Freshwater Bay
1910	*Ellen Beatrice*	Cowes Roads
1910	*Monte Grande*	off Isle of Wight
1911	*Alice*	Portsmouth
1911	*Leonie*	Southsea
1911	*Henry*	Netley
1911	*Puhlin*	Back of the Wight
1911	*Daylesford*	off St Catherine's Point (**243**)
1911	*Shoveller*	Bembridge
1911	*Solent*	off the Needles
1911	*A1*	Bracklesham Bay (**115**)
1912	*Thistle*	Spithead
1912	*Rosina*	Fawley
1912	*L'Aiglon*	Owers Creek
1912	*Bert*	Hayling Bay
1912	*Myosotis*	Gymp Bank
1912	*Romola*	Bembridge Ledge
1912	*Britannia*	Ryde Pier
1912	*Glendoveer*	off St Catherine's Point
1912	*Prima*	Atherfield Ledges
1913	*Olive Branch*	Hill Head
1913	*Water Beetle*	Christchurch Bay
1913	*S.H.B.*	Southampton
1913	*Patience*	Ryde Pier

The 2,123-ton cargo steamer Redesmere (Site 228) fell victim to a U-boat off St Catherine's Point in 1917.

1913	*Maggie III*	off Isle of Wight
1914	*Neath*	Egypt Point
1914	*Balder*	off the Needles
1914	*Niels Juel*	off St Catherine's Point
1914	*Ida*	Culver Cliff
1915	*Triton*	Bramble Bank
1915	*E.B.*	Spithead
1915	*Resource II*	Southampton
1915	*Hermes*	off St Catherine's Point
1915	*Olivine*	off St Catherine's Point
1915	*Erin II*	off Nab Light
1915	*Star of Buchan*	off Nab Light
1915	*Cissie*	off Nab Light
1915	*Velox*	off Bembridge (**123**)
1915	*T.J. and R. No. 17*	off St Catherine's Point
1915	*Louis*	off Isle of Wight
1916	*Algerian*	West Solent (**46**)
1916	*Albion II*	off the Needles (**22**)
1916	*Empress Queen*	Bembridge Ledge (**136**)
1916	*Souvenir*	Brook Ledge
1916	*Jeanette*	off St Catherine's Point
1916	*Charlotte Sophia*	St Helen's Roads
1916	*Margaret Sutton*	off St Catherine's Point
1916	*Sphene*	off St Catherine's Point
1916	*Badger*	off St Catherine's Point
1916	*Cliburn*	off St Catherine's Point
1916	*Barbara*	off St Catherine's Point
1916	*Riguette*	off St Catherine's Point
1916	*Pelagia*	off Bembridge
1916	*Inger*	off St Catherine's Point
1916	*Hendrick*	off Isle of Wight
1917	*Ludlow*	Solent
1917	*Luciston*	Calshot (**49**)
1917	*Ada*	Ryde Pier
1917	*Cuba*	off St Catherine's Point
1917	*Mendi*	off St Catherine's Point (**233**)
1917	*Glynmel*	off St Catherine's Point

1917	*Eastern Belle*	off St Catherine's Point
1917	*Ernest Legouve*	off St Catherine's Point (**244**)
1917	*Lowmount*	off Nab Light
1917	*Elizabeth Hampton*	off St Catherine's Point
1917	*UB-39*	off St Catherine's Point
1917	*Florence Louisa*	off the Needles
1917	*Elford*	off Nab Light (**170**)
1917	*Camberwell*	off Dunnose Point (**183**)
1917	*Milo*	off St Catherine's Point
1917	*Corbet Woodall*	off Nab Light
1917	*Wapello*	off St Catherine's Point (**197**)
1917	*Indutiomare*	off St Catherine's Point
1917	*Bishopston*	off St Catherine's Point
1917	*Ocean Star*	off Nab Light
1917	*Joshua*	Back of the Wight
1917	*Camswan*	Culver Cliff (**167**)
1917	*Redesmere*	off St Catherine's Point (**228**)
1917	*Myrtle Grove*	off the Needles (**29**)
1917	*Oriflamme*	off St Catherine's Point (**216**)
1917	*ML-52*	Sandown Bay
1917	*UB-81*	off St Catherine's Point (**199**)
1917	*Brigitta*	off Nab Light
1917	*Wyndhurst*	off St Catherine's Point
1917	*Apley*	off Nab Light (**173**)
1917	*La Peru*	Niton Cliffs
1917	*Kurland*	off Dunnose Point (**189**)
1917	*Hilda Lea*	off St Catherine's Point
1917	*Espagne*	off St Catherine's Point (**239**)
1917	*Fallodon*	off St Catherine's Point (**202**)
1917	*Westville*	off Back of the Wight (**219**)
1917	*Osaki*	off Isle of Wight
1918	*Mechanician*	Shingle Bank (**8**)
1918	*C.M.B. No. 2*	Portsmouth

The port lamp from the torpedo boat destroyer HMS Boxer (Site 168), which sank in the centre of Sandown Bay in 1918, following a collision.

1918	*Asborg*	off St Catherine's Point (**196**)
1918	*Leon*	off St Catherine's Point (**190**)
1918	*Molina*	off St Catherine's Point (**221**)
1918	*Serrana*	off the Needles (**6** and **12**)
1918	*Aalesund*	off St Catherine's Point
1918	*Rob Roy*	off St Catherine's Point
1918	*Hazard*	East Solent (**104**)
1918	*Boxer*	Sandown Bay (**168**)
1918	*Eleanor*	off St Catherine's Point (**25**)
1918	*Polo*	off Dunnose Point (**187**)
1918	*Borgny*	off the Needles
1918	*Brestois*	off St Catherine's Point
1918	*Braat II*	off St Catherine's Point (**232**)
1918	*Tweed*	off St Catherine's Point
1918	*Londonier*	off St Catherine's Point (**230**)
1918	*Venezuela*	off the Needles
1918	*South Western*	off St Catherine's Point (**237**)
1918	*Azemmour*	off the Needles (**24**)
1918	*New Dawn*	off the Needles (**23**)
1918	*War Knight*	Watcombe Bay (**213**)
1918	*France Aimée*	Princessa Shoal (**134**)
1918	*Highland Brigade*	off Dunnose Point (**198**)
1918	*Luis*	off Dunnose Point (**184**)
1918	*Isleworth*	off St Catherine's Point (**195**)
1918	*UC-77*	off Nab Light
1918	*Michael Clements*	off St Catherine's Point
1918	*P.12*	Culver Cliff (**137** and **158**)
1919	*Violet*	Foreland
1919	*Walcutta*	off Isle of Wight
1919	*U-90*	off St Catherine's Point (**208**)
1919	*Edward Luckenbach*	off Isle of Wight
1920	*UB-21*	Horse and Dean Sand (**111**)
1920	*A2*	Portsmouth
1920	*Spyros*	off St Catherine's
1920	*Heardsman*	off Isle of Wight
1920	*Liffey*	off Isle of Wight
1921	*Imogene*	Shingle Bank

A complete Walker log from HMS P.12, lost in 1918.

1921	*Lois*	Chale Bay
1921	Coastal motor boat	off Isle of Wight
1922	Unknown wreck	Bramble Bank
1922	*Pearl*	Southsea (**87**)
1923	*Anne Marie*	off St Catherine's Point
1923	*Florence Vivian*	East Knoll (**51**)
1924	*Duddon*	Stokes Bay (**74**)
1925	*Excel*	Horse Sand
1926	*Withern*	Langstone Harbour (**93**)
1926	*Weston Maid*	Solent
1926	Unknown wreck	Mother Bank
1926	*Betsy Anna*	off the Needles
1926	*Eugene Schneider*	off St Catherine's Point
1928	*Undine*	Horse Sand
1929	*Penmarch*	off St Catherine's Point
1930	*Menelaos*	Selsey Bill
1932	*Braedale*	off the Needles
1932	*Rainbow*	off Isle of Wight
1933	*New Moss Rose*	Osborne Bay
1934	*Meandros*	off St Catherine's Point
1935	*Betty*	Southampton
1936	*Britannia*	off St Catherine's Point
1939	*Britisher*	Brighstone Ledge
1939	*Bruce*	off Back of the Wight
1939	*Edenwood*	off Nab Light
1940	*Cambrian*	Horse and Dean Sand (**97**)
1940	*Capable*	Nab East (**119**)
1940	*Charde*	Solent
1940	*James No. 70*	Southampton
1940	*Kendal*	Woolston
1940	*Bonaparte*	Southampton
1940	*Ornsay*	Portsmouth
1940	*Westra*	Portsmouth
1940	*Norama*	Southampton
1940	*Caroline Susan*	Dolphin Bank (**10**)
1940	*Campeador V*	off Bembridge (**127** and **139**)
1940	*Crestflower*	off St Catherine's Point (**231**)
1940	*Terlings*	off the Needles (**28**)

Left: The anti-submarine trawler HMS Warwick Deeping (Site 220) sank about 6 miles west of St Catherine's Point after an attack by E-boats in 1940.

1940	*Ajax*	off the Needles (**224**)
1940	*Coquetdale*	off the Needles (**27**)
1940	*Empire Crusader*	off the Needles
1940	*Swordfish*	off St Catherine's Point (**205**)
1940	*Acheron*	off the Needles (**227**)
1940	*Warwick Deeping*	off St Catherine's Point (**220**)
1940	*L'Istrac*	off St Catherine's Point (**234**)
1940	*Her Majesty*	Southampton
1940	*Kingston Cairngorm*	off Isle of Wight
1940	*Kolske 6*	off Isle of Wight
1941	*Portsdown*	Portsmouth (**150**)
1941	*Harbour Launch No. 278*	Portsmouth
1941	*Percy*	Langstone Harbour
1941	*Irishman*	Langstone Harbour (**92**)
1941	*Wilna*	off Nab Light
1941	*Dagmar*	off the Needles
1941	*Ala*	off Nab Tower
1942	*E-boat*	Eastoke Point
1943	*LCT*	Warner Buoy
1943	*Landing craft*	Needs Ore Point
1943	*Kingston Jacinth*	Solent
1943	*LCA No. 553*	Southampton
1943	*LCP (L) No. 136*	Solent
1943	*LCP(M) No.17*	off Back of the Wight
1943	*Sargasso*	off Back of the Wight
1944	*Barge*	Beaulieu River
1944	*LCP (R) No. 895*	Solent
1944	*LCP (L) No. 52*	Solent
1944	*LCP (L) No. 541*	off Isle of Wight
1944	*LCT 809*	off the Needles (**7**)
1944	*Dungrange*	off St Catherine's Point
1944	*Ashanti*	off St Catherine's Point (**229**)
1944	*Prince Leopold*	east of Dunnose Point
1944	*St Enogat*	off St Catherine's Point
1944	*Dumfries*	off St Catherine's Point
1944	Flying boat	Calshot Castle (**31**)
1944	*Gentrice*	off St Catherine's Point
1944	*LC 801*	Portsmouth
1944	*LC 1199*	Portsmouth
1944	*LC 154*	Portsmouth
1944	*Minora*	off Isle of Wight
1944	*Swarthy*	off Isle of Wight
1945	Landing craft	Beaulieu River
1945	*Everleigh*	off the Needles
1945	*Cuba*	east of Dunnose Point (**179**)
1945	*U-1195*	east of Dunnose Point (**192**)
1946	*Islay Mist*	Watcombe Bay
1947	*LCT No. 1068*	Stokes Bay (**58**)
1947	*Varvassi*	Needles Bridge (**18**)

1948	*Hope*	Binnel Point
1951	*Lamorna*	Christchurch Bay
1951	*Volkerak*	Rocken End
1952	*Albatross*	Rocken End
1956	*Carbon*	Compton
1957	*Upstart*	off the Needles (**225**)
1964	*Witte Zee*	off Back of the Wight (**222**)
1965	*Zeemansblik*	Atherfield Ledges
1967	*Roway*	Horse and Dean Sand (**88**)
1967	*Bettann*	off Nab Tower (**132** and **177**)
1967	*Tenace*	off Nab Tower (**191**)
1968	*Lypta*	Portsmouth
1968	*Jgena*	off the Needles
1969	*Beverley Ann*	Hurst Castle
1970	*Diadem of Bursledon*	Horse Elbow Buoy (**95**)
1970	*Enid*	Alum Bay
1970	*Harry Sharman*	Culver Cliff (**157**)
1973	*Nina*	Egypt Point
1973	*Hauler*	Sandown Bay (**156**)
1975	*Estrelita*	Sandown Bay (**164**)
1975	*Gorizont*	off St Catherine's Point
1976	Chain ferry	Calshot (**50**)
1976	*Jo-Anne*	Fort Victoria (**40**)
1977	*Margjagulin*	Gunners Point (**99**)
1977	*Toccatina*	Hurst Castle (**39**)
1977	*Kylin*	off the Needles (**14**)
1978	*Margaret Smith*	off Yarmouth (**42**)
1978	*New Venture*	Sandown Bay (**160**)
1979	*Pool Fisher*	off St Catherine's Point (**241**)
1980	Concrete barge	Shingle Bank (**9**)
1980	*Germa Geisha*	off Nab Tower

Stern lamp recovered from the wreck of HMS Velox (Site 123).

1981	*Millmer*	off the Needles (**13**)
1981	*Sir Jasper*	off Nab Tower (**128**)
1982	*Sargia*	Calshot
1983	*Shallom*	Hayling Island (**116**)
1983	*Spearfish*	off St Catherine's Point
1983	*Teamwork*	off the Needles (**19**)
1990	*Flag Theofano*	Dean Tail (**148**)

The Needles Lighthouse

Index

The bold numbers in parentheses are dive site numbers. There are no page references to the Shipwreck Register (Appendix 3), which should be checked separately.